SNAKES, SANDS AND SILPHIUM

Travels in Classical Libya

Paul Wright

SILPHIUM
PRESS

Produced by Silphium Press, an imprint of
The Society for Libyan Studies
c/o The Institute of Archaeology
31–34 Gordon Square, London
WC1H OPY
www.britac.ac.uk/institutes/libya

ISBN 978-1-900971-12-6

Cover and interior design by Chris Bell
Edited by Michael Leitch

Printed in India by Imprint Digital

To my Father

Fig. 1 Jupiter Ammon, a god of Libya with a temple and an oracle. This image is based on Roman reliefs.

CONTENTS

LIST OF EXTRACTS FROM CLASSICAL WRITERS

The list includes dates when their works first began circulating in public, where known.

Eighth to third centuries BC

First century BC

First century AD

Second century AD

Third century AD

Fourth century AD

LIST OF THEMES

The principal subjects and themes are listed below. More detailed references can be found in the glossary of names at the back of the book.

Ammon: Corippus; Herodotus 2, 6, Lucan 6, Nepos 1, Silius Italicus 2, Strabo 1

Animals: Aelian, Aristotle, Herodotus 7, Lucan 7, Lucian, Pliny 9

Argonauts: Herodotus 6, Pindar

Astronomy: Lucan 6, Manilius

Biography: Eutropius 2, *Historia Augusta*, Plutarch 1, Seneca 1, Suetonius

Cato the Younger: Lucan 2, 5, 6, 7, 8, Plutarch 1, Seneca 1

Cookery: Apicius, Columella 3

Customs: Apuleius, Herodotus 6, Plutarch 2, Synesius 2

Cyrene, foundation: Callimachus 1, Herodotus 4, 5, Pindar

Didactic verse: Lucretius, Virgil 1

Epic verse: Corippus, Homer, Silius Italicus, Virgil 2

Explorers: Herodotus 1, Ptolemy

Fountain of the Sun: Herodotus 6, Lucretius, Mela 2

Geography: Herodotus 6, 8, Lucan 3, 4, Mela, Pliny 1, 2, 3, 4, 5, 6, 7, Strabo, Synesius 3, 4

History: Ammianus Marcellinus, Eutropius, Florus, Herodotus 3, 4, 5, 9, 10, Nepos, Procopius, Sallust, Tacitus, Thucydides

Horses of Cyrene: Oppian, Pindar

Inscriptions: Avidius, Iasucthan

Libyans abroad: Eutropius, Juvenal, Statius, Virgil 3

Local politics: Apuleius, Synesius 6, 7

Lyric verse: Anthologia Latina, Callimachus, Catullus, Juvenal, Martial, Palladas, Pindar, Statius

Medicine: Celsus, Columella 2, Pliny 12, 13

Minerals: Pliny 14

Peoples of Libya: Herodotus 6, Lucan 1, Lucian, Pliny 7, 8, Sallust 1, Silius Italicus 3, 4, 7, Strabo 4, Virgil 1, 3

Philaeni: Mela 2, Sallust 3, Valerius Maximus

Plants: Athenaeus, Pliny 10, 11, 12

Psylli: Celsus 1, Lucan 8, Pliny 8

Rulers: Cornelius Nepos, *Historia Augusta*, Eutropius 2, Herodotus 5, 9, Suetonius

Salt of Ammon: Celsus 2, Columella 2

Science: Celsus, Lucretius, Pliny 12, 13, Seneca 2, Strabo 1

Silphium: Apicius, Celsus 1, Columella, Pliny 13

Snakes: Celsus 1, Aristotle, Lucan 7, Lucian

Syrtes: Lucan 2, Mela 2, Pliny 2, Sallust 2, Strabo 4

Tritonian Lake: Herodotus 6, Mela 2, Pindar

Travellers: Homer 1, 2, Pindar, Seneca 1, Silius Italicus 6, Synesius 1

Vandals: Anthologia Latina, Procopius

LIST OF MAPS AND ILLUSTRATIONS

A Note on the Artists

Jan Crabtree is a figurative artist based in Kingston-upon-Thames who has exhibited widely in South-East England. Her preferred medium is oils but she also works in pencil and pastels.

Paul Fearn is a painter, chiefly of landscapes and still lifes, and also specialises in pencil drawings of wild animals in a popular contemporary style.

FOREWORD

by Professor Andrew Wilson

This book provides a richly variegated glimpse of Libya through Greek, Roman and Byzantine eyes, in freshly translated extracts from ancient authors from Homer to the sixth-century AD poet Corippus. It testifies to the enduring fascination of Libya across the centuries: the Libyan Tourist Board's poster slogan of a few years ago, 'Libya: everything you can imagine, everything you can't imagine' seems really to be the modern version of the ancient proverb recorded by Aristotle: 'Libya is always producing something new'. A few of the writers whose works are excerpted in this book were from or had visited the region, and wrote from personal knowledge, but the majority had never been there, and their writings thus convey a sense of what Libya (both in the sense of the continent of Africa, and the region encompassed by the modern country of that name) meant to their contemporaries around the Mediterranean. The emphasis is on natural wonders, the harsh desert sands of the Sahara, exotic animals (especially snakes), the wonder-plant silphium (used as a medicine, condiment, aphrodisiac, and cattle feed), strange tribal customs, and Libyan recipes; but there are also illuminating accounts of life in the Roman cities of Tripolitania, and of political events. The modern traveller to Libya will find a wealth of interesting material about the region in antiquity, and will enjoy disentangling recognisable facts from garbled exaggeration in the ancient accounts. And at times one is struck by cultural persistences too: Synesius' description of the unstinting generosity of the Libyan peoples of the Marmarica towards him and his shipwrecked companions will strike a heartwarming chord of recognition with anyone who has travelled in Libya and experienced the hospitality afforded to strangers and travellers.

ACKNOWLEDGMENTS

I am very grateful to the publications committee of the Society for Libyan Studies and to Silphium Press for this opportunity to provide a contribution to their work.

In particular, I would like to thank Anthony Layden and Professor Claudio Vita-Finzi, current and former presidents of the Society, and Professor Andrew Wilson and Dr Paul Bennett, current and former chairmen.

In addition I must especially thank Victoria Leitch and Michael Leitch for their editorial control, Professor David Mattingly for reviewing the text and for his suggestions, Dr Philip Kenrick for also reviewing the text and for his financial administration, the late Professor Colin Wells for reviewing the text, Dr John Wright for reading early drafts and for his many comments and suggestions, Primavera Quantrill for much information and advice, Nik Prowse and Michael Crick for their advice, Dr Richard Willmer for reading and commenting on the draft text and for providing photographs of Siwa, and Harun Rathore and Mohan Mukhoty for also examining the text.

Many thanks go to those who provided illustrations for the book: Amina Wright for her photographs of Tripolitania, and Jan Crabtree and Paul Fearn for the artwork they so generously contributed.

Finally, I would like to thank all family and friends who took an interest, and the following in particular for their encouragement and suggestions: Johanna Mitchell, Kevin Wilkinson, Lynne Bell, Luci Spencer, Sally Warren, Derek and Jean D'Arcy, Keith Hathaway, Mark Symms, Andrea Le Mottée, Daniela White, Tim Cullingford and Sarah Greenwood.

INTRODUCTION

Travellers in Libya

This book was originally conceived as the first volume in a series about travellers in Libya. It follows *Travellers in Libya* by John Wright (Silphium Press 2005) which covered the period 1550–1911. These books aim to present the impressions and observations of those who either visited Libya themselves or who recorded the visits of other people. They are intended chiefly for the general reader rather than the specialist and their purpose is therefore to present a selection of material that will be of interest to those visiting Libya or who are in any way curious about this part of the world. They are also, of course, a resource for students and researchers.

The period represented in this book is that of the Ancient World, and more specifically the age of Greece and Rome. Its aim is to provide a useful source of information on how Classical writers perceived Libya, and to include as much as is important or worthwhile on this subject from what remains of Greek and Roman literature. Readers are invited to dip in and enjoy whatever may take their fancy – bold explorers, dangerous animals, uses of silphium, romantic poetry, descriptions of idyllic countryside or baking deserts, the horrors of war, marriage customs, riots, treacherous seas ... a whole variety of unusual things in the texts and illustrations. The compiler's hope is that it may whet the reader's appetite for more of the works of the many authors presented here.

A Definition of Libya

In our age of global positioning systems and international treaty organisations, geography has become a precise science, even when delineating tracts of uninhabited desert waste. The Ancient World had different definitions and, as the first text here dates from the eighth century BC and the last from the sixth century AD, some 1,400 years or so, it is not difficult to appreciate that there was a large shift in the understanding of what constituted Libya even within the period represented by the principal authors whose works appear here.

The Greeks used the term *Libye* to describe the third continent of the Old World, which we would call Africa. They knew little of it other than the parts bordering the Mediterranean Sea and their immediate hinterland. They knew almost nothing of Sub-Saharan Africa and imagined the continent to be a wedge with its point at the Atlas Mountains and its back at the Red Sea. There are various claims in ancient sources about Phoenician explorers hired to sail round the whole of Africa by the Egyptian Pharaoh Necho (who reigned 610–594 BC), or about Hanno the Carthaginian who sailed the coast of West Africa late in the sixth century BC, but certain knowledge of the perimeter of the whole continent was not obtained until the Portuguese discoveries of the fifteenth century AD. Africa, as known to the Ancient World, was therefore little more than the coast opposite the Canary Islands in the Atlantic Ocean clockwise round to Zanzibar in the Indian Ocean, and the hinterland of the continent no more than a few hundred miles inland from the Mediterranean and Red Sea coasts. Where Libya is mentioned in the text, it will normally refer to the whole of North Africa.

The area of the world we are concerned with in this book, however, is essentially the space between the Carthaginian homeland in the west (roughly modern Tunisia) and the kingdom of Egypt, centred on the River Nile, in the east. Our boundary, which need not be too rigidly defined, runs from the Lesser Syrtis (Gulf of Gabès in south-east Tunisia) along the coast to Catabathmos (on the Gulf of Sollum in western Egypt) including all the land south of the coast as far as the Tibesti Mountains of northern Chad; in other words, the eastern part of Greek *Libye*. Readers are referred to the main maps. However, as ancient authors were often vague about what lay beyond the coastal strip, descriptions of tribes and places that may have lain south and west of this area have been included when they seemed relevant, as have some references to the Libyan districts of Egypt.

Ancient Libya

The first inhabitants to leave a distinct record were the pastoral peoples of the Stone Age from about 12,000 years ago, when Libya was a fertile savanna dotted with woods and lakes. The well-known animals and birds of Africa thrived there, as recorded in Saharan rock art. The warming of the world which ended the Ice Age initially made the Sahara wetter. However, from about 5,000 years ago, further climate change turned this savanna into the vast desert of today. Apart from a few very hardy and scattered Berbers and Saharan aboriginals (the ancestors of the modern Tebu), settlement and civilisation became largely confined to the Nile

Valley, the Mediterranean coast and scattered oases. Libya, being the southernmost reach of this coast, and therefore particularly affected by desertification, was only very sparsely populated. Egyptian texts occasionally refer to Libyans, mainly in the context of raids to be guarded against. Some Egyptians themselves migrated westwards and established outlying trading posts and settlements in the oases of Libya, notably at Siwa where the famous oracle of the sky god Amun (Ammon) was established.

The first contacts between non-African travellers and the Libyans began with occasional trading voyages of people such as the Minoan Cretans, early Phoenician traders and Mycenaean Greeks as early as the thirteenth century BC (in the legends of Jason, Menelaus and Odysseus in **Pindar** and **Homer**). A more comprehensive settlement by outsiders began from around the ninth century when Phoenicians from Tyre in Lebanon established Carthage in about 800 BC (although they claimed a much earlier date). Carthage in turn established other colonies and trading posts along the coast of western Libya and the western Mediterranean generally. The Greeks, from around 630 BC, began to colonise North Africa, too, founding Cyrene and other cities in eastern Libya (Cyrenaica), as told in **Herodotus**. After much hostility, a common boundary between the Greek colonies and Carthage was established at the Altars of the Philaeni (best described by **Sallust**). Both civilisations developed agriculture and trade and established their own particular cultures in these distinct spheres of influence.

Cyrenaica was briefly incorporated into the Persian Empire (see **Herodotus**) in the late sixth century BC but soon regained independence and became an important part of the Greek culture that dominated the eastern Mediterranean (**Pindar**). Alexander the Great's conquests once again ended the independence of the Greek colonies in Libya in the 330s BC. On the conqueror's death, they passed to his general Ptolemy and his successors who became rulers of Egypt.

The most significant outside influence on Libya's development, however, was Rome. In three brutal and lengthy wars, Rome wrested control of the western Mediterranean from Carthage. Eventually, in 146 BC, Rome mercilessly destroyed that city, and created a new Roman province, Africa, in the former Carthaginian homeland. Although still retaining their Carthaginian (Punic) culture, the Carthaginian parts of Libya became subject to various Numidian rulers until the Roman civil wars of the first century BC saw the Numidians on the losing side.

In the east, the Kingdom of Cyrene was ceded to Rome on the death of King Ptolemy Apion in 96 BC (described briefly by **Eutropius**) and was, in 74 BC, united to form a new province not with Africa but with Crete, as was consistent with its Greek rather than Punico-Libyan culture.

During the time of Roman administration, the agricultural yields of Libya were improved by efficient water management, advanced farming techniques and powerful market forces. Libyan trade, of some but not vital importance to the Phoenicians and Greeks, was opened to the almost limitless market of the Mediterranean which was now under Roman control. Libyan goods – olives and olive oil, grain, spices, figs, dates and other fruit; wool, horses, and exotic animals for the circus games; slaves; cookware, and commodities such as ivory and gemstones from the deep interior – were exported all over the Roman Empire and beyond, and goods from elsewhere in the empire were imported to the African provinces.

The Romans created a frontier (the *limes*) in the desert regions after imposing their authority through punitive raids against desert peoples such as the Garamantes, under Cornelius Balbus (see **Pliny**), Quirinius (**Florus**) and others. Trade between the Roman Empire and the Garamantes eventually became very substantial and mutually beneficial. Yet the same market forces were also responsible for the supplanting and consequent extinction of the valuable silphium plant by the less useful but more manageable asafoetida (**Pliny**). And so Libya settled down to several centuries of prosperity as an integral part of Roman culture, even supplying Rome with a ruling dynasty when Septimius Severus from Leptis Magna became emperor in AD 193 (see **Eutropius** and the ***Historia Augusta***).

Late in the third century, the administration of the Roman Empire was reformed and western Libya became Tripolitana and Cyrenaica became Libya Superior. From around the beginning of the fifth century, as elsewhere in the Roman Empire, Libya was increasingly subject to the depredations of civil wars as well as invasions from powerful foreign nations and continued raids from Libyans of the interior (**Synesius**). Finally, in 429, the Vandals, a Germanic race who had marched over the western provinces of the empire, settled in the area once ruled by Carthage and established their own kingdom there (life described in the ***Anthologia Latina***). This independence was ended by the swift campaign in 533–534 of the Emperor Justinian I when Tripolitana was reincorporated into the Roman Empire (**Procopius**). And so it remained for a further century until the Arab invasion of the 640s which ended Classical civilisation in Libya and brought Islam and a more Middle Eastern outlook to Libya, which it still possesses today.

Classical Authors and Travellers

It is important to emphasise that this book represents a selection – and a personal selection at that – from the variety of passages on Libya which can be found in those ancient sources which have managed to survive both the destruction of Classical culture by barbarian raids and settlement in the fifth to seventh centuries AD, and European neglect in the Middle Ages. Much that could have been used to make this book has been lost. It is a pity, for instance, that the geographical work of Eratosthenes of Cyrene is largely lost, or that the section on Africa of the Hippocratic treatise *Airs, Waters, Places* is missing. Instead, this book contains the most significant elements of what remains on the subjects associated with ancient Libya and, to a certain extent, with the travellers who went to Libya, but there is inevitably a certain lack of coherence in the jumble of passages – often quite short ones – which we are able to utilise and which are usually taken from their wider context.

Certain themes stand out and recur: the city of Cyrene and its founder, Battus; the temple of Ammon; the many uses of silphium; the poisonous snakes and scorpions, and what to do about them; the sand, and the south wind that blows it; the dangerous shoals of the Syrtes; the native peoples, including the snake-charming Psylli, the dynamic yet impoverished Nasamonians, the Garamantes of the interior; racial tensions; the Severan dynasty...

Other books in this series rely chiefly on eyewitness accounts. The difficulty with the period covered by this book is that few of our writers appear to have travelled to Libya. Exceptions include **Callimachus** and **Synesius** (who both came from Cyrene), the centurions **Avidius** and **Iasucthan** (the latter almost certainly a native Libyan), **Apuleius** (also an African) and possibly **Herodotus, Sallust, Strabo** and **Corippus**, so all other descriptions are related by authors who probably had no direct contact with the land and its peoples and had to rely on reports by others. Our chief travellers (including invaders), whether real or legendary, are Menelaus and Odysseus (in **Homer**), Jason and the Argonauts (in **Pindar**), Hercules (in **Lucan**), Battus (in **Herodotus**), the Philaeni (in **Sallust** and **Valerius Maximus**), Lysander and Agesilaus (in **Nepos**), Cornelius Balbus (in **Pliny**), Cato the Younger (in **Lucan**, **Plutarch** and **Seneca**), Cossus and Quirinius (in **Florus**), the Emperor Vespasian (in **Suetonius**), Septimius Flaccus (or Suellius Flaccus) and Julius Maternus (in **Ptolemy**), the Emperor Septimius Severus (in **Eutropius** and the ***Augustan History***), Belisarius (in **Procopius**) and Iohannes Troglyta (in **Corippus**).

Gods and goddesses (Pallas/Minerva, Triton, Medusa) and legendary heroes (Hercules) appear, too. The modern reader may be surprised at the inclusion of some mythology in what is essentially a travel book. The ancient world was less inclined to make distinctions between the material and the spiritual. To early Greek writers, and the notoriously superstitious Romans, the influence of the gods and the spirits of the dead was an integral part of daily life and thought, the deities looking with favour or disfavour on the activity of the living. Sacrifices of animals and offerings of produce and drink in acknowledgment of the gods' presence and favour were normal everyday activities, and requesting the assistance of these beings was advisable when undertaking anything out of the ordinary, hence the importance of divine oracles such as that of Ammon at Siwa. That said, ancient authors such as Herodotus and Lucan were quite capable of expressing their scepticism of certain mythological tales, and Celsus, for instance, is vociferous in his condemnation of superstition in medical practice.

The large amount of poetry in this volume may also come as a surprise. The classical poet was a seer, divinely inspired to sing truth, and statements by poets were regarded as authoritative. Homer's mention of Libyan lambs with horns budding as soon as born, for example, was the source of much learned discussion by natural philosophers who accepted his statement as fundamentally true, not because they checked facts but because of the authority necessarily imparted by the divine inspiration of the poet. Even rational philosophers like Aristotle discussed such things without raising doubts. Ancient poetry was often characterised by definitions, descriptions and references to places that we would be inclined to regard as prosaic rather than poetic. This characteristic is very helpful in providing information on Libya that would be less forthcoming in a modern poem. The other reason for the abundance of poetry in this collection is that it often represents the height of literary achievement and is therefore more likely to have survived the destruction of much of the rest of Classical civilisation. For the same reason, this collection is necessarily rather literary in nature.

It will not go unnoticed that every item here comes from the cultures of Greece and Rome. The reasons for this are simple. Even less of the written culture of native Libyan peoples survives and it is probable that there was less of it to start with. Carthaginian culture was largely superseded by Rome. Egypt was confidently inward-looking and took little interest in the vast deserts beyond the Nile. Other civilisations of the Near East had contact with Libya only via Egypt, apart from the Phoenicians, but they had become subject to so many Middle Eastern and European empires that their recording of their early discoveries in Libya were stifled. **Tacitus** is one of the few who has something to say on Jewish contacts with Libya.

We therefore have a miscellany of snippets and some longer items. These have been presented here by the date when they first began circulating in public, as far as can be ascertained. So as well as presentations of Libyan geography (**Herodotus, Strabo, Mela, Pliny**) and astronomy (**Manilius, Lucan**), there are also descriptions of Libyan flora and fauna

(**Aristotle, Lucan, Pliny, Athenaeus, Oppian, Aelian**), and history in various guises (but because of the layout of the collection, not necessarily in the exact chronological order of the events described). For a bit of diversion, there are some short passages on goods coming from Libya and their uses in medicine (**Celsus**), agriculture (**Columella**) and cookery (**Apicius**), and comments on Libyans away from home (**Virgil, Statius, Juvenal, Martial** and the ***Augustan History***). Readers are invited to dip in to the text and illustrations at random, and to appreciate the insights, to enjoy the humour, and be informed by the facts as they are presented by our authors. Just two notes of caution: ancient writers had different views on plagiarism, and on accuracy. Copying another author word for word was quite acceptable and normal. Information is not always correct; indeed, any reader seeking facts should not take any statement made by our authors at face value.

Translation

There are many ways to translate and the methods used in this volume merit a few observations. A literal translation – in other words, one that is as close to the vocabulary and phraseology of the original as is possible while not sounding ridiculous in English – is useful when translating for students or scholars who need an accurate rendering. An idiomatic translation, on the other hand, reads well in English but in order to do so may have to compromise accuracy for the sake of that readability. On the face of it, a book like this, aimed at the general reader rather than the specialist, would appear to benefit most from the latter approach.

That said, there is a risk that using a free, idiomatic approach in an anthology such as this, comprising over forty authors writing from the eighth century BC to the sixth century AD, will suffer from the translator's personal style overlying the many different styles and cultural idioms of his sources and so muffling the original voices. To preserve the voices of the individual writers, therefore, a compromise between the two main styles of translation has been attempted, which should enable the sources to express themselves in their own characteristic way but without sounding odd in contemporary English.

There are certain occasions when a translator has to intervene to help the reader along. Sometimes a footnote is needed, but here these have been kept to a minimum to reduce distraction. Cases where words have been added include instances where only a little explanation is needed to clarify the sense. Because these extracts are taken from the wider context of the main work, some words are added on occasion to make the context clearer. For a similar reason, proper names are sometimes substituted for pronouns if it would not otherwise be clear who was being referred to. But generally the original author's text has not been interfered with. A very small number of alternative readings from the standard published texts have been adopted.

Poetry has usually been translated into prose as the aim of this book is to provide information more than to present the sublime. The exception is epigrams which, being lighter in tone, have usually been rendered in various verse forms.

Names

Proper names in works of history, geography or science, which are intended to be informative, are presented in their ancient form, with the modern name bracketed afterwards if it is known, e.g. Oea [Tripoli], but the adding of modern names has been avoided in poetry and oratory as this would detract from the flow. The glossary will be of help here, especially when reading poetry in the Alexandrian tradition (**Callimachus, Catullus, Virgil**), which is wilfully obscure.

Greek names are given the Latinised spelling that is traditional and familiar in English rather than a modern scholarly transliteration from the original Greek or other language (e.g. Heracles not Herakles, Nectanebo not Nakhtnebef). Place names have many different spellings among the authors so, for ease of reference, these have usually been presented as one form: Ammon in preference to Hammon, Barca for Barce, Leptis for Lepcis, Sabratha for Sabrata, and so on. The glossary gives details of variant forms.

Weights, measures and distances are given their nearest metric equivalent. However, as such measurements are based upon the ancient texts, they may not necessarily correspond accurately with actual distances or measures.

The transliteration of modern North African place names is a vexed issue, which is why the ancient name has normally been kept in the translation. A glance at different editions of contemporary atlases will reveal many different spellings in Roman script of the same Libyan place names. Therefore, in the glossary, and where the modern name is mentioned after the ancient name, the modern names are presented in the form in which they have become best known in English, usually from the period of direct British involvement in Libya in the mid-twentieth century. So, for instance, Sollum and Augila are preferred to Salum and Awjilah. Readers are referred to the maps.

One thing needs to be said about regional names. Libya, Egypt, Mauritania and Ethiopia are all sovereign states at the time of writing, and

Africa is the name of the continent in which they are found. These modern names bear only a little relation to the entities identified by those names in the Ancient World. In simple terms, *Libya* was the continent (bounded by the Atlantic Ocean in the west, the Mediterranean Sea in the north, the River Nile in the east, and an unknown southern limit beyond the tropics). *Africa* corresponded roughly to modern Tunisia and north-eastern Algeria, and *Mauretania* to Morocco and north-western Algeria. *Egypt* was chiefly the Nile Valley from the delta upstream to northern Sudan, and *Ethiopia* was Sub-Saharan Africa which fell into a Western and an Eastern division (the latter including modern Ethiopia). The archaic forms *Ægypt* and *Æthiopia* have been used so that the reader is always reminded of the difference. Ancient *Mauretania* is spelled with a middle *e* not *i*, and *Africa* will normally be designated by its Roman province name (e.g. *Africa Proconsularis, Africa Nova*) or some other indication of its locality. The area of Libya focused on in this book is the space between the Carthaginian and Egyptian homelands, although this is one portion of ancient Libya as a whole. Where the continent of Libya (i.e. Africa) is intended, it should usually be clear from the context.

For the reader

Because of the many references to places, people and things about whom little is now known, there are two glossaries at the back. One is a **Glossary of technical terms**, another a full **Glossary of names**, which doubles as the index. Words which are in the glossary of technical terms are marked with an asterisk in the text (*).

Because of the apparent random order of passages, readers who are seeking information on specific themes may find assistance in the **thematic index**, although it is impossible to be exhaustive. Readers seeking more of the same from classical authors will find a list of **suggestions for further reading** and an **index of extracts** to the passages included here. There is also a **list of other references** to Libyan matters in these ancient authors, and in a handful of others, which have not been included in the text.

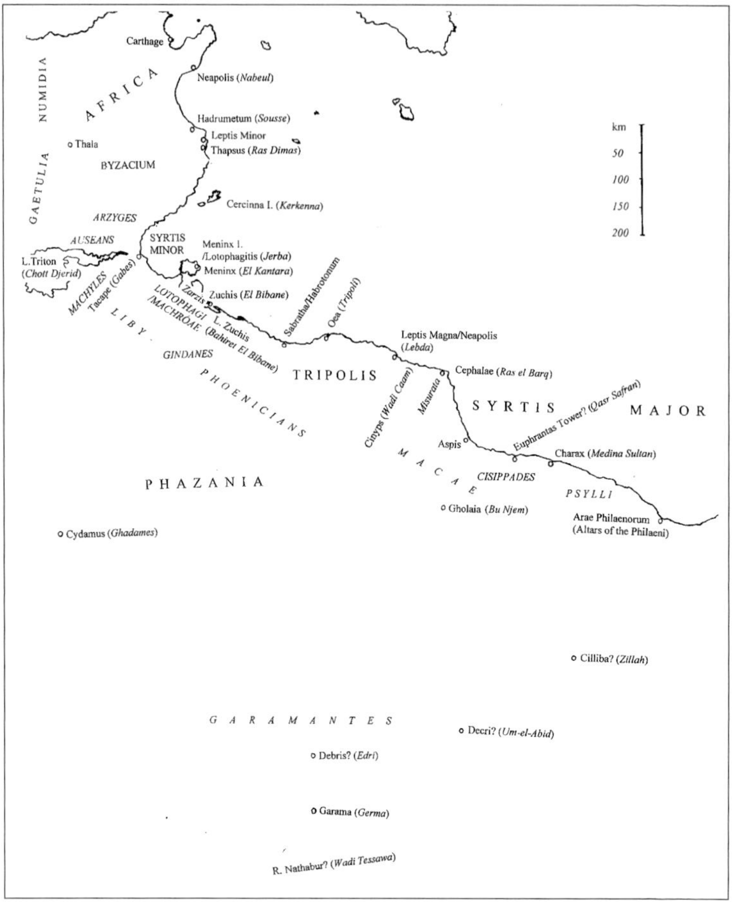

Fig. 2 (above) Map 1: Africa, Tripolis and Phazania. Note that tribal designations are approximate as they could vary over the centuries.

Fig. 3 (top right) Map 2: Cyrenaica and Ægypt.

Fig. 4 (bottom right) Map 3: Tripolis (detail).

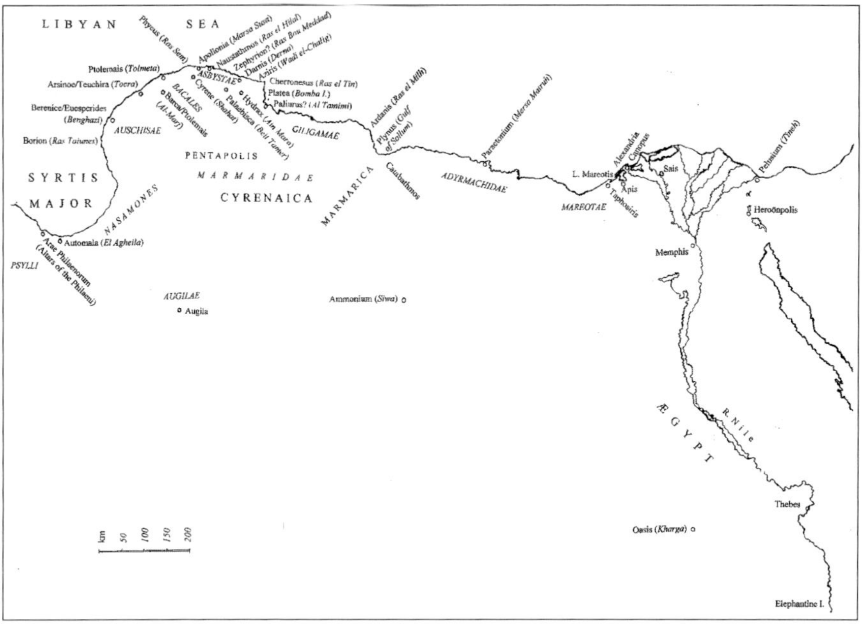
LIBYAN SEA
Phycus (Ras Sem)
Apollonia (Marsa Susa)
Naustathmos (Ras el Hilal)
Zephyrion? (Ras Bou Meddad)
Darnis (Derna)
Aziris (Wadi el-Chalig)
Ptolemais (Tolmeta)
Arsinoe/Teuchira (Toera)
Berenice/Euesperides (Benghazi)
Borion (Ras Taiunes)
ASBYSTAE
Cherronesus (Ras el Tin)
Platea (Bomba I.)
Paliurus? (Al Tamimi)
BACALES
Barca/Ptolemais (Al-Marj)
Cyrene (Shahat)
Palaebisca (Beit Tamer)
Hydrax (Ain Mara)
AUSCHISAE
GILIGAMAE
Ardanis (Ras el Milh)
Plynus (Gulf of Sollum)
Catabathmos
PENTAPOLIS
MARMARIDAE
CYRENAICA
MARMARICA
SYRTIS MAJOR
NASAMONES
Automala (El Agheila)
Arae Philaenorum (Altars of the Philaeni)
PSYLLI
AUGILAE
Augila
Ammonium (Siwa)
Paraetonium (Mersa Matruh)
ADYRMACHIDAE
MAREOTAE
L. Mareotis
Alexandria
Canopus
Apis
Taphosiris
Sais
Pelusium (Tineh)
Heroönpolis
Memphis
ÆGYPT
R. Nile
Thebes
Oasis (Kharga)
Elephantine I.
km 50 100 150 200

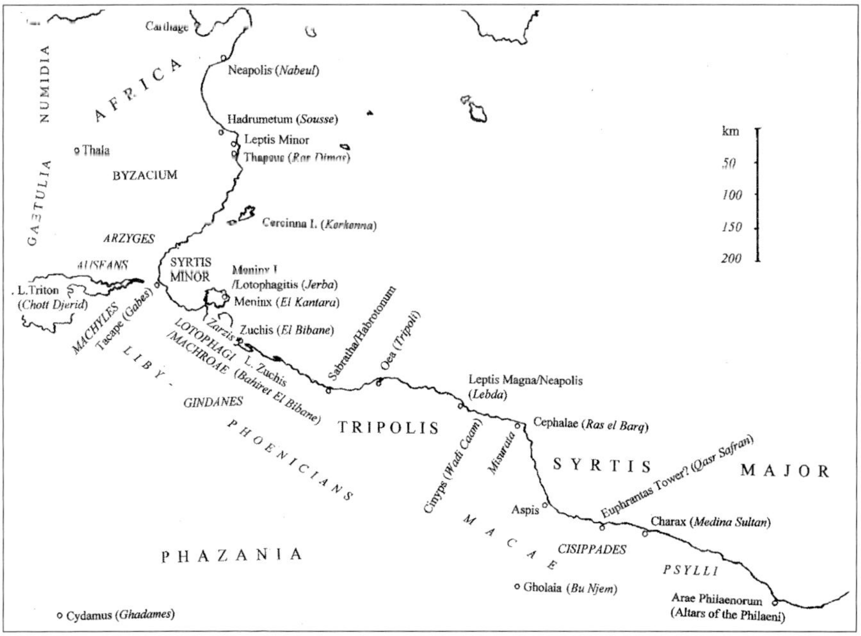
Carthage
NUMIDIA
AFRICA
Neapolis (Nabeul)
Hadrumetum (Sousse)
Leptis Minor
Thapsus (Ras Dimas)
Thala
BYZACIUM
GAETULIA
Cercinna I. (Korkenna)
ARZYGES
AUSEANS
SYRTIS MINOR
Meninx I./Lotophagitis (Jerba)
Meninx (El Kantara)
L.Triton (Chott Djerid)
MACHYLES
Tacape (Gabes)
Zarzis
Zuchis (El Bibane)
LOTOPHAGI /MACHROAE
L. Zuchis (Bahiret El Bibane)
LIBY-PHOENICIANS
GINDANES
Sabratha/Habrotonum
Oea (Tripoli)
Leptis Magna/Neapolis (Lebda)
Cephalae (Ras el Barq)
TRIPOLIS
Cinyps (Wadi Caam)
Misurata
SYRTIS MAJOR
Euphrantas Tower? (Qasr Safran)
Aspis
Charax (Medina Sultan)
MACAE
CISIPPADES
PSYLLI
Gholaia (Bu Njem)
Arae Philaenorum (Altars of the Philaeni)
PHAZANIA
Cydamus (Ghadames)
km 50 100 150 200

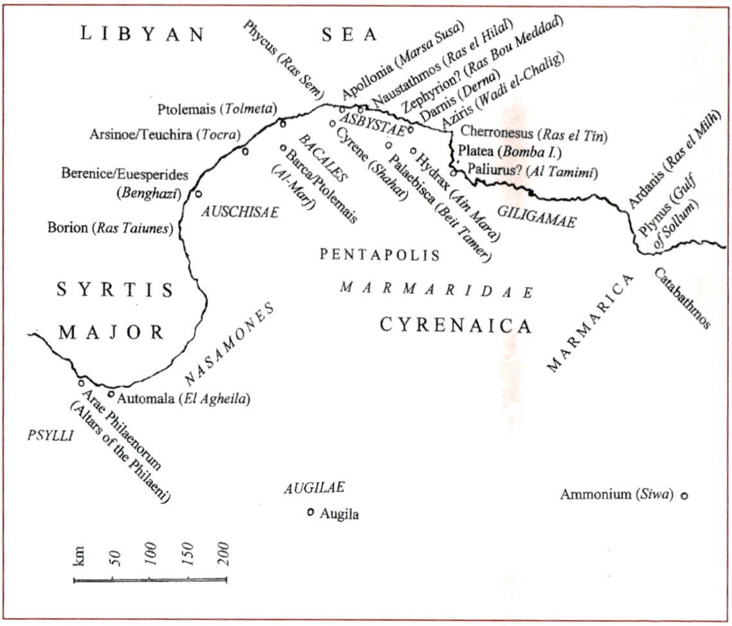

Fig. 5 Map 4: Cyrenaica (detail).

EIGHTH TO THIRD CENTURIES BC

HOMER

Western literature is traditionally considered to begin, fully developed, with Homer, one of the greatest of poets. His birthplace and dates have been the subject of debate for the best part of three millennia but contemporary scholarship is inclined to put the writing of his works in the eighth century BC, although it is almost certain that they were composed orally some time earlier. The *Iliad* describes episodes in the later stages of the War of Troy; the *Odyssey* recounts the troubled return of Odysseus from that war to his home in Ithaca.

The two extracts below, both from the *Odyssey*, describe (1) how Menelaus, king of Sparta, having been driven off course on his way home from the Trojan War, wanders in Libya, among other places; and (2) how Odysseus, also on his return journey, is blown off course and finally arrives in the Land of the Lotophagi (or Lotus-Eaters), traditionally associated with the Libyan coast. There has been much discussion over the centuries as to what the lotus fruit may have been, without any firm conclusions, but, if real, it may have been the jujube.

Such passages hint at an increased trade and contact between the Eastern Mediterranean civilisations and the Libyans in the first half of the first millennium BC.

1 Menelaus's wanderings bring him to Libya

I wandered over to Cyprus, Phoenicia and even to Ægypt; I went to the Æthiopians and the Sidonians and the Erembians; and to Libya where the lambs grow horns as soon as born and the ewes give birth three times in the course of the year.[1] There neither king nor shepherd wants for cheese or meat, or sweet milk either, for the sheep yield milk all the year round.

2 Odysseus in the Land of the Lotus-Eaters

For nine days I was borne along from there by destructive winds on the fish-infested sea, but on the tenth we reached the Land of the Lotus-

1 Many ancient authorities commented on these statements. See, for example, Aristotle below.

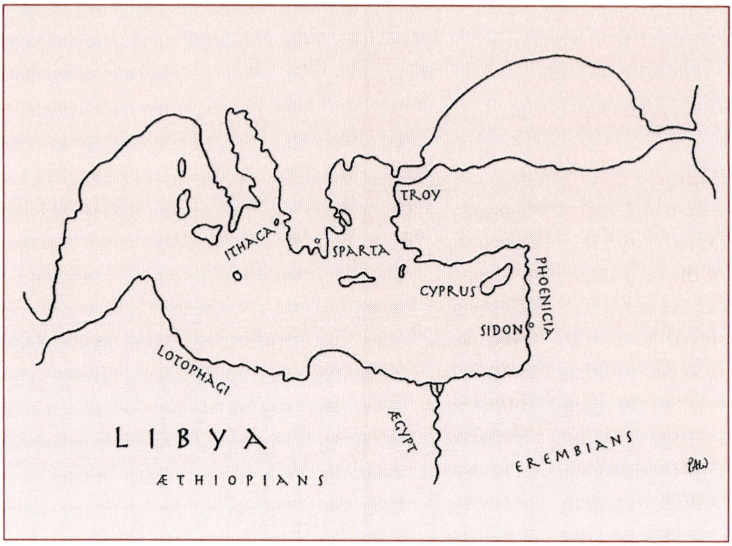

Fig. 6 Map 5: The World according to Homer.

Eaters, who eat a food from a kind of flower. There we disembarked to draw water and our crews had a meal by the swift ships. When we had eaten and drunk I sent some of my company to find out what men – who eat bread – there might be there. I detailed two men, with a third as herald.

They went at once and soon mingled with the Lotus-Eaters who had no thought of killing my comrades but gave them lotus to eat. Those who ate the honey-sweet fruit of the lotus lost any wish to bring back news or return home but wanted to stay there with the Lotus-Eaters, feeding on lotus, and to forget all about their return home.[2]

Though they wept, I brought them back to the hollow ships by force, and dragged them under the benches and bound them fast; and then I commanded the rest of my comrades, who were trustworthy, to embark with speed on the swift ships for fear that some of them might eat lotus and forget about going home. So they went on board at once, took their places at the tholes* and, in due order, struck the grey sea with their oars.

2 Herodotus 6, Pliny 10 and Athenaeus below say that the Lotus-Eaters also made wine from the lotus, which may have held more attractions for Odysseus's sailors than the fruit alone.

PINDAR

Born in Cynoscephalae, a village in Boeotia, probably in 518 BC, Pindar was to be hailed by many as Greece's finest lyric poet, mainly for his famous odes dedicated to victors in the various religious sporting festivals of the Greek calendar.

The Pythian Games in honour of the god Apollo were held at Delphi, site of his oracle. In 462 BC a team sent by king Arcesilaus IV of Cyrene won the chariot race and Pindar wrote his longest poem *(Pythian IV)* in celebration. Much of the poem is an excuse to present the legend of Jason and the Argonauts, but the opening concerns the founding of Cyrene. Pindar's version is given in preference to Apollonius Rhodius's lengthier telling of the legend.

In a culture where cities regularly spawned colonies, foundation myths were important. Pindar is here giving a history of Cyrene and its ancestral link to Euphemus, one of the heroes on the *Argo*, the legendary vessel which made Greece's first overseas expedition and was the first Greek ship to land in Libya. In addition, the mention of the sorceress Medea of the land of Colchis (the *Argo*'s destination), who was a healer, hints at Cyrene's destiny in supplying silphium, an important ingredient in ancient medicine; and Poseidon, god of the sea and father of Eurypylus who welcomed the Argonauts to Libya, was also god of horses, for which Cyrene was famous, as this sporting victory attested. Arcesilaus, descendant of Cyrene's founder, is celebrated and flattered and, at the end of the poem, asked to take back to Cyrene an exile, Damophilus, who may have commissioned the poem.

In the extract below Medea declares that had Euphemus been able to take a clod of earth (a symbol of sovereignty), offered in Libya as a gift for visitors, to his home near Cape Taenarum, Greeks would have colonised Libya sooner than they did when they eventually founded Cyrene from Thera where the clod washed up.

The same victory is also celebrated in Pindar's *Pythian V.* Telesicrates of Cyrene's victory in the race in armour at the Pythian Games of 474 BC is the subject of *Pythian IX*, which gives the legend of the girl Cyrene which is also told by Callimachus (1).

The history of the founding of Cyrene can be found in Herodotus 4, and the *Argo*'s time in Libya is also mentioned in Herodotus 6.

Cyrene's destiny

FOR ARCESILAUS [IV] OF CYRENE, WINNER IN THE CHARIOT RACE

Today, Muse, you must stand beside a friend, the king of Cyrene of good horses, so that when Arcesilaus has his triumph you may swell the gale of songs due to Leto's children and to Pytho where once the priestess who sits beside the gold eagles of Zeus, when Apollo was not absent, ordained that Battus would be leader of fruitful Libya and that he should straight away leave the holy island to found a city of fine chariots on a white breast of the earth and to fulfil in the seventeenth generation the word of Medea spoken at Thera, which the queen of the Colchians, the bold child of Aeëtes, breathed from immortal lips. This she spoke to the demigods sailing with Jason the warrior:

'Hear, O sons of high-hearted men and gods. I tell you that from this sea-beaten land the daughter of Epaphus shall one day be planted with a root to give rise to cities of renown at the place where Zeus Ammon was founded. Instead of short-finned dolphins they shall take swift horses, and instead of oars they shall ply reins and storm-footed chariots. That clod of earth, offered as a guest-gift by a god in the likeness of a man, which Euphemus, alighting from the prow at the outflow of Lake Triton, once took, and Father Zeus, son of Cronus, confirmed with a peal of thunder, will bring to pass that Thera shall become mother-city of mighty cities.

'When he came upon us we were hanging the bronze-jawed anchor, swift *Argo*'s bridle, against the ship. By my counsel we had drawn up our sea-timbers ashore and for twelve days we had borne it from Ocean across ridges of desert land. The solitary god then appeared, having donned the radiant semblance of a venerable man, and he began friendly words, as well-meaning men do when first offering strangers a meal. But the excuse of our sweet way home did not permit us to stay. He said that he was Eurypylus, son of the immortal Holder and Shaker of Earth, and he understood that we were in a hurry. Straight away he took a clod of earth in his right hand, willing to offer whatever guest-gift he could. Nor did the hero refuse it but leapt on the shore and pressing hand into hand he took the divine clod of earth.

'But I hear that it was washed off the ship into the sea by a wave in the evening, borne by the watery deep. Often indeed did I bid the servants, who lighten our labours, to keep it safe but their minds forgot and now the immortal seed of spacious Libya has been dispersed upon this island before the appointed time. For if the royal son of Poseidon, ruler of horses, whom Europa, Tityus's daughter, bore on Cephisus' banks, had

Fig. 7 Coin of Cyrene bearing an image of Nike, the goddess of victory, in a chariot.

come home to holy Taenarum and cast it beside the subterranean mouth of Hades, then the blood of the fourth generation of our sons after him would have taken that wide continent with the Danaans, for then they would have set out from great Lacedaemon, from the Gulf of Argos and from Mycenae. But now, lying with foreign women, he will gain a chosen race who, blessed by the gods, will come to this island and beget a man to be lord of the dark-clouded plains. When later he goes down to the shrine at Pytho, Phoebus, in his house full of gold, will admonish him by oracles to convey many men in ships to the land of the son of Cronus that is fertile from the Nile.'

Medea's words ran thus and the godlike heroes bowed their heads, silent and motionless, listening to her wise counsel. O happy son of Polymnestus, it was you the oracle of the Delphic Bee foretold in these words, exalted with spontaneous cry, three times bidding you hail and revealing you to be the destined king of Cyrene, when you were asking what help there would be from the gods for your stammering tongue. And even now, later in time, as in the bloom of red-blossomed spring, the eighth generation flourishes in Arcesilaus. To him Apollo and Pytho have given glory in chariot racing from the hands of the Amphictyons. I shall for my part commend to the Muses him and the all-golden fleece of the ram, for the Minyans sailed to find it when the god-given honours of their house were planted.

HERODOTUS of Halicarnassus

Herodotus was dubbed 'the Father of History' by Cicero. His *Histories (Historiae)*, an account of the wars between Persia and Greece, is the first significant Greek work in prose. Not merely a history, his book is full of geographical and anthropological digressions that make fascinating, if meandering, reading.

Herodotus was born at Halicarnassus in Caria (now Bodrum in Turkey) in 484 BC, according to Aulus Gellius. He lived at Samos and Athens and died at the Greek colony of Thurii in Southern Italy some time in the 420s BC. It seems he recited some of his *Histories* at Athens in 445, to much acclaim.

During his life, which coincided with the greatest period of Greek history, he travelled extensively throughout the Eastern Mediterranean, visiting Ægypt (probably via Cyrene), Asia Minor, Syria and Eastern Europe. His curiosity about the cultures of his age and the geography of the world were partly what encouraged his travelling, and the stories he heard form an important part of his book, although some of the more unlikely sounding ones have long branded him the 'Father of Lies' (Plutarch's criticism *On the Malice of Herodotus*, for example, is still extant); furthermore, his lack of condemnation of foreign practices led to his being called a 'philobarbarian'.

Herodotus's integrity has, however, been reviving of late, especially as he himself will often state that his source is hearsay and he cannot vouch for it. (Take the first extract, for example: Herodotus hears from some Cyrenaeans that the king of the Ammonians once met some Nasamonians who knew some young men who sent some of their number deep into the interior of Africa. Herodotus's sources may or may not be reliable, but he is reporting the story transmitted by them because it may help to draw conclusions about the source of the Nile.)

Herodotus is our most significant contributor and is here allowed to speak for himself with the minimum of comment. Many other authors here have relied on him as a source.

1 *Nasamonian explorers and the Libyan Nile*

The course of the Nile, then, is known not only in Ægypt but as far beyond it as a four months' journey by land or water, for calculation shows that it takes that time to travel from Elephantine to the land of the Deserters. At that point the river flows from the west and the setting sun. Beyond this, no-one has knowledge of its course with certainty, for that country is uninhabited because of the heat.

I did, however, hear a story from certain men of Cyrene who told me that they had gone on a visit to the oracle of Ammon and that, in the course of a conversation with Etearchus, king of the Ammonians, they came to the subject of the Nile and how no-one knew its source. Etearchus told them that some Nasamonians had once come to him (these are a Libyan people who inhabit the Syrtis and the country a little to the east of the Syrtis). When the Nasamonians were asked if they could give any information concerning the uninhabited parts of Libya, they told him that there had grown up among them certain licentious young men, sons of their chieftains, who, when they had come to manhood, planned all sorts of wild adventures. Among other things they chose five of their number by lot to explore the deserts of Libya and try to see if they could penetrate further than anyone had done before.

The whole coast of Libya along the sea to the north, from Ægypt to Cape Soloeis, which is the end of Libya, is inhabited by many tribes of Libyans, except for that portion which is possessed by Greeks and Phoenicians. In the region away from the sea and the inhabited coast, Libya is

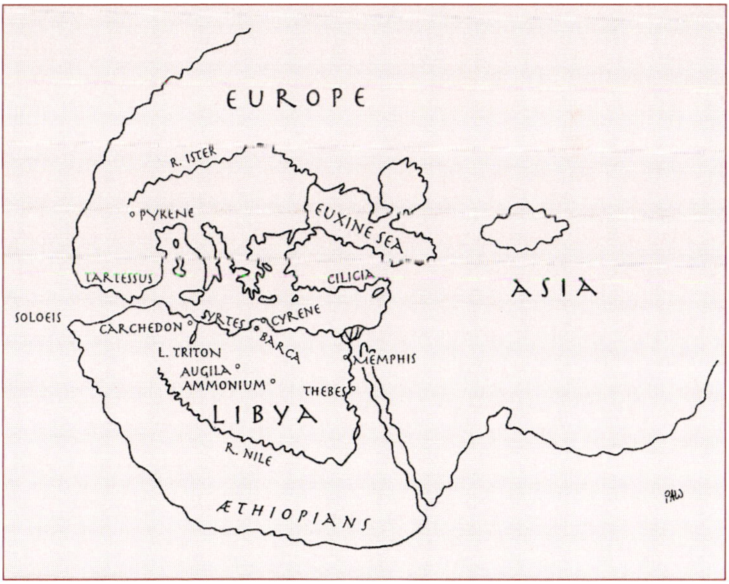

Fig. 8 Map 6: The World according to Herodotus.

full of wild beasts; and further inland than the wild beast region there is a sandy desert, entirely waterless and lifeless.

The story, then, was that the young men, sent off by their companions with a good supply of water and provisions, travelled first through the inhabited region and, passing this, they came to the region of wild beasts. Then they made their way through the desert, which they proceeded to cross towards the west. After crossing over a wide extent of sand for many days they at last saw trees growing in a plain. They approached to pick the fruit on the trees and as they were doing this they were attacked by little men of a stature shorter then average, who seized them and carried them off. The Nasamonians could not understand these men's language nor could they understand the Nasamonians. They were led through vast marshes and, having crossed these, they came to a town where all the people were the same height as their captors, and black in colour. A great river, in which crocodiles could be seen, flowed past the town from the west towards the sunrise.

I have said enough about the story told by Etearchus the Ammonian, except to add that he said that the Nasamonians returned home – as the men of Cyrene told me – and that the people whose country they had reached were all sorcerers.

Respecting the river which ran past their town, Etearchus supposed it to be the Nile, and reason prefers that view.[1] For the Nile flows from Libya and divides it in the middle; and, judging the unknown from the known, I conclude that it rises at the same distance from its mouth as the Ister [the Danube] does. For the River Ister has its source in the country of the Celts [i.e. Western Europe] and the city of Pyrene and flows through the middle of Europe, dividing it in two. [...] The Ister, then, flows through the whole of Europe and ends in the Euxine Sea [the Black Sea]. As it flows through country that is inhabited, its course is well known; but no-one can say anything about the source of the Nile, for Libya, through which it flows, is uninhabited and desert. All that I could possibly learn about its course by inquiry I have stated here. It enters into Ægypt. Ægypt lies more or less opposite the mountainous part of Cilicia, from where it is a five days' journey for a man travelling light by direct route to Sinope on the Euxine, and Sinope lies opposite the place where the Ister falls into the sea. I reckon, therefore, that the course of the Nile as it traverses the whole of Libya is equal in length to the Ister.

I have now said enough about the Nile.

1 The river could not have been the Nile but may have been the Niger.

2 Why Zeus Ammon has horns

The Thebans, and those who follow their practice, give the following origin for their custom of abstaining from sacrificing sheep. Heracles, they say, wished above all things to look upon Zeus but Zeus did not want to be seen by him. Heracles persisted and in the end Zeus devised a plan. He skinned a ram and cut off its head and covered himself in the fleece and showed himself to Heracles thus. This is why the Ægyptians give images of Zeus the head of a ram. The practice has passed from the Ægyptians to the Ammonians who are joint Ægyptian and Æthiopian colonists and speak a language combined from both of theirs. Since the Ægyptian name for Zeus is *Amun*, it seems to me that the Ammonians also got their name from it.[2]

Fig. 9 Ammon, a bearded god with the horns of a ram, based on a Greek marble bust.

3 Libyan episodes in the Persian invasion of Africa

Cambyses laid siege to Memphis and after a while it surrendered. The neighbouring Libyans were alarmed by what had happened in Ægypt and gave themselves up without resistance, agreeing to pay tribute and sending him gifts. The people of Cyrene and Barca, having the same fear as the Libyans, did likewise. Cambyses received the gifts of the Libyans favourably, but was displeased with the gifts from Cyrene; I suppose they were considered too little – the Cyrenaeans has sent only 500 silver minae[3]. He snatched the money with his own hands and scattered it among his army. […]

2 This story probably reverses the true relationship with a Libyan ram-headed god, and has later been associated with Zeus.

3 It is impossible to give an exact equivalent in modern currency but this would have been about a day's pay for 100,000 servicemen, which probably explains Cambyses' reaction since Herodotus says that the detachment sent to attack Ammonium alone numbered 50,000, although this number is improbably high.

After this Cambyses planned three military expeditions: one against the Carthaginians, another against the Ammonians, and the third against the long-lived Æthiopians who dwelt in Libya near the Southern Sea [the Indian Ocean]. [...]

When he had come to Thebes on his march, he detached about 50,000 men from his army and ordered them to reduce the Ammonians to slavery and burn down the oracle of Zeus. Then he himself went on towards Æthiopia with the rest of his forces. [...]

Those he sent to march against the Ammonians started from Thebes with guides and it is known that they reached the town of Oasis [Kharga], which belongs to Samians said to be of the Aeschrionian tribe, seven days' journey across the sand desert from Thebes. This place is called the Island of the Blessed in Greek. It is said that the army came as far as this but no one can report anything further of them, except the Ammonians and those who heard it from them. They neither reached the Ammonians nor ever came back. But the Ammonians themselves say about this that when the men left Oasis and marched across the sand and had reached about midway between Oasis and themselves, while they were having their breakfast a powerful and violent wind arose from the south, burying them in the heaps of sand it was bearing along, so that they disappeared completely.[4] This is what became of this army, according to the Ammonians.

4 *The Greeks colonise Libya*

They say Grinnus, the son of Aesanius, a descendant of Theras and king of the island of Thera, went to Delphi, bringing a hecatomb* on behalf of his city. He was accompanied by other citizens, among them Battus, son of Polymnestus, a member of the Minyan family of the Euphemides. When Grinnus, king of the Theraeans, consulted the oracle about various matters, the Pythian priestess gave him an answer that he should found a city in Libya. 'Lord,' he replied, 'I am too old and too inactive to undertake this. Command one of these younger men instead,' and as he spoke he pointed to Battus. For the time being, nothing further happened. When they had returned, they ignored the oracle as they did not know where Libya was and did not dare to send a colony out into the unknown.

After this, no rain fell on Thera for seven years and all but one of the trees on the island withered. The Theraeans again sent to Delphi and the Pythian priestess reminded them of the colony they had to send to

4 Seneca 2 discusses this event in scientific terms.

Libya. So since there was no other solution to their plight, they sent messengers to Crete to inquire whether any Cretan or foreigner living there had ever travelled to Libya. In their wanderings about the island, the messengers came to the town of Itanus where they met a fisher of murex* named Corobius who told them that he had once been blown off course by winds to Libya, to an island called Platea. They hired this man and took him with them to Thera. A small party sailed from Thera to reconnoitre. Guided by Corobius to the island of Platea, they left him there with provisions for a specific number of months, and sailed back with all speed to bring news of the island to the Theraeans. But they were away for longer than the time they had agreed upon and Corobius had no provisions left when a Samian ship bound for Ægypt, whose captain was Colaeus, was driven off course to Platea. The Samians heard the whole of Corobius's story, left him enough food for a year, then, anxious to voyage to Ægypt, they sailed from the island, but an easterly wind drove them off course and did not abate until they had passed through the Pillars of Heracles [Straits of Gibraltar] and by some guiding providence came to Tartessus. This trading entrepôt had not yet been exploited at that time. Consequently they returned home having made a greater profit on their cargo than any Greeks of whom we have accurate knowledge, except Sostratus of Aegina, son of Laodamas – no-one can compare with him. The Samians took the tenth part of their profits, amounting to six monetary talents,* and made a bronze vessel shaped like an Argive wine-bowl with gryphons' heads projecting round the rim. This they placed as an offering in the temple of Hera, supported upon three colossal kneeling figures in bronze seven cubits high [3 m]. The help given to Corobius by the Samians was the origin of the close friendship between the Cyrenaeans and Theraeans and the Samians.

When the Theraeans who had left Corobius on the island reached Thera, they announced that they had established a settlement on an island off Libya. The Theraeans resolved to send men from all their seven districts to join the colony, one of every two brothers to be chosen by lot to go, and Battus was to be their leader and king. So they manned two penteconters* and sent them to Platea.

This is what the Theraeans say. In the sequel of the story the Theraean and Cyrenean accounts agree, but concerning Battus the Cyrenaeans tell a completely different story from the Theraeans. They tell it thus.

There is a town in Crete called Oaxus over which Etearchus ruled as king. He had a daughter named Phronime whose mother had died, so he married a second wife who had no sooner entered his house than she thought fit to be a proper stepmother to Phronime, ill-treating her and contriving all manner of nastiness against her. At last she accused her of lewd conduct and persuaded her husband to believe that the charge was true. Convinced by his wife, he devised a most sinful thing against his daughter. Living at Oaxus there was a Theraean merchant, Themison. Etearchus made this man his guest and friend [by formal declaration] and got him to swear an oath that he would do him whatever service he requested. As soon as Themison had taken the oath Etearchus fetched his daughter and, putting her into his hands, he told him to take her away and throw her into the sea. Themison was very angry at being deceived by oath in this way and renounced his friendship and then, to free himself of the obligation under which the oath had laid him, he sailed away with the girl. When on the open sea he tied a rope about her, lowered her down into the sea, drew her up again and sailed with her to Thera.

There a distinguished Theraean man, Polymnestus, took Phronime and made her his concubine. In due course, she bore him a son who stammered and spoke with a lisp. According to the Theraeans and Cyrenaeans, the boy was given the name Battus ['Stammerer']. However, I imagine that he was given some other name[5] and changed it to Battus after coming to Libya because of the words spoken to him by the oracle at Delphi and the honourable office which he held, for the Libyans call a king *battus*; and this, I think, is why the Pythian priestess called him this in the Libyan language in her prophecy: she knew that he was to be a king in Libya. For when he had grown to manhood, he went to Delphi to consult the oracle about his speech defect and the Pythian priestess gave him this answer to his question:

> 'Battus, you come for a voice, but Phoebus Apollo
> Sends you to Libya, nourisher of flocks, to found a colony',

just as if she had said in Greek, 'O King, you come for a voice ...'. He replied, 'O Lord, I did come for advice about my speech but you have spoken of other matters, bidding me to colonise Libya, something impossible. How shall I get the power or the men?' This is what he said, but the god was not persuaded to give him any other response, and when he found that the same answer was given as before, he left her still speaking and returned to Thera.

But afterwards both he and the rest of the Theraeans continued to suffer bad luck and, ignorant of the cause of their misfortunes, they sent to Delphi to inquire about their present difficulties. The Pythian priestess replied that things would go better for them if they would join Battus

5 Some writers, as in Callimachus 1, called him Aristoteles.

in founding a settlement at Cyrene in Libya. At this, the Theraeans sent Battus off with two penteconters.* [*The Cyrenean and Theraean accounts now converge.*] He and his men sailed to Libya but, not knowing what to do, they returned to Thera. The Theraeans, however, shot at them as they came to land and would not allow them ashore and ordered them to sail back. So, compelled to do so, they settled on an island off the Libyan coast which, as I have already said, is called Platea. The island is said to be the same size as the city of the Cyrenaeans is now.

They lived here for two years but, as nothing went right for them, leaving one man behind, the rest sailed to Delphi to enquire of the oracle, stating that although they were living in Libya, they were no better off than before. Then the Pythian priestess gave this reply:

> 'Do you know Libya, nourisher of flocks, better than I who have been there
> When you have not? Then I wonder greatly at your wisdom.'

When Battus and his men heard this, they sailed back again for it was plain that the god would not let them off until they colonised Libya itself. Calling at the island and taking the man whom they had left there, they made a settlement on the mainland of Libya opposite the island at a place called Aziris [Wadi el Chalig]. It is enclosed on both sides by the most beautiful valleys and a river flows on one side of it.

They lived here for six years but in the seventh the Libyans persuaded them to leave, saying they would lead them to a better place. So the Libyans moved them from their settlement and led them towards the west, so calculating the timing of the journey that the Greeks would not see the best district in the country, called Irasa, as they passed through it in the night. They brought them to a spring called the Fountain of Apollo and said to them: 'Greeks, here is the right place for you to settle, for here there is a hole in the sky [i.e. it rains].'

5 *Cyrene under the Battiad dynasty*

During the lifetime of Battus [I], the founder of the colony, who ruled for forty years, and of his son Arcesilaus [I], who ruled for sixteen, the Cyrenaeans living there remained the same in number as the original settlers. But in the reign of the third king, Battus [II], called the Fortunate, the Pythian priestess urged all the Greeks to sail to Libya to live with the Cyrenaeans, for the Cyrenaeans invited them to share in a distribution of land. This was the oracle:

'He who comes to lovely Libya too late for the division of land
Will regret it one day, I predict.'

So a great multitude gathered together in Cyrene, and the neighbouring Libyans found themselves cut off from large tracts of their lands. They and their king, Adicran, being robbed of their territory by the Cyrenaeans and their overbearing attitude, sent messengers to Ægypt and put themselves under the rule of Apries the Ægyptian king. He assembled a large army of Ægyptians and sent it against Cyrene. The Cyrenaeans marched out to Irasa and, near the spring called Theste, engaged the Ægyptians and defeated them. The Ægyptians had had no previous experience of Greek fighting and held them in contempt, and thereby were routed so severely that few of them returned home to Ægypt. For this disaster the Ægyptians blamed Apries and revolted against him.

This Battus [II] had a son Arcesilaus [II], who, on becoming king, quarrelled with his brothers until they left him and went to another district of Libya where they founded a city on their own which was then and is still now called Barca [Al-Marj]. While they were establishing it, they persuaded the Libyans to revolt from the Cyrenaeans. Then Arcesilaus made war against the Libyans who had received his brothers and revolted. These Libyans, fearing him, fled to the eastern Libyans. Arcesilaus pursued them until he came to Leucon in Libya where the Libyans resolved to attack him. In the battle, the Cyrenaeans were so comprehensively beaten that as many as 7,000 hoplites* were slain there. After this blow, Arcesilaus fell ill and, after taking some medicine, was strangled by his brother Learchus who in turn was cunningly killed by Arcesilaus's wife, whose name was Eryxo.

The kingship passed to Battus [III], son of Arcesilaus [II], who was lame and walked with a limp. Their misfortunes prompted the Cyrenaeans to send to Delphi to inquire what ordering of their government should best secure prosperity for themselves. The Pythian priestess told them to bring an arbitrator from Mantinea. So the Cyrenaeans sent this request and the Mantineans gave them their most reputable citizen, whose name was Demonax. This man arrived in Cyrene and, after making himself acquainted with all the facts, divided the people into three tribes. The first division consisted of the Theraeans and neighbouring inhabitants, the second of the Peloponnesians and Cretans, and the third of all the islanders. Moreover, he set aside certain lands and priesthoods for the king, Battus, but put all the other things which had belonged to the kings into the hands of the people in common.

During the lifetime of this Battus these arrangements remained in force, but in the reign of his son Arcesilaus [III] there arose a great disturbance about the privileges. For Arcesilaus, son of Battus the Lame and Pheretima, refused to abide by the ordinance of Demonax of Mantinea and demanded the restoration of his ancestral rights. In the civil strife which followed he was defeated and fled to Samos while his mother took refuge at Salamis in Cyprus. At that time Salamis was ruled by Euelthon, the same one who dedicated the remarkable censer* at Delphi, which is in the treasury of the Corinthians. Pheretima came to him and asked him for an army which would restore her back to Cyrene; but Euelthon was willing to give her anything but an army. While she accepted what he gave her, and said that they were fine gifts, it would be better to give her the army she requested. She repeated this every time he presented a gift to her. At last Euelthon sent her a golden spindle and a distaff, with some wool for them. Pheretima again uttered the same words as before; Euelthon replied that these were the gifts suitable for women, not armies.

Meanwhile Arcesilaus was in Samos collecting all the men he could by the promise of grants of land. Having mustered a large army, Arcesilaus sent to Delphi to consult the oracle about his return. The Pythian priestess gave him this answer:

> 'Under the rule of four named Battus and four named Arcesilaus, for eight generations of men, [Apollo] Loxias grants the kingship of Cyrene. He advises you not to attempt ruling beyond this. As for you, return to your country in peace. If you find a kiln full of jars, do not fire the jars but send them away with a fair wind. If you fire the kiln, do not enter the place surrounded by water. If you do, both you yourself and the finest of bulls will die.'

This was the reply given by the Pythian priestess to Arcesilaus.

So he returned to Cyrene with the men from Samos. He retook control of power, forgot the oracle and demanded that his political opponents stand trial for his exile. Some of them left the country for good; others fell into his hands and were sent away to Cyprus to be killed. These last were blown off course to Cnidus where the Cnidians rescued them and sent them off to Thera. Others found refuge in a high tower, the private property of Aglomachus, and Arcesilaus piled wood around the place and burnt them alive. After the deed was done he realised that this was what the Pythian priestess meant when she warned him not to fire the jars if he found them in the kiln. He stayed away from the city of the Cyrenaeans on purpose, fearing the prophesied death and thinking that Cyrene was the place surrounded by water. He had a wife, his blood relation, who was the daughter of the king of the Barcaeans called Alazir, and he went to stay with him. But the men of Barca and some of the exiles from Cyrene sought him out as he frequented the market place and killed him, and his father-in-law Alazir also. So Arcesilaus, whether wittingly or unwittingly, missed the meaning of the oracle and so fulfilled his destiny.

While Arcesilaus was living in Barca after working his own ruin, his mother Pheretima enjoyed his privileges at Cyrene, managing the business of government and taking her seat in the council. But when she heard of her son's death at Barca she fled to Ægypt, for Arcesilaus had done Cambyses, the son of Cyrus, good service – for it was Arcesilaus who had put Cyrene under Cambyses and agreed a rate of tribute. On her arrival in Ægypt, Pheretima presented herself as a suppliant before Aryandes, entreating him to avenge her, claiming that her son had met his death on account of his pro-Mede stance.

This Aryandes had been appointed governor of Ægypt by Cambyses. Later he was put to death for attempting to rival Darius [I]. He had seen and heard that Darius wished to leave a memorial of himself such as no king had ever left before. Aryandes imitated his example till he got his reward. Darius had refined gold to the greatest possible purity and struck coins from it and Aryandes, as ruler of Ægypt, did the same with silver – to this day the purest silver coinage is the Aryandic. But when Darius heard that he was doing this, he had him executed on a different charge, that of rebellion.

But at this time Aryandes took pity on Pheretima and gave her all the Ægyptian forces, on both land and sea. He appointed Amasis, a Maraphian, general of the army and Badres, of the tribe of the Pasargadae, to command the fleet. Before despatching the expedition, Aryandes sent a herald to Barca to inquire who it was who had killed Arcesilaus. The Barcaeans replied that they all took responsibility, for many injuries had been done to them at his hands. When he heard this Aryandes sent his troops with Pheretima. This, then, was the motive which served as a pretext for the expedition, but its real object, I imagine, was the subjugation of Libya. For the races of Libya are many and various and few of them were subjects of the [Persian] king; the great majority cared nothing for Darius.

6 The peoples of Libya

The Libyans inhabit their lands in the following order.

Starting from Ægypt, the first Libyans are the Adyrmachidae. For the most part they follow Ægyptian customs but they dress like the rest of the Libyans. Their women wear a bronze ring on each leg and grow their hair long. When they catch lice on their bodies they bite them back and throw them away. They are the only Libyans to follow this practice and also the only ones that show the king all the young women who are about to be married; whichever of them pleases the king loses her virginity. The Adyrmachidae extend from Ægypt to the harbour called Plynus [Gulf of Sollum].

Next to them are the Giligamae who inhabit the country to the west as far as the island of Aphrodisias. In between lies the island of Platea [Bomba] which the Cyrenaeans settled, and on the mainland is the Port of Menelaus, and Aziris [Wadi el Chalig] where the Cyrenaeans lived. The region of silphium begins here; the silphium extends from the island of Platea to the mouth of the Syrtis [Gulf of Sidra]. The customs of this people are much like those of the others.

Next to the west of the Giligamae are the Asbystae who live inland of Cyrene. The Asbystae do not extend to the sea for the Cyrenaeans inhabit the sea coast. They use four-horse chariots more than any other Libyans and seek to imitate the Cyrenaeans in most of their customs.

Next to the west of the Asbystae are the Auschisae who live inland of Barca and touch the sea at Euesperides [Benghazi]. In the middle of the territory of the Auschisae lives the little tribe of the Bacales who touch the sea near Tauchira [Tocra], a town of the Barcaeans. Their customs are the same as those of the people inland of Cyrene.

Next to the west of the Auschisae are the Nasamonians, a populous tribe, who leave their flocks on the coast in summer and go up country to a place called Augila to gather dates. The palm trees grow in abundance and to a great size there and all of them bear fruit. They hunt locusts which, when caught, they dry in the sun and afterwards grind them and sprinkle the powder on milk and drink it. It is the custom for each man to have many wives; their relations are in common, in a manner resembling the Massagetae. When a staff is set up outside, they are lying together. When a Nasamonian man first marries, it is the custom for the bride to lie with each of the guests in turn on the wedding night and each man

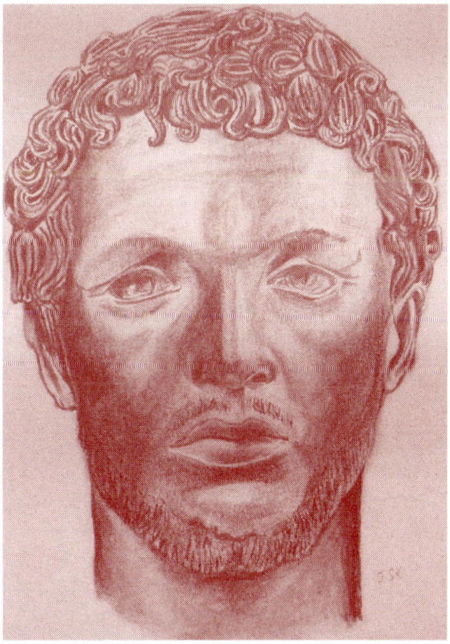

Fig. 10 Head of an African, based on a Greek bronze bust from Cyrene, c. *300 BC.*

then gives her some gift he has brought from home. Their practices in the matter of oaths and divination are as follows. They swear by the men of their country who are reputed to have been most just and best and they lay their hands upon their tombs. For divination they go to the tombs of their own ancestors and, after praying, lie down to sleep and take as oracles whatever dreams come to them. When they make pledges to one another, each drinks from the other's hand; and if they have no liquid available they take dust from the ground and lick it up.

Neighbouring on the Nasamonians are the Psylli who perished in the following way. The south wind blew and dried up the water in their storage cisterns so that the whole country within the Syrtis became waterless. They took counsel and together decided to make war on the south wind (I repeat the story the Libyans tell), and when they reached the desert the south wind blew and buried them. Having been utterly destroyed, the Nasamonians have their land.[6]

Inland towards the south, in the area full of wild beasts, live the Garamantes. They avoid all contact and interaction with men, possess no weapons of war and do not know how to defend themselves.

These live inland of the Nasamonians. The Macae inhabit the sea coast to the west. They cut their hair to the form of a crest, letting it grow in the middle of their heads and shaving it close on either side. In war they carry ostrich skins as shields. The River Cinyps [Wadi Caam], rising from a hill called the Hill of the Graces, flows through their country to the sea. The Hill of the Graces is thickly wooded, unlike the rest of Libya I have described so far, which is bare of trees. It is two hundred stadia [35 km] from the sea.

Fig. 11 The Graces, personifications of kindness, charm and beauty. This relief of the Roman period is from the theatre at Sabratha.

Next to the Macae are the Gindanes whose woman wear many leather anklets. It is said that they put one on for every man they have slept with, and she who wears the most is reputed the best as she has been loved by the most men.

6 See Pliny 8 for more on the Psylli.

Jutting out into the sea from the land of the Gindanes there is a headland [Zarzis Peninsula?] inhabited by the Lotophagi [the Lotus-Eaters] who live entirely on the fruit of the lotus. The lotus fruit is about as big as a mastic berry and has a sweet taste like the fruit of the date palm. The Lotophagi also make wine from it.

Next along the coast to the Lotophagi are the Machyles who also make use of the lotus, but to a lesser extent than the aforementioned people. Their country reaches as far as a great river called the Triton, which empties into the great Tritonian Lake. In this lake is an island called Phla. It is said the Lacedaemonians were advised by an oracle to establish a settlement on the island.

The following story is also told. Jason, when he had finished building the *Argo* at the foot of Mount Pelion, put on board, besides the usual hecatomb,* a bronze tripod and set sail round the Peloponnese so as to get to Delphi. But when he was off Cape Malea a north wind caught him and carried him to Libya where, before he could sight land, he found himself in the shallows of the Tritonian Lake. He was perplexed at finding no way out. Triton, the story goes, appeared to Jason and told him to give him the tripod; in return he would show him the channel and send them safely away. Jason was persuaded and Triton showed him the passage through the shallows and set the tripod up in his own temple. But first he prophesied over it to Jason's companions all these details: that when a descendant of the *Argo*'s crew should carry off the tripod, then, by fate, a hundred Greek cities would be built around the Tritonian Lake. When the indigenous Libyans heard of this prophecy, they hid the tripod.

Next to the Machyles are the Auseans. Both these and the Machyles live round the Tritonian Lake and the River Triton forms the boundary between them. The Machyles let their hair grow long on the backs of their heads, the Auseans in front. They keep an annual festival in honour of Athena at which the young women are divided into two teams and fight each other with stones and cudgels. They say that they are fulfilling the rites in honour of their native goddess, whom we call Athena, that have come down to them from their ancestors. If any young women die of their wounds, they call them 'false maidens'. Before they set them to fight they choose the most beautiful girl and dress her up in a Corinthian helmet and a Greek suit of armour. Then they put her in a chariot and drive in a circuit around the lake. What they dressed their young women with before the Greeks settled near them, I cannot say. I suppose they dressed them in Ægyptian armour for I maintain that both the shield and the helmet came to the Greeks from Ægypt. They say that Athena is the daughter of Poseidon and the Tritonian Lake and that she had some quarrel with her father and gave herself to Zeus who made her his own daughter. They have sexual relations with women in common and do not live together as couples but promiscuously like beasts. When a woman's child is sufficiently grown, the men assemble within three months and the child is assigned to the one whom it most resembles.

I have now described all the nomadic Libyans who live along the coast. Further inland from them is the region of Libya full of wild beasts, and beyond that wild beast region is a ridge of sand stretching from Ægyptian Thebes to the Pillars of Heracles. Along this ridge at intervals of about ten days' journey are hills formed of large lumps of salt and on top of each hill a spring of cold fresh water gushes up from the middle of the salt. Around them dwell people who are furthest towards the desert and inland from the wild beast region.

The first of these, ten days' journey from Thebes, are the Ammonians who have a temple derived from that of Theban Zeus; for the image of Zeus has a head like a ram, as I mentioned before. They have another spring of water besides this one whose water is warm at dawn, cooler at market time and very cold by noon, and it is then that they water their gardens. As the day advances, the coldness abates until, at sunset, the water is warm again. It increases its heat and, bubbling up, it boils as midnight approaches. After midnight passes it gets cooler till dawn. This is called the Fountain of the Sun.

At a distance of ten days' journey along the ridge of sand away from the Ammonians is a hill of salt like the Ammonian one, and water. Men live round about it. This place is called Augila and it is here that the Nasamonians come to gather their dates.

Ten days' journey again from Augila there is another salt hill and water spring and many fruit-bearing date-palms as in the other places, and the people living here are called the Garamantes, a great people who lay soil over the salt and sow their seeds in it. From there is the shortest route – thirty days' journey – to the Lotophagi. Among them are found oxen that walk backwards as they graze. The reason for this is that their horns curve forwards so that they are unable to move forwards seeing that their horns would stick into the ground. In other ways they are like other oxen except for the thickness and toughness of their hides. These Garamantes hunt the Æthiopian Troglodytes in four-horse chariots, for the Æthiopian Troglodytes are the swiftest on foot of any men of whom we have heard any information. The Troglodytes eat snakes and lizards and other such reptiles. Their language is unlike any other on earth – it sounds like the squeaking of bats.

[*Further to the west are the Atarantes and the Atlantes.*]

I am able to tell the names of the inhabitants on the ridge as far as the Atlantes but no further. The ridge extends as far as the Pillars of Heracles and even beyond. There is a salt mine at intervals of ten days' journey, with people living there whose houses are all built of blocks of salt, for no rain falls in these parts of Libya; for if there were rain, the walls of salt could not stand. The salt dug there is both white and purple in colour. Beyond the ridge, towards the south and in the interior of Libya, is a desert, without water, animals, rain, woods or any drop of moisture.

So from Ægypt to the Tritonian Lake the Libyans are nomads who eat meat and drink milk, but they abstain from cows' flesh for the same reason as the Ægyptians, and they do not breed pigs. The women of Cyrene also think it wrong to eat cows' flesh because of the Ægyptian Isis[7] whom they honour both with fasts and with festivals. The Barcaean women abstain from eating pigs as well as cows.

This region is like this. West of the Tritonian Lake the Libyans are no longer nomads nor do they follow the same customs nor treat their children in the way the nomads do. For many of the Libyan nomads – whether all of them I cannot say with certainty – when their children are four years old, burn the veins on their heads, or sometimes those of their temples, with an oily piece of sheep's wool. They do this to prevent them from being troubled for the rest of their lives by phlegm flowing from their heads. They say that this is why they are so healthy. It is indeed true that the Libyans are the healthiest people known to us but whether this is through this practice I cannot say for sure, but they are certainly the healthiest. If convulsions are brought on when they are burning the children, the remedy they have discovered is to treat them by sprinkling with goat's urine. I am only repeating what the Libyans themselves say.

The nomad's sacrificial rites are as follows. They begin by cutting off the ear of the sacrificial victim, and throw it over their house. Having done this, they twist back the victim's neck. They sacrifice only to the Sun and the Moon. This sacrificing is common to all the Libyans but the inhabitants around the Tritonian Lake sacrifice chiefly to Athena and, after her, to Triton and Poseidon.

It was from the women of Libya that the Greeks derived the dress and the aegis* of statues of Athena. For, excepting that the garments of the Libyan women are of leather and that the tassels of their aegises* are made of leather thongs instead of snakes, in everything else it is the same. What is

7 The Ægyptian god Osiris and the goddess Isis, his sister and wife, were represented by the ox and the cow. After Osiris had been murdered by his brother Seth, Isis requested his priests to choose an animal to represent him and to accord it special veneration. The ox was chosen since the god had shown the Ægyptians how to plough with that animal. Isis naturally took the cow as her symbol and, as moon goddess, was often depicted wearing a crown of two cow horns, similar to crescent moons and usually embracing the full moon between them. The Ægyptians accordingly abstained from beef.

more, the name itself shows that the dress of the statues of Pallas came from Libya. For over their dresses Libyan women wear goatskins shorn of hair, with tassels dyed with red madder, and it was from these goatskins [*aegeae*] that the Greeks got their word *aegis*. Furthermore, for my part I think that the ceremonial cry, *ololuge* [like *hallelujah*], also originated there, for Libyan women often make these cries, and very beautifully. And it was from the Libyans that the Greeks learned to yoke together four horses to a chariot.

The nomads bury their dead in the manner of the Greeks, except the Nasamonians. They bury them in a sitting position and take care to make the dying sit up and not let them die lying down on their backs. Their houses are made of asphodel stalks twined around reeds. They can be carried about. Such are the customs of these tribes.

7 Unique fauna

The eastern region of Libya, where the nomads live, is low-lying and sandy as far as the River Triton, but westward of this the land of the cultivators is very mountainous and wooded and full of wild beasts. For this is where huge snakes are found, and lions and elephants, and bears and asps and horned asses [kudu?] and the dog-headed men [baboons?] and the headless men who have their eyes in their chests [gorillas?], at least according to what the Libyans say, and the wild men and wild women [apes?] and a great number of other unfictitious creatures.

None of these are in the nomads' country but there are other animals: white-rumped antelopes, gazelles, *bourbaliës* antelopes, asses – not the horned sort but a different, undrinking, kind (for they do not drink,

Fig. 12 The jerboa, or dipodes (Jaculus jaculus).

in fact) – oryxes whose horns are used for making the curved sides of lyres and whose size is about that of an ox, foxes, hyenas, porcupines, wild rams, *dictyes* and *thoës* [both jackals?], panthers, *boryes* [unknown], land-living crocodiles three cubits long [1.5 m] similar to lizards, ostriches, and little snakes each with a single horn. All these are found here together with those found elsewhere, except for deer and wild boar; deer and wild boar are not found at all in Libya. However, there are three kinds of mice here: one kind is called the *dipodes* ('two-footed') [the jerboa], another the *zeguriës* (which is a Libyan word meaning 'hills' in the Greek language), and the third the *echines* ['bristle-haired']. There are also weasels which are found in the silphium, very like those of Tartessus. This many, then, are the wild animals of the land of the Libyan nomads as far as we have been able to learn by our inquiries.

8 The inhabited and fertile parts of Africa

These are the Libyans we can name and most of them, then as now, cared nothing for the king of the Medes. I can add this much about this country: four nations inhabit it and no more, as far as our knowledge goes, of which two are indigenous and two are not. The Libyans and the Æthiopians are indigenous, the former living in the north and the latter in the south. The Phoenicians and the Greeks, however, are immigrants.

It seems to me that Libya [i.e. Africa] can not be compared for goodness of soil with either Asia or Europe except the Cinyps – the region is called the same name as its river [Wadi Caam]. This region is equal to any land in the world for Demeter's crops, for the soil here is black and well watered by springs. It has no fear of drought nor is it harmed by drinking excessive rain (for it does indeed rain in this part of Libya). The yield of the harvest is the same measure as in Babylonia. The soil is also good in the region inhabited by the Euesperidans; in the best years it yields a hundredfold but the Cinyps yields three hundredfold.[8]

The country of Cyrene, which is the highest of that part of Libya inhabited by nomads, has three remarkable seasons. First, the crops by the sea coast ripen and are ready for harvesting and picking. When these are gathered in, the crops of the middle region above the coast, which they call the Bounoi ('the Hills'), are ripe for gathering. When the crops of this middle country have been harvested, the crops in the highest tract are ripe and ready, so the last harvest comes in by the time the first has all been

8 Herodotus [I, 193] and others noted that the annual corn yields of Babylonia were a remarkable 200–300 times the sowing.

eaten and drunk. Thus the Cyrenaenans have an eight-month harvest. Enough, then, about these matters.

9 *Pheretima's revenge*

When the Persians sent by Aryandes from Ægypt to assist Pheretima arrived at Barca [Al-Marj], they laid siege to the city, demanding the surrender of those who were responsible for the murder of Arcesilaus [III]. But the people as a whole were guilty of the deed and so refused. So they besieged Barca for nine months, digging mines leading to the walls and making violent direct assaults. A metalworker discovered the mines with a bronze shield in this way: carrying the shield round the inner circuit of the walls he tapped it on the ground inside the city. The bronze of the shield rang hollow on the ground over the mines but in other places the shield was dead. Here, therefore, the Barcaeans dug countermines and killed the Persian sappers. That is how the mines were discovered. The Barcaeans beat off the direct assaults.

When much time had passed and many had fallen on both sides, not least the Persians, Amasis, the commander of the land forces, devised a plan. Realising that the Barcaeans could not be conquered by force but that they might be taken by guile, he dug a wide trench by night and laid weak planks over it, which he covered over with earth level with the ground surrounding it. When day came he invited the Barcaeans to talks with him, and they gladly agreed. At length they had an agreement. They swore the agreement over the hidden trench, that their treaty should stand so long as the ground beneath their feet stood firm; the Barcaeans promised to pay a fair sum to the king [of Persia] and the Persians should do no further harm to the Barcaeans. After the oath, the Barcaeans, trusting to it, came out of the city and opened all their gates and let within the walls any of their enemies who wished to enter. But the Persians broke down the hidden bridge and ran into the fortifications. They broke it down so that they might keep the oath which they had sworn to the Barcaeans, that it should stand as long as the ground remained firm. But the bridge was broken; the oath no longer held.

The Barcaeans who were the most guilty were delivered by the Persians to Pheretima, who impaled them round the walls. She cut off the breasts of their wives and placed them round the walls in the same manner. She told the Persians to treat the remainder of the Barcaeans as their booty, except those of the House of Battus and those not accessory to the murder. To these Pheretima entrusted the city.

So the Persians enslaved the rest of the Barcaeans and set off on their way home. When they appeared before the city of Cyrene the Cyrenaeans let them pass through in fulfilment of a certain oracle. As the army was passing through, Badres, the commander of the naval forces, recommended their seizing the city but Amasis, the commander of the land forces, would not consent since they had been sent to take the Greek city of Barca alone. When they had passed through and encamped on the hill of Lycaean Zeus they regretted that they had not taken Cyrene. They attempted to enter it a second time but the Cyrenaeans would not allow them to. Then fear fell upon the Persians even though no-one was fighting them and they fled a distance of sixty stadia [10 km] before they encamped. But, having established the camp, a messenger came from Aryandes ordering them to return home. The Persians asked the Cyrenaeans to give them provisions for the journey and, having obtained them, they departed for Ægypt. But the Libyans then harried them and slew the stragglers for the sake of their clothing and equipment until they came to Ægypt.

The furthest point in Libya this Persian army reached was Euesperides. The Barcaeans taken as slaves were sent from Ægypt to the king, and King Darius gave them a village in Bactria to live in. They gave this village the name Barca and it was still an inhabited place in Bactria down to my own time.

But Pheretima herself did not end her life well, for just after she had taken her revenge on the Barcaeans and returned to Ægypt from Libya, she died a horrible death: her body teemed with worms while she was still alive. Thus the anger of the gods is drawn down upon people whose vengeance is excessively violent.

Such was the great vengeance which Pheretima, descendant of Battus, took on the Barcaeans.

10 A failed colony

Now Cleomenes, it is said, was not right in his mind – indeed he was on the verge of madness – but Dorieus was the leading man among his youthful peers and confidently assumed that he would become king by virtue of his manly qualities. With this disposition of mind Dorieus was indignant when, on the death of Anaxandrides, the Lacedaemonians followed their custom and made the eldest son, Cleomenes, king. Dorieus could not bear to be subject to Cleomenes' rule and asked the Spartans for a body of men and took them away to found a colony. But he neither consulted the Delphic oracle on the land he should go to, nor did anything else that was customary, but he sailed in a rage to Libya with men from Thera as guides. Arriving there, he settled by the River Cinyps [Wadi Caam] in the most beautiful district in Libya, but in the third year he was driven out by the Macae and the Libyans and also the Carthaginians, and returned to the Peloponnese.

THUCYDIDES of Athens

Considered one of the greatest historians, Thucydides lived in the fifth century BC and was a prominent citizen in the great age of Athenian democracy. His *History of the Peloponnesian War* of 431–404 BC was written shortly after the events, often from first-hand knowledge (he was a general in the war).

In this short passage Thucydides describes how Spartan forces bound for the reinforcement of Sicily (414 BC) are unintentionally diverted to Libya by a storm.

Libyan diversion

Meanwhile Gylippus and Sicanus returned to Syracuse. Sicanus had failed to gain Agrigentum because the party friendly to the Syracusans had been driven out while he was still at Gela; but Gylippus brought a large army from Sicily as well as the hoplites* who had been sent in merchant ships from the Peloponnese in the spring and had arrived at Selinus from Libya. They had been driven to Libya by the weather and the Cyrenaeans had given them two triremes* and pilots. On their voyage along the coast they had joined the people of Euesperides [Benghazi] who were being besieged by the Libyans. They defeated the Libyans and sailed on to Neapolis [Nabeul], a Carthaginian market town and the nearest point to Sicily, the voyage taking only two days and one night; there they crossed and came to Selinus.

ARISTOTLE of Stagira

Born in 384 BC, Aristotle became a leading pupil of the great philosopher Plato and, after tutoring the young Alexander the Great, set up the Lyceum in Athens where he lectured on a wide variety of topics. His Peripatetic School, as it became known, was one of the five chief schools of Greek philosophy. His importance gradually waned in antiquity but he had the most profound influence on the Renaissance.

Aristotle's works contain a significant amount of material on the natural world; indeed, he may be regarded as one of the first true scientists. Here are some notes on animals specific to Libya, from his *Historia Animalium (History of Animals)*, which may be compared to similar observations in Herodotus 7 and Pliny 9.

Some characteristics of Libyan animals

Cicadas. Cicadas are not found where there are no trees. This explains why they are not found in the open country in the district of Cyrene but are abundant near the city and especially where there are olive trees because these do not produce much shade. [...]

They lay their eggs in uncultivated land, boring a hole with the pointed organ they have at their rear, as locusts do; for locusts also lay in uncultivated lands, which explains why they are numerous in Cyrene.

Remoras. In the sea between Cyrene and Ægypt there is a fish called the phtheira ['the louse'], which accompanies the dolphin. It gets extremely fat because it enjoys an abundance of food when the dolphin is out hunting.

Absent animals. There were formerly no croaking frogs in Cyrene. In all Libya there is neither wild boar nor stag nor wild goat.

Horned sheep. In Libya, the horned rams are born with horns, and not only the males, as Homer says,[1] but the others, too.

Snakes. In Libya the snakes, so it is said, grow to unimaginable size, for some say that when they sailed there they saw the bones of many oxen

1 Homer, *Odyssey*, IV, 85, which is in the first extract from Homer, above.

Fig. 13 Dolphin, from the theatre at Sabratha.

which had evidently been devoured by snakes and, as they were putting out to sea, the snakes chased their galleys at speed and, overturning one galley, threw some of the crew into the sea.

Variety of Libyan animals. In general, wild animals are fiercest in Asia, those of Europe are the boldest and those of Libya are the most varied in form; in fact, there is a proverb that Libya is always producing something new. For it seems that, through lack of rain, animals of different species meet at the water holes and mate there and produce young if their periods of gestation are the same and if their sizes are not too dissimilar. They become gentle towards each other because of the need to drink. For, contrary to other animals, they want to drink more in winter than in summer for they are not accustomed to drinking in the summer since there is usually no water then. And the mice die if they drink. Other animals are also produced from the mix of different breeds, just as in Cyrene the wolves mate with the dogs and produce young.

Snakebites. The bites of snakes vary greatly. For in Libya is found the asp from which they make a septic drug and which is deadly. In the silphium is also found a small snake for the bite of which the remedy is said to be a certain stone which is taken from the tomb of one of the ancient kings, and they dip it in wine which they drink.

Swan song. Swans are web-footed and live near ponds and marshes. They live easily, have gentle temperaments, care for their young and grow very old. [...] They sing, especially at their deaths, for then they fly out to sea, and people sailing along the coast of Libya have come across many of them on the sea singing in mournful tones and have seem some of them dying.

CALLIMACHUS of Cyrene

Callimachus is the first of our writers to come from Libya and is probably the most famous citizen of Cyrene. Born very late in the fourth century BC (probably no earlier than 305), Callimachus moved from Cyrene to work as a librarian (though never director) of the great library at Alexandria where he compiled a catalogue of the works available there. He is, however, chiefly known as a highly influential poet of exquisite refinement and originality, his many poems characterised by perfect versification and obscure cultural references, including many allusions to his home town. He was at the forefront of the great literary controversy that arose between his 'Alexandrian' school and the epic poets, notably Apollonius Rhodius, as to whether the future of poetry lay in expansive epics or crafted gems. His famous saying 'a big book is a big bore' neatly sums up his view.

The problem for the modern reader, though, is to understand the many allusions that are part of his style. The first passage below, from his *Hymn to Apollo (Hymn II)*, is of interest in explaining the divine inspiration behind the founding of his home city of Cyrene. The text, with its references to many of the local features and practices of Cyrene, is presented here without a commentary as this would be longer than the poem itself. Therefore, readers who seek an explanation for the names will find them in the Glossary. Making the reader look things up is part of Callimachus's aim.

The second poem is a poignant and more intimate epigram describing a tragedy in Cyrene.

1 *Praise the god Apollo, founder of Cyrene*

Men who plan cities follow Phoebus, for Phoebus is always pleased by the founding of cities, and Phoebus himself lays their foundations. Phoebus was four years old when he set up his first foundation in fair Ortygia, near the round lake.

Phoebus also revealed my fertile city to Battus and in the form of a raven, auspicious to our founder, guided his people in Libya and swore to grant city walls to our kings, and Apollo's oath is always true.

O Apollo! Many call you Boedromius, and many Clarius. Everywhere you have many names. But I call you Carneius – this is the usage of my ancestors.

Fig. 14 According to one legend, the city was named after Cyrene, a princess who slew a lion with her bare hands. The event was commemorated in many statues.

Sparta, Carneius, was your first foundation; then second was Thera; but third was the city of Cyrene. From Sparta the sixth generation from Oedipus brought you to the colony of Thera, and from Thera vigorous Aristoteles set you up in the Asbystian land and built you a splendid sanctuary and in the city he established an annual festival where many bulls fall on their haunches for the last time, O Lord.

Hië! *Hië*! Carneius! Much invoked are you. In spring, your altars bear as many flowers as the Horae bring forth in all their colours when the Zephyr breathes dew; and in winter, the sweet crocus. Ever eternal is your fire nor does its ash ever feed on the coals of yesterday.

Phoebus certainly rejoiced greatly when the girded men of Enyo danced with the fair-haired Libyan women when the appointed season of the Carneian festival came round. But the Dorians were not yet able to reach the springs of the Cyre, but lived in Azilis with its thickly wooded vales. The Lord himself saw these and showed them to his bride as he stood on the craggy hill of Myrtussa where Cyrene, the daughter of Hypseus, slew the lion, the destroyer of the cattle of Eurypylus. Apollo has not seen another dance more divine nor, remembering his previous abduction, has he given so many benefits to any city as he has to Cyrene. Nor have the children of Battus honoured any other god more than Phoebus.

2 *A double tragedy at Cyrene*

We buried Melanippus in the morning; and, as the sun sank low,
We did the same for the young girl, Basilo.
She died by her own hand, having no desire
To live, once she'd placed her brother on the pyre.
Aristippus' emptied home thus saw a double woe
And all Cyrene stood with heads bowed low.

FIRST CENTURY BC

LUCRETIUS

Titus Lucretius Caro

Lucretius was most likely a Roman aristocrat, born around 98 BC, who seems to have had the standard legal and political education of his class. His one known work, not quite finished, which was published shortly after his death around 55 BC, is the long didactic poem *De Rerum Natura (On the Nature of Things)*. It is a forceful exposition of Epicurean scientific theory.

Lucretius's style demonstrates a remarkable blend of evidence-based science with poetic imagery and turn of phrase, but suffers from Latin's lack of a scientific vocabulary. His phraseology can be peculiar as a result of this restriction as well as the requirements of his metre.

With regard to the passage below, the reader should bear in mind that Epicureans held that all matter was made up of tiny particles *(atomoi)* which could not be reduced further. Fire grows from specific particles much as plants grow from seeds, and objects radiate particles from their surfaces.

An explanation of the properties of the Fountain of the Sun

There is said to be a spring within the sanctuary of Ammon that is cold by the light of day and warm in the night time. People wonder excessively at this spring and some think that it grows hot from the intense heat of the sun beneath the earth when night has cloaked the earth in dreadful darkness. This is very far removed from true reasoning. In fact, when the sun, touching the exposed substance of the water, has been unable to warm it from the region above – although the light above enjoys such an intensity of heat – how can it, when underneath the earth of a substance so dense, boil the liquid and fill it with warm vapour, especially when it can barely force its radiation through the walls of houses with its burning rays?

What, then, is the reason? Undoubtedly because the earth has a looser texture around the spring than other ground has, and there are many seeds of fire near the body of water. So, when night has covered the earth with its dew-bearing waves, the earth immediately becomes cold within and coalesces. It is for this reason that, as though it were being squeezed in the hand, it forces out into the spring whatever seeds of fire it possesses, which warm the feel of the liquid and the vapour. Then when the risen sun has separated the soil with its rays and has loosened it by mixing in its warming heat, the atoms of fire return again to their former places and all the heat of the water withdraws into the earth. Because of this the spring becomes cold in the light of day.

Besides, the water's fluid is agitated by the rays of the sun and it loses its density in the daylight through the shimmering heat. And so it is that it discharges whatever seeds of fire it is holding, just as it often sheds the cold which it contains within itself and melts its iciness and loosens its bonds.

CATULLUS

Gaius Valerius Catullus

Catullus was one of Rome's foremost lyric poets who combined intense personal feelings with the studied linguistic and metrical skill derived from Callimachus's Alexandrian school of poetry. He is best known for his liaison with a wealthy and intelligent married woman whom he calls Lesbia, but not a great deal else is known of his life: born into a wealthy family from Verona around 84 BC, he knew – and insulted – Julius Caesar, was deeply affected by the death of his brother, and accompanied the governor of Bithynia & Pontus in 57–56 BC, dying a couple of years after his return.

One of his famous and beautiful Lesbia poems is given below because of its Libyan references. It shows typical Alexandrian erudition in the context of a love poem. The juxtaposition here of a request for an infinity of kisses with images of smelly silphium, sweating gods and ancient tombs is a noteworthy example of the style, as are the nonce-words.

Countless kisses

How many kissings, you ask me, my Lesbia,
    Might be enough and to spare?
A number as large as the sandgrains of Libya
    At silphiumacious Cyrene – there
Twixt Jove, sultry and hot, at his shrine
    And Battus's tomb, the old king –
Or as stars in the silence of night that shine
    On mankind's secretive loving.
Kissing kisses so many is our excessive pleasure
    And enough for my mind in its frenzy,
So inquisitive folk cannot count their full measure,
    Nor tongues curse us in their envy.

Fig. 15 Silver drachma coins of Cyrene of the late fifth century BC depicted a silphium seed pod, which was shaped like a heart. Certain ancient beliefs held that the heart was the seat of the emotions and there is some speculation that the design on this coinage may be where the love-heart symbol originates.

SALLUST

Gaius Sallustius Crispus

Sallust, born around 86 BC, became a Roman senator and lived in the lively times that ended the Roman Republic. He held a number of important offices of state and became governor of Africa Nova (formerly the Kingdom of Numidia), from which his interest in North African history may have stemmed. He retired from political life after Julius Caesar's assassination, established his famous villa and gardens in Rome, the Horti Sallustiani, and dedicated his remaining time to writing history. He died in 35 BC.

As well as a history of Rome he wrote two historical monographs, one on the conspiracy of Catiline, the other on the war between Rome and Jugurtha, king of Numidia, in 112–105 BC, which was first circulated around 41 BC.

Numidia, corresponding approximately to Algeria, lies outside the scope of this book, but in places Sallust feels the need to describe the wider geography, environment, peoples and history of the surrounding area. Two passages are of relevance to our part of Libya: the first on the general geography and peoples of North Africa; the other on Leptis Magna, a description of the Syrtes, and the story of the Philaeni. Sallust's account of this last, in which he implies that the Greeks were incompetent or unlucky, is worth comparing with the neutral version of Mela 2 and Valerius Maximus's anti-Carthaginian version.

Sallust's style is terse and his vocabulary somewhat archaic. His geography is poor and he frequently has to admit his ignorance. Nevertheless his works and style were greatly admired in antiquity and influenced other authors.

1 *Africa and its peoples*

My subject seems to call for me to describe the geography of Africa in a few words and to touch upon those peoples with whom we have had wars or alliances, except that these regions and races are seldom visited because of the heat or the rough terrain and also the deserts, so I cannot easily report on these with certainty. Everything else I shall relate in the fewest possible words.

In dividing up the earth's circle the majority reckon Africa as a third part. A few state that there are only Asia and Europe, and that Africa is in Europe. Its boundary in the west is the strait between our sea [the Mediterranean] and the Ocean [the Atlantic]; in the east, a broad slope which the natives call Catabathmos.

The sea is rough and harbourless. The soil is abundant in arable crops, good for livestock, poor for trees. There is a scarcity of water from the sky and on the ground.

The race of men there is healthy in body, fast-running and able to endure exertion. The majority are carried away by old age, save for those killed by the sword or wild animals, for disease rarely overcomes any of them. Add to this the very many dangerous kinds of animals. But I shall relate in the fewest possible words which men originally inhabited Africa and who came subsequently or in what way they mingled amongst themselves, although it is contrary to that tradition asserted by the majority, even though it was translated for me from Carthaginian books which were said to be by King Hiempsal; at any rate the inhabitants of that land themselves think that the events are believable. Still, the truth of the matter will rest with my authorities.

In the beginning, the Gaetulians and Libyans inhabited Africa. They were rude and uncivilised, their food was the flesh of wild animals and they grazed the ground in the manner of cattle. They were governed neither by common usage nor by law or anyone's dominion. Unsettled and nomadic, they had their homes where nightfall forced them to. [...]

[Sallust now relates how Medes, Persians and Armenians who accompanied Hercules to Spain sailed across to Africa after his death and settled in Numidia and Mauretania.]

Moreover, the Libyans joined the Medes and Armenians, for they lived nearer the African Sea – the Gaetulians more to the south, not far from the realms of burning heat – and they soon dwelt in towns. Being separated from Hispania [Spain] only by a strait, they began to barter goods with them. The Libyans gradually corrupted their name, calling the Medes Moors in their own language. [...]

Towards Catabathmos, therefore, which is a place that divides Ægypt from Africa, first along the sea coast is Cyrene, a colony of the Theraeans; and in turn the two Syrtes and Leptis between them; then the Altars of the Philaeni, which place the Carthaginians held to be the frontier of their empire in the direction of Ægypt; then other Punic cities.

2 *Leptis and the Syrtes*

But at the same time as the capture of Thala [108 BC], envoys came to Metellus from the town of Leptis, begging him to send a garrison with a commanding officer there. A certain Hamilcar, a power-hungry man of high birth, was eager for revolution. Neither the authority of their officials nor the laws were effective against him. Unless he hurried there, the safety of these allies of Rome would be in the utmost danger. For the people of Leptis, since the very beginning of the Jugurthine War, had sent word to Bestia the consul,* and afterwards to Rome, to seek friendship and an alliance. Then, when this had been obtained, they always remained conscientious and dependable and had diligently executed all the orders from Bestia, Albinus and Metellus. Therefore they easily obtained what they were seeking from the general. Four cohorts of Ligurians were sent to them with their commander, Gaius Annius.

That town was founded by Sidonians whom I understand to have come to those parts by ship as fugitives because of political disturbances. Besides this, the site is between the two Syrtes whose name is derived from their nature, for they are two gulfs nearly at the furthest end of Africa, unequal in size but alike in their properties. Nearest to the shore they are very deep; elsewhere they are deep or, alternatively, shoals according to the weather, whatever is brought about by chance. For whenever the sea begins to swell and to be aroused by the winds, the waves sweep mud and sand along and even large rocks. In this way the appearance of these places changes in time with the winds. They are called the Syrtes from this sweeping.[1]

It was only the language of that city which changed through intermarriage with the Numidians. Most of their laws and way of life are Sidonian, which they preserved more easily there because they lived far from the king's centre of authority; between them and the populous Numidia there were many desert regions.

3 *The story of the Philaeni*

But since we have come to these parts because of the affairs of the people of Leptis, it seems appropriate to recall the honourable and extraordinary deed of two Carthaginians; the place reminds me of this.

At the time when the Carthaginians were ruling most of Africa, the Cyrenaeans were also great and powerful. The land between them was

1 From the Greek *surein*, to sweep. Probably false etymology.

sandy and uniform in appearance. There was neither river nor mountain which might mark their boundary, a fact which occupied them in great and lengthy war between them. After the armies on both sides had been routed and put to flight many times, and the fleets likewise, and they had considerably weakened each other, fearing that soon another power might attack the victors and the vanquished when both exhausted, they made a solemn promise during a truce that on a certain day envoys should set out from home, and the common frontier of both peoples would be in that place between them where they met.

Accordingly, two brothers sent from Carthage called the Philaeni hastened to proceed with their journey. The Cyrenaeans went more slowly. I do not really know whether this happened from laziness or chance, but in those parts a storm is as likely to cause delay as it would do on the sea. For when the wind has risen through places that are flat and bare of vegetation, it stirs sand up from the ground and when this is in motion it usually fills mouths and eyes with great force. With one's sight thus obstructed, one's journey is delayed.

As soon as the Cyrenaeans saw that they were considerably behind, and feared punishment at home because they had botched the business in hand, they resolved to accuse the Carthaginians of having set out from home before the appointed time, to confuse the issue, and finally to prefer anything than to go away beaten. But when the Carthaginians sought other terms so long as they were fair, the Greeks gave the Carthaginians this choice: either they be buried alive there where they claimed the boundary for their people or else the Greeks would, on the same terms, advance to any place that they wanted. The Philaeni, having agreed the terms, sacrificed their lives for their country; and so they were buried alive. The Carthaginians dedicated altars to the Philaeni brothers on that spot, and other honours to them were established at home.

CORNELIUS NEPOS

Nepos was born in Cisalpine Gaul (Northern Italy), probably at Ticinum (Pavia), around 99 BC and moved to Rome where he spent much of his time writing books on a variety of subjects – mainly history, geography and biography. He was known and admired by the literary circle of his time and Catullus dedicated his collection of poems to him. He died around 24 BC. His only work to survive (and then only in part) was the *De Viris Illustribus (Lives of Illustrious Men)*. These extracts are taken from the short biographies of military men, which were probably first circulated around 35–34 BC.

1 *The priests of Jupiter Ammon take a dim view of Lysander's attempt to bribe them*

And so they resented the ten-man authority established by him. For this reason, inflamed with anger, he drew up plans to abolish the kings of the Spartans. But he understood that he could not accomplish this without the support of the gods, because the Spartans had been accustomed to refer all matters to oracles.

First he tried to bribe the Delphic oracle. When he was unable to do this, he approached Dodona. Rejected from here, too, he stated that he had taken vows which he should fulfil to Jupiter Ammon, reckoning that the Africans would be more easily bribed by him.

When he had travelled to Africa in this hope, the high priests of Jupiter greatly disappointed him, for not only could they not be bribed but they even sent envoys to Sparta to make a complaint against Lysander because he had attempted to bribe the priests of the sanctuary.

Having been arraigned on this charge and acquitted by the verdicts of the jurors, he was sent with auxiliary forces to the Orchomenians and was killed by the Thebans near Haliartus.

2 *Agesilaus dies in Libya and his body is embalmed in an unusual way*

When Agesilaus was returning from Ægypt, having been presented with two hundred and twenty monetary talents* by the Pharaoh Nectanebo, which he was to give to his people as a gift, and had come to a port which is called the Port of Menelaus, situated between Cyrene and Ægypt, he died in the grasp of sickness.

Thereupon his courtiers, so that they might be able to convey him to Sparta more easily, actually poured wax around him because they did not have honey;[1] and thus they brought him back home.

1 Spartan kings who died abroad were traditionally embalmed in honey to help preserve their bodies for their funeral at home.

VIRGIL

Publius Vergilius Maro

Rome's greatest poet, born in 70 BC, was invited to join the circle of Maecenas, the patron of many poets of the early empire. His three great works are: the *Bucolica (Pastorals)*, better known as the *Eclogae (Eclogues, or 'Selections')*, a collection of nominally pastoral poems published in final form in 38 BC; the *Georgics*, a didactic poem on farming (29 BC); and the *Aeneid*, an epic on the origins of Rome. He died in 19 BC with the last work still needing revision, but it was circulated in public soon after his death. Like Homer, Virgil's influence on subsequent Western literature has been incalculable.

Our first short extract, from the *Georgics*, describes the nomadic pastoralist of the Libyan deserts, whom Virgil contrasts to the frozen Russian and compares to the legionary on the march.

The name Libya appears many times in the *Aeneid* but Virgil is usually referring to the part of the continent near Carthage. In the second passage below, however, Virgil places the new Carthaginian state in the context of a wider Libya. The founding queen, Dido, exiled from Tyre after her husband's murder by her own brother, is counselled by her sister Anna to ignore her many native Libyan suitors and instead marry the poem's hero, Aeneas of Troy, whose fleet has been blown onto Carthaginian shores in a storm sent by the jealous goddess Juno. This advice will have disastrous consequences not only for Dido but for future Roman–North African relations. In Virgil's day, the major African states of Carthage, Numidia and Ægypt had all finally been reduced to provinces of the new Roman Empire. Although the Dido episode is both fictitious and anachronistic, it is important in the context of Rome's perception of herself and the wider world, and serves as background to the glorification of Rome under its first emperor, Augustus, which is the poem's underlying purpose. Indeed, later in the poem (VI, 794–795) Virgil presents a prophecy that Augustus 'will extend the empire beyond both the Garamantians and the Indians'. A sequel to this episode may be found in Silius Italicus 5.

The third passage is from the *Moretum (Herb Salad)*, a charming idyll attributed to Virgil though unlikely to have been by him, which describes a peasant making his breakfast of bread with a herb salad, aided by his good Libyan servant.

1 Libyan pastoralists

How shall I present to you the shepherds of Libya in verse? How shall I present their pastures and the villages they inhabit with the dwellings scattered here and there? Often, day and night, and a whole month continuously, the flock is put to graze and goes into the vast deserts devoid of any lodgings, so far does the plain extend. The African herdsman carries everything with him, his roof and hearth and weapons, his Amyclaean dog and Cretan quiver.[1]

2 Fatal advice

Anna replies: 'O you who are more beloved to your sister than life itself, surely you are not going to waste the whole of your youth mourning alone and will know neither sweet children nor the rewards of Venus? Do you think that ashes or the buried shades of the dead bother about that? Granted that no suitors persuaded you in your suffering, neither those of Libya nor formerly those from Tyre. Iarbas has been shunned and the other chieftains whom the land of Africa, rich in triumphs, sustains. You would not also fight a love that pleases, surely? And does it not occur to your mind whose lands you have settled in? You are surrounded on one side by the cities of the Gaetulians, a race unconquerable in war, and the unbridled Numidians and the inhospitable Syrtis; on the other side by a region made desert from drought and the Barcaeans raging far and wide. Shall I speak of those hostilities arising from Tyre, and our brother's threats? ... For my part I think that the Ilian ships held this course with the wind, the gods being marriage winesses and Juno being favourable. Sister, what a city you will see here, what realms will arise with such a spouse! In how many things will Punic glory exalt itself with weapons from Teucer accompanying us!'

3 Characteristics of a Libyan woman

Occasionally he calls Scybale. She was his sole attendant. Her race was African, her whole figure bearing witness to her native land: frizzled of hair, swollen in lip and swarthy in colour, broad of chest, her breasts hanging loose, narrower in the belly, thin in the leg, her ample feet of generous size.

---

1 Not literally; the epithets are used to convey an idea of quality. Amyclae in the south of Greece bred fine dogs; Cretans were traditionally renowned for their archery.

STRABO of Amasia

Born to a well-connected family of Pontus around 64 BC, Strabo came to Rome for the first time in 44 BC, the year of Julius Caesar's assassination, and also travelled extensively in Ægypt and the Near East. He wrote the lengthy *Historical Sketches*, now lost, and also the *Geography*, which describes much of the known world in some detail. It may have been first circulated around 7 BC but was subsequently revised. Strabo died some time after AD 21.

Two extracts here, 2 and 3, are descriptions of the continent of Africa, from two different parts of the *Geography*, and both different in their conclusions. These are followed by a more detailed description of Libya's coastline, with some information on the interior.

The first extract, however, shows Strabo using an example from Eratosthenes of Cyrene, an important predecessor of his who made a significant contribution to ancient geography and astronomy, but whose work is now largely lost. The example of the temple of Ammon at Siwa in the Libyan Desert is used to question whether the sea once flowed much further inland. Strabo's work, as well as a description of places, is a promotion of the science of geography, and it is problems such as this which he feels this science may be able to answer.

1 The temple of Ammon may once have been on the coast

How does it come about that in many places inland, two or three thousand stadia [300–500 km] from the sea, are found large quantities of mussel, oyster and scallop shells and salt water lakes? Eratosthenes says, for instance, that in the vicinity of the temple of Ammon and along the road to it, which is three thousand stadia [500 km] long, a large deposit of oyster shells and many salt beds and jets of salt water bubbling up are still found. Besides these they show pieces of wreckage from sea-going ships which they say have been cast up through some fissure, and dolphins on small columns bearing the inscription of the sacred envoys of Cyrene. [...]

Perhaps the temple of Ammon, too, was formerly on the sea but now it is in the interior because the sea has flowed away. Strato conjectures that the oracle of Ammon became celebrated and renowned because of its being so near the sea and that its present distinction and fame could not be explained by its being currently so far from the sea.

2 The appearance of Africa

After Asia comes Libya which lies next to Ægypt and Æthiopia. The shore opposite us forms a straight line from Alexandria almost to the Pillars [Straits of Gibraltar], except for the Syrtes and occasionally some moderate indentations of gulfs and the projections of the headlands that form them; but its coast on the Ocean from Æthiopia to a certain point is almost parallel to the former, but then its southern parts narrow into a sharp headland which extends slightly beyond the Pillars and gives it the shape of a trapezium.

As others relate, and also as Gnaeus Piso (who was governor of this province) told me, Libya is like a leopard's skin, for it is dotted with settlements surrounded by waterless, desert land. The Ægyptians call these settlements *auases* [i.e. oases]. It has some other peculiarities beside this, which divide it into three distinct parts.

Most of the coast opposite us is extremely fertile, especially Cyrenaea [i.e. Cyrenaica] and the territory around Carthage as far as Maurusia [i.e. Mauretania] and the Pillars of Heracles. The coastline of the Ocean offers moderate conditions for living but the central region which produces silphium is mostly barren, stony and sandy, and the same applies to the straight strip of land aligned with this which runs through Æthiopia, Troglodytica, Arabia and Gedrosia occupied by the Ichthyophagi [the Fish-Eaters].

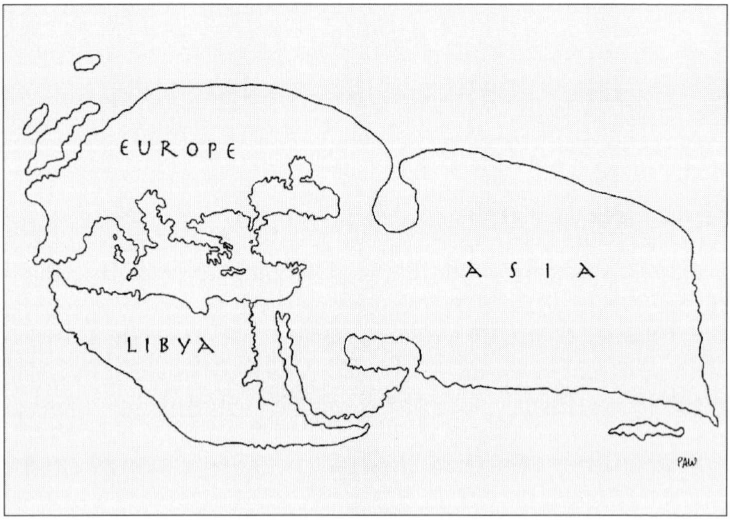

Fig. 16 Map 7: The World according to Strabo.

Most of the peoples of Libya are not known to us, for it has only rarely been entered by armies or by travellers, and few of the natives from far away visit us and their information is untrustworthy and incomplete. But here is what they say. The most southerly peoples they call Æthiopians. More towards us are mainly the Garamantes, the Pharusii and the Nigritae. Still closer are the Gaetulians. Near the sea or on the coast next to Ægypt, and even as far as Cyrenaea, are the Marmaridae. Beyond Cyrenaea and the Syrtes are the Psylli, the Nasamones and certain of the Gaetulians, and then the Asbystae and Byzacians as far as Carthage.

3 The continent of Africa

Next let me describe Libya, which is the final part of this *Geography* as a whole. I have said much about this country before but I must now comment on what is appropriate, adding what has not been said before.

The writers who have divided the inhabited world according to continents have divided it unequally, for a threefold division implies a division into three equal parts but Libya is so far from being a third part of the inhabited world that even if it were added to Europe it would not appear to be equal to Asia. Perhaps it is even smaller than Europe and in resources it is much inferior, for a large part of the interior and its Ocean coast is desert, and it is dotted with small settlements, which are scattered and mostly inhabited by nomads. Besides the desert, its being a nursery of wild animals keeps men out of areas that could be inhabited. It also comprises a large part of the torrid zone. All the coast opposite us between the Nile and the Pillars, and particularly that which belonged to the Carthaginians, is prosperous and inhabited but even here there are some parts destitute of water as they are around the Syrtes, the Marmaridae and the Catabathmos.

Libya is the shape of a right-angled triangle when imagined drawn on a plane surface, having for its base the coast opposite us from Ægypt and the Nile to Maurusia and the Pillars. The side perpendicular to this is formed by the Nile as far as Æthiopia and which I extend to the Ocean. The hypotenuse of the right angle is the whole of the Ocean coast between Æthiopia and Maurusia. As the part at the very vertex of the above-mentioned figure, lying within the torrid zone, is inaccessible (I speak from conjecture), I cannot therefore state its greatest breadth.

Although in a previous part of this work I have said that the distance, as one goes from Alexandria southwards to Meroë (the royal capital of the Æthiopians) is about ten thousand stadia [1,600 km], and from there in a straight line to the borders between the torrid zone and the inhabited world it is three thousand more [500 km]. The greatest breadth of Libya may be put down as the same, thirteen or fourteen thousand stadia [2,500 km], its length a little less than double this sum. These are my general remarks on Libya but let me describe its various parts beginning with its western and more famous ones.

4 *A detailed description of Libya*

Adjacent to these islands is the Little Syrtis [Gulf of Gabès], which is also called the Syrtis Lotophagitis [i.e. the Syrtis of the Lotus-Eaters]. The circuit of this gulf is one thousand six hundred stadia [300 km] and the breadth of the entrance six hundred [100 km]. At each of the headlands which form the entrance are islands close to the mainland, Cercinna [Kerkenna] just mentioned and Meninx [Jerba], which are nearly equal in size. Meninx is held to be the land of the Lotophagi [Lotus-Eaters] mentioned by Homer and certain tokens of this are pointed out: an altar of Odysseus and the fruit itself, for the tree called the lotus grows in abundance in the island and its fruit is delicious. There are several towns on it, one of which bears the same name as the island [i.e. Meninx (El Kantara)]. On the coast of the Syrtis itself are several small towns. In the recess of the gulf is a very large market town [i.e. Tacape (Gabès)] with a river that flows into the gulf. The effects of the flow and ebb of the tides extend this far and at the right moment the inhabitants of the neighbourhood rush at a run to catch fish.

The Zuchis [Bahiret El Bibane] which follows the Syrtis is a lake four hundred stadia [75 km] in circuit with a narrow entrance and on it is a city with the same name [Zuchis (El Bibane)] containing purple dye factories and establishments for all kinds of salting. Then there is another much smaller lake, and after this the city of Abrotonum [Sabratha] and some others. Next after these is Neapolis, which is also called Leptis [Magna]. From here to Locri Epizephyrii [Locri, Italy] is three thousand six hundred stadia [650 km]. Next is a river [the Cinyps] and afterwards there is a kind of wall which the Carthaginians built to bridge over some gorges which extend far into the interior. There are some places here without harbours although the rest of the coast has them. Next comes a high, wooded headland which marks the beginning of the Great Syrtis [Gulf of Sidra] and is called Cephalae [Ras El Barq]. From Carthage to this headland is a little more than five thousand stadia [900 km].

Inland from the coast from Carthage to Cephalae and to the land of the Masaesylians lies the territory of the Libophoenicians, which extends to the mountainous country of the Gaetulians where Libya proper [i.e. Western Libya (Algeria)] begins. Inland from the Gaetulians is the territory of the Garamantes, lying parallel to the former and from where the Carthaginian stones are brought.[1] The Garamantes are said to be nine or ten days' journey distant from the Æthiopians who live on the Ocean, and fifteen from Ammon. Between the Gaetulians and the coast of our sea there are many plains but also many mountains, great lakes and rivers, some of which sink into the earth and vanish from sight. The inhabitants are very simple in their way of life and in their dress but they have many wives and many children and in other respects are like the nomadic Arabs. Both their horses and their cattle have longer necks than those of other countries. The breeding of horses is attended to with great care by their kings so that every year the foals number one hundred thousand. The sheep are fed on milk and meat, particularly near Æthiopia. This is my account of the interior.

The Great Syrtis has a circuit of about three thousand nine hundred and thirty stadia [700 km]; a diameter to its inmost recess of one thousand five hundred [250 km] and a breadth at the opening of about the same. The difficulty with both this and the Little Syrtis is that the deep water has shallows in many places and so it happens that, during the ebb and flow of the tides, vessels can end up in the shallows and remain stuck and escape is rare. Therefore sailors keep at a distance when sailing by the coast, taking care not to be caught off their guard and driven into these gulfs by the wind. Yet the risk taking disposition of man induces him to try anything and particularly sailing along a coast.

Now, on entering the Great Syrtis, on the right after passing Cephalae, is a lake about three hundred stadia [50 km] in length and seventy [10 km] in breadth which flows into the gulf and has small islands and an anchorage at its entrance. After the lake follows a place called Aspis and the finest harbour in the Syrtis. Adjacent to this is the Euphrantas Tower, the boundary between the former territory of Carthage and Cyrene under Ptolemy. Then there is another place called Charax [Medina Sultan] which the Carthaginians had as a trading centre, conveying wine there and in exchange loading silphium juice and silphium from merchants who brought them clandestinely from Cyrene. Then there are the Altars of the Philaeni and, after these, Automala [El Agheila], a fort with a garrison situated in the inmost recess of the whole gulf. The parallel through this gulf is a thousand stadia [175 km] more to the south than the one through Alexandria and under two thousand stadia [350 km] more than the one through Carthage, but it would coincide with the parallel which passes through Heroönpolis situated in the

1 See Pliny 14.

recess of the Arabian Gulf [the Red Sea] and through the interior of the territory of the Masaesylians and the Maurusians.

The rest of the coast to the city of Berenice [Benghazi] is one thousand five hundred stadia in length [250 km]. Inland from this length of coast, and extending as far as the Altars of the Philaeni, are the so-called Nasamones, a Libyan people. The intervening distance has only a few harbours, and watering places are rare. Then there is a headland called Pseudopenias on which Berenice is situated near a Lake Triton in which is a small island with a temple to Aphrodite on it. There is also the Harbour of the Hesperides and the River Lathon flows into it. On this [north] side of Berenice is a small promontory called Borion [Ras Taiunes] which with Cephalae forms the entrance of the Syrtis. Berenice lies opposite the headlands of the Peloponnese, Ichthys [Cape Katakolo] so called, and also Zacynthus, a distance of three thousand six hundred stadia [650 km]. Marcus Cato set out from this city round the Syrtis in thirty days at the head of an army of more than ten thousand men which he had divided into units on account of the watering places. He marched on foot in deep sand and blazing heat. After Berenice comes a city, Tauchira [Tocra], also called Arsinoe; then the former Barca [Al-Marj], now called Ptolemais [Tolmeta], then a headland, Phycus [Ras Sem], which is low-lying but extends further towards the north than the rest of the Libyan coast; it is opposite Taenarum in Laconica at a distance of two thousand eight hundred stadia [500 km]. There is also a small town which bears the same name as the headland. Not far from Phycus, at a distance of about one hundred and seventy stadia [30 km], is Apollonia [Marsa Susa], the port of Cyrene, one thousand [175 km] from Berenice and eighty [15 km] from Cyrene, a big city situated in a trapezoidal-shaped plain as I saw it from the sea.

Cyrene [Shahat] was founded from Thera, a Laconican island, whose ancient name was Calliste, as Callimachus says,

> Calliste was its name before, and Thera later on;
> Mother of my fatherland, and for its horses famous.[2]

The port of Cyrene is situated opposite Criu Metopon [Cape Krio], the western cape of Crete, two thousand stadia [350 km] away. The crossing is made with the Leuconotus [the South-South-West Wind]. Cyrene is said to have been founded by Battus, whom Callimachus claims was his ancestor. It flourished thanks to the quality of its land, for it is the best for breeding horses and fine crops, and it has had many notable men

2 This is an isolated fragment of poem known only from Strabo.

who were able to defend its freedom and strenuously resist the foreigners living inland. So in ancient times the city was independent but later it was attacked by the Macedonians (who had occupied Ægypt and so increased their power) under Thibron, the murderer of Harpalus. Having been subject to kings for some time it came under the power of the Romans and now forms one province with Crete. In the district of Cyrene are Apollonia, Barca, Tauchira, Berenice and other small towns nearby.

Bordering on Cyrenaea [i.e. Cyrenaica] is the region which produces silphium and the Cyrenaean juice which is drawn off the silphium. It nearly disappeared when the foreign peoples, who are nomads, invaded the country for some malicious motive and destroyed the roots of the plant.

Famous people from Cyrene were Aristippus the Socratic philosopher, who also laid the foundations of Cyrenaic philosophy, and his daughter named Arete who succeeded him at the school and in turn was succeeded by her son Aristippus, who was called Metrodidactus ['Mother-Taught'], and Anniceris, who is believed to have reformed the Cyrenaic sect and to have introduced the Annicerian sect in its place. Callimachus was also a Cyrenaean, and Eratosthenes, both of whom were held in high esteem by the kings of Ægypt, the former being a poet and a zealous man of letters, the latter excellent above all others not only in these things but also in philosophy and mathematics; and also Carneades who, by common consent, was the best of the Academic philosophers; and Apollonius Cronus the teacher of Diodorus the Dialectician, who was also called Cronus because some transferred the epithet of the teacher to the pupil.

After Apollonia the rest of the Cyrenaean coast as far as Catabathmos, two thousand two hundred stadia [400 km] long, does not offer much when sailing along the coast, for there are few harbours, anchorages, settlements and watering places. Among the best-known places along the coast are Naustathmos [Ras el Hilal] and Zephyrion with an anchorage, and another Zephyrion, and a headland called Cherronesus [Ras el Tin], which has a harbour. This headland is opposite Cyclos in Crete, the distance being one thousand five hundred stadia [250 km] from the south-west. Then there is a temple of Heracles and above it a village, Paliurus; and then the Port of Menelaus, and Ardanis [Ras el Milh], a low-lying headland with an anchorage; then a large harbour, opposite which rises the Cherronesus in Crete; the distance between them being about three thousand stadia [500 km], for almost the whole of Crete, which is narrow and long, lies opposite and parallel to this coast. After the large harbour is another harbour, Plynus [Gulf of Sollum], and above it is Tetrapyrgia. The place is called Catabathmos. Cyrenaea extends this far. The remainder to Paraetonium [Mersa Matruh] and from there to Alexandria I have described in my account of Ægypt.

The barren and dry country deep in the interior above the Syrtis and Cyrenaea is occupied by Libyans, first the Nasamones, then the Psylli and some Gaetulians, then the Garamantes; and still more towards the east, the Marmaridae who border on Cyrenaea for a long way and extend as far as Ammon. It is said that people walking from the inmost recess of the Great Syrtis from about the neighbourhood of Automala in the direction of the winter sunrise [i.e. east-south-east], arrive at Augila on the fourth day. This place resembles Ammon, producing palm trees and being well watered. It is situated beyond Cyrenaea, to the south. For a hundred stadia [18 km] the land produces trees; for another hundred it is only sown with crops as trees do not take root because of the aridity. Beyond this is the region which produces silphium. Then follows the uninhabited country and the country of the Garamantes. The region which produces silphium is narrow, long and dry, extending about three thousand stadia [500 km] in length heading towards the east, and three hundred [50 km] or a little bit more in breadth, at least the part which is known. For we may suppose that all places lying one after the other on the same parallel have the same climate and plants, but since various deserts intervene we do not know all these places. Similarly, we do not know all the regions beyond Ammon, nor the oases as far as Æthiopia, nor can we state what the boundaries of either Æthiopia or Libya are, still less the parts which border on the Ocean.

FIRST CENTURY AD

VALERIUS MAXIMUS

Apparently from an impoverished background, Valerius Maximus (whose first name is unknown) found patronage with Sextus Pompeius and accompanied his patron to the Province of Asia, of which Pompeius was governor in AD 27. Evidently a great admirer of Livy and Cicero, Valerius culled many examples of noteworthy actions and speeches from their works and those of other authors to provide ease of reference. His *Memorable Deeds and Sayings (Facta ac dicta memorabilia)*, first circulated in the early AD 30s, hold these examples up as illustrations of specific virtues and vices or practices and customs.

The story of the Philaeni is also told in Sallust 3 and Mela 2, but here Valerius insists that the Carthaginians cheated. Interestingly, though, Valerius uses their action to illustrate love for one's country, rather than using their alleged dishonesty as an example of vice. The somewhat overblown style is characteristic.

The Philaeni's sacrifice

When there was a very obstinate dispute between Carthage and Cyrene concerning the size of their territories, it was finally resolved that young men would be sent out from both sides at the same time and that the place at which they met would be regarded as the boundary of both peoples. But two Carthaginian brothers, the Philaeni by name, anticipated this agreement by dishonesty, widely advancing their boundaries by hastening their pace before the appointed hour. When the young men of the Cyrenaeans had realised this, after complaining for a long time about the trick, they finally tried to dispel the injury by the severity of their terms. For they said that this boundary would be fixed as things were if the Philaeni would submit to having themselves be buried there. But the result did not accord with their plan, for without a moment's hesitation, they gave their bodies up to them to be buried in that land. Since they preferred the boundaries of their homeland to be more protracted than their own lives, they lie honourably, the Punic Empire having been broadened by their spirits and their bones.

Where are the lofty city walls of proud Carthage? Where is the maritime glory of her famous harbour? Where is her fleet terrifying all the coasts? Where are her many infantry units? Where is her cavalry of such size? Where is her arrogance not satisfied with the vast extent of Africa? Fortune divided all these between the two Scipios. But not even the destruction of their fatherland extinguished the memory of the outstanding deed of the Philaeni. There is nothing immortal, therefore, except virtue, which can be acquired by human will and personal valour.

CELSUS

Aulus Cornelius Celsus

Celsus may have been born around 25 BC. He wrote an encyclopaedic work, probably during the reign of the Emperor Tiberius (AD 14–37). Originally the work included books on agriculture, medicine, war, rhetoric, philosophy and law but, apart from a few fragments, only the books on medicine have come down to us. Celsus is believed to have been a layman rather than a doctor, although professional distinctions were not as acute then as they are now. His *De medicina (On Medicine)* is a digest of medical knowledge up to his time and seems to be intended chiefly as a practical guide for domestic use by heads of households. With his clear, elegant style and sound structure and knowledge, this 'Latin Hippocrates' or 'Medical Cicero' did for medicine among the Romans what Cicero had done for philosophy.

These extracts are included to illustrate remedies sourced from Libya, one effective (salt of Ammon), one bogus (Psylli). Libya specifically supplied silphium and products derived from it, which were used in many dietary recommendations and medical remedies, such as those for snakebites in the first passage below. It also supplied the high-quality salt which was found in abundance around the temple of Jupiter Ammon and was used in poultices and salves.

1 Remedies for snakebites, especially African ones; and why the Psylli are charlatans

Even reptiles' bites do not require a treatment that is very different, although ancient writers often varied in these matters so that for different kinds of snake some advised unique kinds of remedy and others advised other remedies; but in all things the same remedies are especially useful.

First, therefore, the limb should be bound above a wound of this sort, but not very tightly lest it become numb. Then the venom should be drawn out. A cupping-glass does this best. And cutting all around the wound beforehand with a lancet is not inappropriate, so that more of the infected blood is drawn out straight away. If there is no cupping-glass (which, however, can hardly be the case) then use any similar vessel which can do the same thing. If you do not even have this then a man should be summoned to suck out the wound. Those who are called Psylli do not have a special skill, by Hercules! but a presumption reinforced by practice. For the venom of a reptile is actually like certain hunters' poisons, which the Gauls in particular make use of: they harm in a wound but not when swallowed. That is why the snake itself can safely be eaten but its bite kills. And if a snake has been stupefied, which quacks bring about with certain drugs, anyone who places a finger into its mouth is not bitten; there is no harm in the saliva. Consequently, everyone who, following the example of a Psyllus, sucks out the said wound will himself be safe and keep the injured person safe.[1] He should consider this beforehand, lest he die: that he has not had an ulcer on his gums or palate or another part of his mouth. [...]

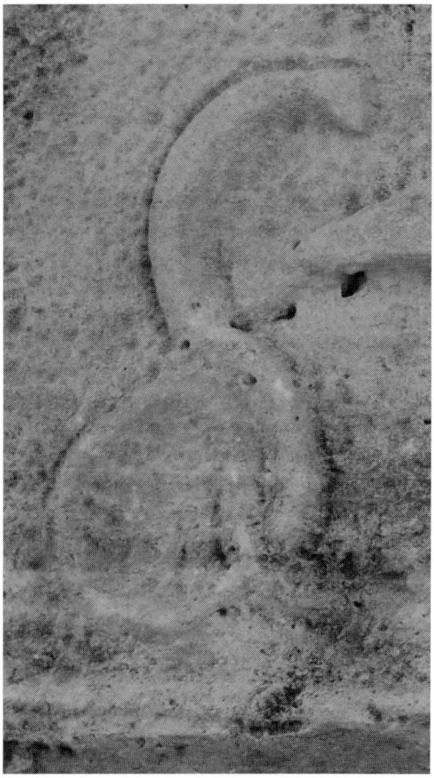

Fig. 17 A striking snake, detail from a relief sculpture from Leptis Magna.

These remedies are universal against all bites. However, experience itself has taught that someone who has been bitten by an asp ought preferably to drink vinegar. [...]

Certain established aids in the case of certain other reptiles are also sufficiently known. [...] And, indeed, in respect of the sting of a scorpion or spider, garlic well mixed with rue and ground with olive oil should be placed on top. [...]

But if a *cerastes* [a horned viper] or a *dipsas* or a *haemorrhois* has struck, use poley-germander, dried, which should equal an Ægyptian bean in size as it needs to be divided into two draughts so that a little rue can be added to it. Trefoil also, and wild mint, and panacea with vinegar are equally useful. And costus and cassia and cinnamon are also appropriately taken in draughts.

Against the bite of a *chelydrus*, however, panacea or silphium – 3½ scruples (1 drachm) [4 g] to be used – or else leek juice should be taken with half a pint [250 ml] of wine, and a lot of savory should be eaten. Moreover, goat

1 The actual practices of the Psylli are descibed in Lucan 8.

dung boiled with vinegar should be laid over the wound; or barley meal with the same; or rue or catnip pounded with salt, with honey added. The last is also equally efficacious on the wound which a *cerastes* has made. [...]

But in truth these kinds of reptiles are not only from foreign parts but are also more pernicious and arise especially in very hot places.

2 *A remedy for inflammation of the eye*

Salt of Ammon, or any other salt at all – the best possible – should be ground in such a way that olive oil may gradually be added to it until its density becomes that of skin scrapings. Then this should be mixed with barley meal which has been boiled down with mead.

But it should easily be clear to anyone, after reviewing all the things which doctors have published, that there is hardly any defect of the eye, of those which have been described above, which cannot be dispelled by remedies that are simple and also handy.

MELA

Pomponius Mela

Born in Baetica (Southern Spain) possibly as early as 24/23 BC, Mela is known for one work, his *Chorographia (Description of Places)*, also known as the *De situ orbis (On the Layout of the World)* or just the *Geography*, which was first circulated in AD 43 or 44 and takes the form of a periplus, or sea journey, around the main countries of the world. With few measurements of distance, little fine detail and a more direct engagement of the reader, it is more readable than Strabo and is an improvement on early geographical descriptions such as those of Eratosthenes. Mela also appears to have benefited from Rome's administrative tallies (the census which opens Luke's gospel is a well-known example), which by this time covered almost all Mediterranean lands. Mela's book is the earliest surviving geographical work in Latin. He seems to have intended it as a model for a longer book which, in the event, he never wrote.

The extracts here provide a summary of the geography of Africa (part of his opening description of the continents), followed by greater detail on regions and peoples of Libya. (Mela also describes a journey around the outer coast of Africa which does not fall within the parameters of this book but which may be of further interest to the reader.)

1 The African continent

The continent of Africa is bounded by the Nile on its eastern side and by the sea on the other sides. It is, in fact, smaller than Europe because it does not lie opposite Asia at any point and does not lie opposite Europe along all of its coastline. It is, however, longer than it is wide, and widest where it borders on the river. As it progresses from there, rising to higher ground chiefly in the middle, so it extends curving towards the west and gently brings itself to a point; and that is why it is narrower by degrees in its extent and narrowest there where it ends.

For as far as it is inhabited it is exceptionally fertile but because the largest part of it is uncultivated and is either covered by barren sands or is uninhabited because of the aridity of the sky and the land, or is infested by the kinds of animals that are numerous and vicious, it is more desolate than populous. The sea by which it is surrounded we call the Libyan in the north, the Æthiopian in the south and the Atlantic in the west.

In that part which borders on the Libyan Sea nearest to the Nile is the province which they call Cyrene. Then there is the Province of Africa, the name applied to designate the continent as a whole. The Numidians and the Moors occupy the other parts, but the Moors are exposed to the Atlantic Sea. Beyond are the Nigritae and the Pharusii as far as the Æthiopians who occupy both the remainder of this side and all the side which faces the south as far as the borders of Asia.

But on those sides that are washed by the Libyan Sea are the Libyan-Ægyptians and the White Æthiopians and the populous and numerous Gaetulian people. Then lying unoccupied is a region utterly uninhabitable throughout its extent. Next we understand that the Garamantes are the first towards the east, afterwards the Augilae and the Troglodytes; and the Atlantes are the furthest towards the west. In the interior, if you wish to believe it, the Aegipanes and the Blemmyae and the Gamphasantes and the Satyrs, scarcely really men but more half-beast, wandering here and there without hearth and home, occupy the land rather than dwell in it.

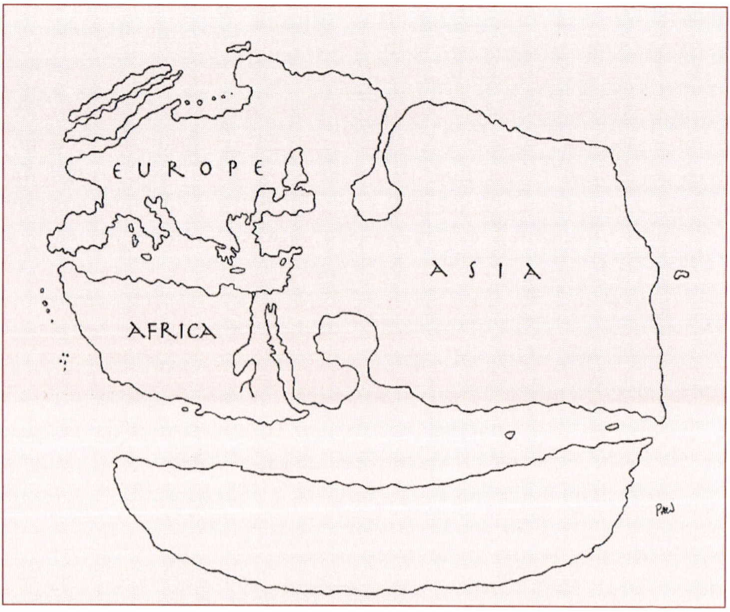

Fig. 18 Map 8: The World according to Mela. Note that the continent of Libya is known to him as Africa, and, thanks to his sea-based approach to geography, now has a better defined shape and islands. Note also the imagined southern continent.

2 A journey along the coast

The Syrtis [Gulf of Gabès] is a gulf. Where it receives the open sea it is almost a hundred miles [65 km] across; where it surrounds it, three hundred [200 km]. It is truly harbourless, and dreadful because of the shallow waters of its numerous shoals and even more dangerous because of the alternating motions of the sea as it ebbs and flows.

Beyond this, the huge Lake Triton [Chott Djerid] receives a river, itself called the Triton, and from where Minerva's epithet was derived, she having been born there, as the inhabitants declare. And they impart some truth to this story because they celebrate the day they think is her birthday with public shows of young women fighting it out amongst themselves.

Beyond is the town of Oea [Tripoli] and the River Cinyps [Wadi Caam] that tumbles down through very fertile fields, then the other Leptis [i.e. Leptis Magna] and a Syrtis [Gulf of Sidra] equal in name and nature to the earlier one but in other respects almost as much again in extent where it has its opening and more spacious where it curves. Borion [Ras Taiunes] is its headland and, starting from there, the country – which they say the Lotophagi [the Lotus-Eaters] occupied – extends along a harbourless shore as far as Phycus [Ras Sem]; this is also a headland.

The Altars derive their name from the Philaeni brothers who permitted themselves to be buried alive here – an extraordinary deed and most deserving of recollection. They were sent from Carthage against the Cyrenaicans by an arrangement to put an end to a war over their borders which had already been waged for a long time and to the great detriment of both sides. When what they had previously decided did not last, they agreed anew that the boundary lines would be established in the place where envoys met each other after being sent out from either side at a specified time, so whatever was on the nearer side would fall to their fellow countrymen.[1]

From there to Catabathmos is the Province of Cyrenaica and in it are the Oracle of Ammon of renowned credibility, and a spring which they call the Fountain of the Sun and a certain rock sacred to the South Wind. When this is struck by the hand of man that wind rises up unrestrained and, raising the sands as if they were the waters of the sea, it rages in the same way as it would over the waves. In the middle of the night the spring boils and then, gradually cooling off, it becomes cold in the daytime; then it is accordingly colder as the sun climbs, is especially frigid during the middle of the day, then assumes warmth a second time and is hot in the

1 See Sallust 3 and Valerius Maximus for more detailed accounts of this story.

first part of the night and is accordingly hotter as it proceeds; when it is the middle of the night, it boils again.[2]

On the coast are the headlands of Zephyrion and Naustathmos [Ras el Hilal], the port of Paraetonium [Mersa Matruh], the cities of Hesperia [Benghazi], Apollonia [Marsa Susa], Ptolemais [Tolmeta], Arsinoe [Tocra], and Cyrene [Shahat] itself, its name being given to the region. The Catabathmos valley, descending into Ægypt, bounds Africa.

Accordingly, the coastal regions are inhabited by natives conditioned to our own customs, except that certain ones are distinguished by their languages and by the worship of their gods whom they preserve from their forefathers and worship in the manner of their forefathers. In fact, there are no cities located in the vicinity, yet there are dwellings which are called *mapalia*. Their way of life is harsh and devoid of refinements. Their chiefs are clothed in woollen mantles, the common people in the skins of wild and domestic animals. Sleeping and feasting are done on the ground. Their vessels are made from wood or from bark. Their drink is milk and the juice of berries. Their food is usually the flesh of game for they spare what they can from their flocks because they alone are fruitful.

3 *The strange peoples of the interior*

Those inland live more roughly. They are unsettled and also follow their flocks; and as the flocks are drawn by their fodder, so they and their huts move on; and when daylight fails, there they spend the night. Although they are dispersed randomly in family groups and have no law, they do not deliberate over anything communally. However, because each man has several wives at the same time and, because of this, many children and relations, they are not few in number.

Of those who are mentioned as being beyond the deserts, the Atlantes curse the sun both while it is rising and while it is setting as being destructive to them and their fields. Individuals do not have names. They do not eat animals. Nor is it granted to them to have visitations in their sleep such as are granted to the rest of mankind.

The Troglodytes do not possess wealth, they shriek rather than speak, they go down into caves and feed on reptiles.

There are also herds among the Garamantes and these graze with their necks awry for, when bending forward, their horns get in the way of the ground. No one has a specified wife. From those children who are born from this promiscuous and confused intercourse and are uncertain

2 See Lucretius for a scientific explanation of the properties of this spring.

of their parents, they recognise those whom they care for as their own by their likeness in appearance.

The Augilae think that the spirits of the dead are the only gods. They swear oaths by them, they consult them as oracles and, when they have thrown themselves on burial mounds after praying for what they want, the spirits bring dreams instead of responses. There is a religious rite for their women on the night on which they marry: to be accessible to the debauchery of all who come with a gift, and at that time to have lain with the most men is the greatest honour; for the rest of the time their chastity is conspicuous.

The Gamphasantes are naked and know nothing of weapons. They do not know how to avoid missiles or how to throw them and for this reason they flee anyone who encounters them, and they do not submit to encounters or conversations with others except those whose nature is the same.

The Blemmyae are missing their heads; their faces are on their chests.

There is nothing of that which is human in the Satyrs except a certain likeness.

The Aegipani have that appearance which is widely known.

These are the things concerning Africa.

SENECA THE YOUNGER

Lucius Annaeus Seneca

Son of Lucius Annaeus Seneca the Elder and uncle of the poet Lucan, Lucius Annaeus Seneca the Younger came to Rome in childhood from Corduba in Baetica (Cordoba, Spain) where he had been born around 4 BC. He was arguably the foremost philosopher of the first century, writing philosophical dialogues and other prose works, as well as drama, epistles and a satire. He was tutor to the young Nero and, on his protégé's becoming emperor, was appointed a personal minister. He chose to retire in AD 62 and was then – probably wrongly – implicated in Piso's conspiracy of 65 and, like many of the alleged conspirators, took his own life.

His influence on Renaissance essayists and dramatists was profound, but his overly sententious style, rather like that of his contemporary thinker, St Paul, has often grated – 'like dining on nothing but anchovy sauce', Lord Macaulay famously declared – particularly as his life did not always conform to his Stoic ideals. In the first extract, from one of his letters, Seneca shows how Cato's march through Libya is an example of Stoic endurance. This may be compared to Lucan's and Plutarch's assessments below and is included in this collection in preference to Lucan's many passages extolling Cato's virtues.

Seneca also wrote a work on natural history, the *Naturales Quaestiones (Natural Questions)* in which he discusses the nature of the storm that destroyed Cambyses' army, as described in Herodotus 3 above.

1 A Stoic in Libya

You see that men can put up with toil: through the middle of the deserts of Africa Cato led an army on foot. You see that thirst can be borne: in burning hills without any supply train, dragging the relics of a conquered army, clad in mail, he bore the scarcity of liquid and, as often as there was the opportunity for water, he drank last of all. You see that honour and disgrace can be despised: on the same day on which he was rejected in an election, he played with a ball. You see that stronger power need not be feared: he challenged both Pompey and Caesar; no-one else dared to offend one of them unless he lay under obligation to the other. You see that death can be as much despised as exile: he imposed exile upon himself, and death, and war in the meantime.

2 *Do sandstorms produce thunder and lightning?*

Certain people, among whom is Asclepiodotus, consider that thunder and lightning can also be emitted by the collision of certain bodies. [...]

Once Cambyses sent an army to Ammon which the sand, stirred up by the south wind, covered and then buried like falling snow. It is probable that there was also thunder and lightning at the same time from the friction of the sand rubbing against itself.

COLUMELLA

Lucius Iunius Moderatus Columella

Columella wrote the most comprehensive treatise on farming of the Roman period, the *De Re Rustica (Country Matters)* probably in the early AD 60s. Although born in Gades (Cadiz, Spain) he moved to Italy where he owned several farms.

Columella mentions several products of Libya: varieties of fig and grape, jujubes (tuber-apples), grain, salt of Ammon and, of course, silphium and asafoetida. He also mentions how asses may be used to plough loose soils such as those of Libya. The following extracts illustrate uses of silphium and salt of Ammon for the benefit of the arboriculturist, the veterinarian and the housewife.

1 How to sweeten pomegranates

The pomegranate is duly planted in spring right up to the first of April. If it bears fruit that is sour or not so sweet, it can be improved in this way: the roots should be moistened with pig and human manure and with old human urine. This method both renders the tree productive and makes the fruit wine-flavoured in the earliest years, and also makes it sweet and soft-seeded afterwards. Quite a short time ago I dissolved Cyrenaic silphium in wine and smeared it on the topmost extremities of the tree. This has improved the sour taste of the fruits.

2 Libyan products for vets

Defects of the eyes are generally cured with honey. For if they have swollen up, wheat flour is sprinkled with honeyed water and is laid on them. Or if there is a white film on the eye, Hispanian or Ammoniac or even Cappadocian rock salt finely ground and blended with honey diminishes the defect. In the same way, ground cuttle shell is useful and should be blown into the eye through a tube three times a day. Also useful is the root which the Greeks call *silphion* [silphium] and which in our idiom the people call *laserpitium* [laserwort]. To whatever sized weight of this, ten parts of salt of Ammon are added and these, ground together, are similarly poured in; or the same root pounded and anointed with mastic oil purges the defect.

3 A quick digestive

DIGESTIVE MIXTURE

3 ounces [75g] of pepper, white if available, black if not;
2 ounces [50g] of celery seed;
1½ ounces [35g] of laserwort root, which the Greeks call *silphium*;
one sixth of a pound [50 g] of cheese.

These are pounded and sieved, mingled with honey and preserved in a new jar. Then when it is needed, whatever sized quantity seems right should be diluted in vinegar and fish sauce.

Fig. 19 Silphium, as depicted on the reverse of a bronze coin of Cyrene. Silphium was a frequent symbol on Cyrenean coinage.

LUCAN

Marcus Annaeus Lucanus

Though born (in AD 39) at Corduba in Baetica (now Cordoba, Spain), Lucan was brought to Rome as a baby and enjoyed the typical education of a wealthy Roman. He benefited from his family connections: Seneca the Elder, the noted writer on rhetoric, was his grandfather; Seneca the Younger, tutor to the young Emperor Nero, was his uncle. His friendship with Nero led to his being given official appointments at an age earlier than the law allowed. However, after the younger Seneca's dismissal in 62, Lucan found the Emperor's favour greatly diminished. Implicated in the conspiracy of Piso against Nero in 65, Lucan chose to commit suicide rather than be executed.

The young poet flourished in the literary and artistic climate fostered by Nero. His only surviving work is the *Bellum Civile (Civil War)* or *Pharsalia*, which is probably incomplete, although he evidently wrote and recited other works.

Lucan's poem describes the civil war between Julius Caesar and the Roman senate which had taken place a hundred years before his time. His aim seems to be to shock the reader into adopting a position in the politics of that time by emphasising the horrors of war through vivid, lurid or macabre imagery and rhetorical energy, and to present the noble Stoic philosophy of Cato as a contrast to the usurping violence of Caesar. He shows off his often obscure learning, such as astronomical observations or the many species of snakes to be found in the Libyan desert, and includes much technical vocabulary as a result.

His reputation has fluctuated greatly. He is now regarded as inferior to other Roman poets, especially those of the Augustan age, but he was admired by Statius and Martial who wrote for the generation after him, and later by poets such as Dante and Shelley. His contribution to our theme is, however, significant. Here we find: (1) the nations of Juba's kingdom; (2) a description of, and explanation for, the Syrtes; (3) some divinities and legends associated with Libya; (4) the geography and environment of Libya, and how the Romans are exploiting it; (5) the desert wind and the reason why it is so powerful; (6) the geography of Ammonium (Siwa) and the Tropic of Cancer; (7) the many species of venomous animals, both real snakes and mythical reptiles; and (8) the practices of the Psylli of Libya.

It is important to note that, although Lucan's geographic and scientific descriptions are based on fact, his dramatic and often strained style demands great exaggeration. Cato's march, though a renowned logistical exercise of note to military historians, is expanded by Lucan into a catalogue of hardships two months long, crossing the length and breadth of Libya, which contrasts with Strabo's statement that it took a month, and Plutarch's more sober account of a week's journey over a more restricted area. The histrionics have been largely excluded here, as well as the speeches and the character of Cato (for which see the summary in Seneca). Cato's philosophical doubts about the oracle of Ammon may be compared to the pious paganism in Silius Italicus 2 and the Christian condemnation in Corippus.

1 *Juba's Libyan empire*

All of Africa which had yielded to the Roman cohorts was then under the authority of Varus who, although confident in the power of Latium, nevertheless called forth Juba's troops from every quarter; the Libyan peoples and the furthest cohorts of the world accompanied their king.

His land was more extended than that of any other lord. To what extent were his territories the vastest? Atlas in the neighbourhood of Gades bounded them at its western point, Ammon bordering on the Syrtes bounded them on the meridian. But where it established its flanks, a burning tract of the desert kingdom separated the Ocean and the dried up parts of the Hot Zone.

The peoples matched its size. So many attended the camp: the Autololes, and the roving Numidians, and the Gaetulians always equipped with horses without accoutrements; and then the Moors of the same colour as the Indians, the destitute Nasamonians, swift Marmaridae united with the swarthy Garamantians, and the Mazacians who would equal the arrows of the Medes when they hurled quivering javelins; and the nation residing in Massylia which, riding bareback, turns mouths unaware of bridles with lightweight switch; and the African hunter, accustomed to wander in villages devoid of commerce and to cover furious lions with his roomy garments as soon as he has no confidence in his weapon.[1]

1 Pliny, in his *Natural History* (VIII, xxi, 54), explains how Gaetulians first discovered how to catch lions by throwing cloaks over them. This became one of the showpieces in the Roman arena.

2 The perils of Libya I: the Syrtes

And now, through the business of warfare and by a series of tasks, Cato resolved to engage minds unskilled in tolerating the quiet life. First the army was wearied on the sands of the sea shore. The next task was against the city walls and ramparts of Cyrene – having been shut out, he avenged himself without wrath and for Cato the only penalty with respect to the vanquished was for Cato to have vanquished them. After that it was decided to attack the territories of Libyan Juba bordering upon the Moors, but Nature opposed the march by putting the Syrtes in the middle: bold vigour expected Nature to submit to it.

Nature either left the Syrtes undetermined between ocean and land when she was giving its first form to the world (for the ground neither sank completely to where it might receive the waters of the deep, nor did it protect itself from the sea, but the place lies inaccessible through the condition of the locality, sometimes taking one form, sometimes another, the sea broken by shoals and the land separated by the deep, and the waves resound, stretched out behind many beaches; to such an extent has Nature given up and required nothing useful of this part of herself); or, some time ago the Syrtis was fuller of the ocean and completely inundated, but the fierce Titan, pasturing his sunbeams on the depths, drew up the surface of the sea in the neighbourhood of the Burnt Zone; even now the depths still oppose Phoebus who dries; presently, as soon as destructive time has brought his rays, the Syrtis will be dry land; for water already shallow flows above, and the surface of the sea, about to disappear, is departing on all sides.

3 Lake Triton and the Garden of the Hesperides[2]

As tradition has it, this lake is loved by the god whom the sea hears sounding his braying notes all over the shore through a shell filled with the wind, and by Pallas when, new-born from her father's head, the first of the lands she came to was Libya – for it is nearest to the sky, as its very heat proves – and

2 In this mythological passage, the trumpeting sea god is Triton. Pallas, Greek goddess of wisdom and warfare, was born from her father Zeus's head. The River Lethon is associated with the River Lethe of the Underworld, from which dead souls drank to forget past lives. The Garden of the Hesperides (the Ladies of the West) contained trees of golden apples which were picked by Heracles/Hercules, descended from Alceus, as one of his twelve labours imposed by King Eurystheus of Argos. The places mentioned were associated both with an area west of the Gulf of Gabès (the Chott Djerid and the Atlas Mountains) and locations near Cyrene. Lucan maintains the geographic uncertainty.

Fig. 20 Hercules, the powerful Greek hero, was set various tasks, including collecting the golden apples from the Garden of the Hesperides in North Africa. This relief, from the forum of Leptis Magna, shows a number of his labours.

she saw her looks in the calm waters of the pool and set her feet on its edge and called herself Tritonis after this water beloved to her. Near to it the noiseless River Lethon flows along bringing forgetfulness, as tradition has it, from the water courses of the Underworld; and the Garden of the Hesperides, once the charge of an unsleeping dragon, now impoverished with its green boughs stripped. He who disparages that tradition from time of old, who exhorts poets to write facts, is a grudge.

There was a golden orchard and boughs laden with riches and tawny buds, and a band of young women as guards of the glittering thicket, and a serpent, doomed never to close its eyes in slumber, entwining the trees bent crooked by gold metal. Hercules, descendant of Alceus, robbed the trees of their value and the grove of its purpose and, leaving the branches forlorn without their burden, returned to the Argive king, carrying the gleaming fruits.

4 The poverty of Libya

Libya is the third region of the world, if you wish to believe all the talk of the multitude; but if you went by the winds and the sky it would be one region with Europe. For the banks of the Nile are not further away from Gades (from where Europe shuns Libya and, by curving away, the shores have made room for the Ocean) than the Scythian Tanais is. But the greater region of the world has gone into making Asia alone. For although the first two bring forth Zephyr, the West Wind, the other, bordering on the left side of Boreas, the North Wind, and the right side of Notus, the South Wind, goes into the east, sole mistress of Eurus, the East Wind.

That part of the land of Libya which is fertile is inclined towards the west, but even this is not broken up by any water courses. It receives northern rains from the scarce northerly Aquilones, and its fields revive during fair weather for us. Libya is not violated for any resources, it is not melted down for copper or gold; the land is completely undefiled, with no reproach for its soils. To its inhabitants, Maurusian hardwoods were riches so small they did not know a use for them but lived satisfied with the foliage and shade of the citrus tree. Our axes have come to the grove unacquainted with them, and we seek dishes on the table from the furthest ends of the earth.

But all that coast encloses the shifting Syrtis and far beneath the immoderate light of day, near to the scorched sky, it burns up the corn crops and kills Bacchus and, crumbling away, is not held fast by any roots. That vital temperateness has vanished and the land is not under the care of Jupiter. Nature languishes idly and, with its sands undisturbed, it does not feel the Earth's seasons. However, it is so inactive it only puts forth scattered weeds which the Nasamonians – a hardy, naked people – gather.

They occupy the lands nearest the sea. The savage Syrtis nourishes them through the losses of mankind, for the wrecker is a threat on the sands of the shore and he knows wealth even when no ship reaches the harbours. In this way – through shipwrecks – do the Nasamonians have dealings with all the world.

5 The perils of Libya II: the wind

Stern virtue commands Cato to go this way. There his soldiers, unconcerned about the winds and not fearing any storms on land, suffered the anxieties of the sea. For the Syrtis catches the Southerly Auster more violently on the dry shore than on the sea, and it is more harmful to the land. When it has risen, Libya does not break it with mountains standing over against it, nor disperses it when beaten back by cliffs nor weakens it from a tornado into calm breezes; nor does it fall on woods and, bending the aged oaks, is it deprived of its vigour. All the land is exposed and, unimpeded, Auster drives the Aeolian fury through all the sands and violently impels clouds without rain into a twister with whirling dust. A very large portion of the soil is removed and hangs in the vortex that is never set free. The needy Nasamonian sees his possessions flying about on the wind and his home smashed to pieces, and the Garamantian is unroofed;

huts, caught by the gables, fly about. The dust has as much mastery of the atmosphere as fire which carries its plunder no higher and can rise as much with its smoke and profane the light of day. Then, too, more violently than usual, it attacked the Roman column and the unsteady soldier could not stand firm on the sands, even those on which he was treading being carried off.

If Libya were rocky with a solid structure and an unyielding mass it might confine the Southerly Auster in eroded caverns and would shake the earth and move the world from its foundation; but because, with its loose sands, it is easily disturbed, it remains stable by resisting nowhere, and the lowest ground stands firm because the topmost ground takes flight. [...]

When Southerly Notus was tormenting the earth in this way the Roman soldiers lay prostrate and were frightened of being carried off. They had drawn their clothing tight and inserted their hands into the soil and lay there, not only by their weight but through effort; even in this way they were hardly motionless in the Southerly Auster who rolled huge mounds of sand over them and covered the men with earth. Soldiers were barely able to raise their limbs held fast by the great mass of dust. Even those standing were bound by a large mound of sand poured over them and were held by the rising soil, unable to move.

6 *Cato feels no need to consult the oracle of Jupiter Ammon*

He had come to the temple, the only one among the peoples of Libya. It belongs to the savage Garamantians. Oracular Jupiter lives there, so they say, but he neither brandishes thunderbolts nor is similar to our god, but is Ammon with crooked horns. The peoples of Libya have not built rich sanctuaries there, nor do treasure chambers gleam with Eastern gems. Although the multitudes of the Æthiopians and the prosperous tribes of Arabs and the Indians may have only Jupiter Ammon, the god is poor, occupying sanctuaries which no riches have profaned throughout eternity, and the deity of the customs of yesteryear has protected the temple from Roman gold.

A wood, the only one that flourishes in the whole of Libya, proves that the gods above are in those places. For everything that separates with its dry sand the burning territory of Berenice from warm Leptis has no knowledge of foliage. Ammon alone has contributed a wood. The reason for the trees in the place is a spring which binds the looseness of the soil and unites the subdued sands with its water. Here, too, nothing stands in the way of Phoebus. When the summer solstice stands at its highest, the day is in equilibrium. A tree scarcely shields its trunk, so short is the shadow brought together in the centre by the rays. It has been discovered that this is the place where the circle of the upper solstice strikes the middle of the circle of the constellations.[3] But for you, whatever people you may be, separated by the burning heat of Libya, your shadow falls towards the Southerly Notus; for us it goes towards the Great Bear. For you the sluggish Little Bear climbs, you think the dry Plough is immersed in the deep and have no constellation overhead ever free from the sea, and either pole is far away, and the speed of the constellations carries away everything in the middle of the sky. They do not pass by obliquely nor does Scorpio rise more steeply than Taurus, or Aries give his appointed times to Libra, or Virgo bid Pisces to sink slowly; Sagittarius is equal to Gemini, and moist Capricorn the same as burning Cancer, and Aquarius's Water Jar is not elevated more than Leo.

Fig. 21 A sundial, depicted in a Roman relief from the theatre at Sabratha.

Large crowds which the East had sent stood before the doors and, through the prophecy of horned Jupiter, sought destinies not yet experienced. But they gave precedence to

3 Lucan here describes the Tropic of Cancer ('the circle of the upper solstice') crossing the Zodiac. He goes on to describe the phenomenon of shadows falling to south or north, although this observation belongs more strictly to the equator than the tropic. For Europeans, constellations such as the Great Bear (which includes the Plough) and the Little Bear are circumpolar, in other words they never seem to set but move slowly round the North Pole; for the people of the tropics they will appear to set in the sea. Again, whilst in Europe the signs of the Zodiac appear to pass by at a greater or lesser angle to the zenith (i.e. overhead) as the year progresses, and so some signs appear to move faster than others, in the tropics the Zodiac passes quickly directly overhead from horizon to horizon, each sign occupying a near equal amount of space and time when passing by. Lucan lists the constellations in their opposite pairs.

the Latian general, and his comrades entreated Cato to put to the test the divine powers famed all over the Libyan world, that he might judge a reputation that had endured so long. Labienus gave the most encouragement to examine fate through the voice of the gods. [...]

Cato, filled with the god whom he bore concealed in his soul, gave vent from his heart to words worthy of being from those sanctuaries: 'What do you bid me seek, Labienus? Whether I might want to die in war a free man rather than see despotism? Whether there is no difference if life is short or our time is of long duration? Whether violence, that is of no account, may hurt a good man and fortune waste its threats when virtue is standing against it; and is it enough to want things that are laudable and virtue never to grow by success? We know this and Ammon will not implant this deeper in us. We all cleave to the gods above and, even when the temple is silent, we do nothing without the aid of the god. And the godhead acted with no maxims and the creator told us whatever it is permitted to know as we were being born. Did he choose these barren sands so that he might prophesy to a few, and did he bury the truth in this dust? Is there an abode of the god save the land and the sea and the air and the sky and virtue? What do we seek besides the gods above? Jupiter is all that you see, all that affects you. Let the unsure desire soothsayers, and those who are always doubtful about future events. It is not oracles that make me sure, but certain death. The timid and the brave must fall – it is enough that Jupiter has said it.'

Fig. 22 The few remains of the original Temple of Ammon at Siwa.

Fig. 23 Head of Medusa, one of several gorgon heads in the forum at Leptis Magna.*

Having given utterance in this manner, he went away from the altars, preserving the honour of the temple and leaving Ammon, untested, to the crowds.

7 The perils of Libya III: the deadly snakes

Now the radiance grew more intense and they trod the region beyond which, from the middle of the sky onwards, the gods have created no other for mortal men, and water was scarcer. A single spring, abundant in water, was found in the middle of the sands but which a throng of snakes was occupying, the place scarcely able to contain them. Parched asps were on the edge, dipsads thirsted in the midst of the waters. [...]

Why the Libyan environment, abounding in forms of death, overflows with so many curses, or what Nature in secret has blended in its harmful soil, our trouble and labour have not been able to find out, except that, instead of the true reason, a tale spread all over the world has deceived generations.

[Having cast doubt on the myth as a source of fact, Lucan proceeds to tell the story anyway: how the hero Perseus slew the snake-haired gorgon Medusa in Libya and how her gore soaked into the land and so gave rise to a multitude of deadly snakes.]*

Here this poison made a head first stir out of the dust and raised the deadly asp with its swelling nape, there the blood and a drop of the dense venom fell more plentifully; in no reptile is it more concentrated. Needing warmth, this snake does not go into the cold region of the world of its own accord but traverses the sandy deserts as far as the Nile. But – will we feel shame in profit? – Libyan forms of death from over there are desired over here, and we have made the asp an item of merchandise.

Moreover, the enormous *haemorrhois* unfolds its scaly coils – it will not let blood stay within its wretched victims; and the *chersydrus*, born to live on the changeable shore of the Syrtes; and the *chelydrus*, hauling itself along in a track that smoulders; and the *cenchris* forever sliding in a straight line – this one is coloured with more marks on its variegated belly than the serpentine marble of Thebes, ornamented with little spots; and the *hammodytes*, indistinguishable from the dried up sands; and the twisting backbone of the *cerastes*; and the *scytale*, it alone shedding its skin with the hoar frost still sprinkled about; and the parched *dipsas*; and the noxious *amphisbaena* turning one head towards its twin; and the *natrix*, desecrator of water; and the flying *iaculus*; and the *parias*, content to furrow a way with its tail; and the voracious *prester* stretching wide its frothing mouth; and the corroding *seps* that destroys the bones along with the body; and the basilisk, giving vent to its hisses and frightening all the other pests – inflicting harm even before its venom does, it drives the whole multitude far away from itself and lords it in the vacated desert.

You dragons, too, shining in golden splendour, who crawl as deities in all lands, doing harm to none, fiery Africa makes you deadly. You move the airs on high with your wings and, following entire herds, you encircle

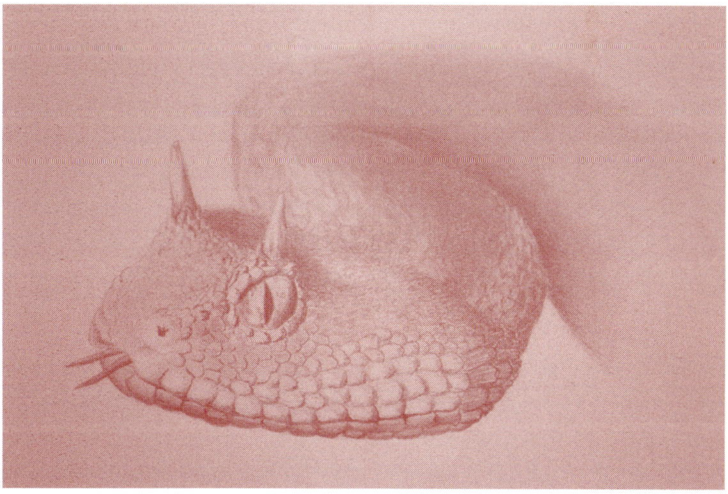

*Fig. 24 The horned desert viper (*Cerastes cerastes*).*

huge bulls, rending them with a blow; not even the elephant is safe in his bulk; you offer all things up to destruction and you do not need poison for your awful killings. [...]

Who would have thought the scorpion possessed doom or the power of an early death? Threatening with its segments, and fierce with its sting straight up, it took away the glory of Orion whom it had conquered, as the sky has been called to witness.

Who would fear to tread on your lair, *salpuga*? The infernal sisters give you rights over their threads of life.[4]

8 *The Psylli come to the aid of the Roman army*

So neither bright day nor dark night gave them rest. To the wretched men the ground on which they lay was suspect. For neither heaped-up leaves made their couches, nor did their beds rise on straw, but their bodies, exposed to death, were rolled up together on the ground and with their warmth they attracted the pests that were chilled by the night's cold and for a long time, between their limbs, the snakes' food kept them warm, harmless, with their poison inactive. [...]

With difficulty did Fortune, tired of so much danger, give late succour to the wretched men. A unique race inhabits those lands, unharmed by the ferocious bites of the reptiles: the Psylli of Marmarica. Their tongues are the equal of potent herbs, their very blood is safe and has the power not to let any poison in, even without using incantations. The nature of their locality has bidden them be unharmed by the reptiles they mingle with. It benefited them to have placed their abode in the midst of poisons. Peace with death was granted to them.

They have so much confidence in their blood. Whenever a small child has been born into the world, if they fear that there has been a union of love with a foreigner, they put the dubious offspring to the test with a deadly asp. And in the same way that Jupiter's bird, the eagle, when it has brought its unfledged children forth from the warm egg, turns them towards the sunrise – the ones who can endure the rays and withstand the daylight with eyes straight ahead are retained in the employment of heaven; those who have yielded to Phoebus are neglected – in that way a Psyllus has assurance of his race if the infant is one who is not afraid of touching snakes and if it is one who plays with the reptile given him.

4 The *salpuga* was a species of venomous ant. In Greek myth, the infernal sisters were the Fates who spun a thread representing the lifetime of each human being. Death came when the thread was cut.

And this race is not satisfied only with its own safety: a Psyllus is on the alert for foreigners and is present for all peoples against harmful monsters.

At that time they followed the Roman standards. As soon as the commander ordered the tents to be set up, they first purified the sands which the extent of the rampart enclosed, by incantation and words to banish the snakes. Medicinal fire surrounded the perimeter of the camp. Here dwarf elder crackled and foreign galbanum plants exuded juice; and tamarisk not rich in foliage and Eastern costus and potent panacea and Thessalian centaury and sulphurwort and thapsia from Eryx made noise in the flames. And they burnt larch, and southernwood offensive to reptiles with its smoke, and the horns of a deer born far away.

In this way night was safe for the men. But if anyone attracted misfortunes from a pest by day, then the marvels of that race were magic and great was the fight of the Psylli with the poison that had been taken. Now he would first indicate with his saliva the limbs that had been bitten, which restrained the venom and kept it within the wound; then, with an uninterrupted murmuring, he would breathe a great many incantations with his frothing tongue and the rapidity of the wound would not allow him breaths nor would death allow him to be silent for the shortest time. Often, indeed, the destruction implanted in the black marrow fled, charmed out; but if the venom listened to this more slowly and, after being lured and ordered to go out, it resisted, then, leaning over the pale-coloured wounds, he would lick them, extracting the poisons with his mouth and would drain the limbs with his teeth and, victorious, he would spit death out from the cold body. And it would now be evident to the Psylli, even by the taste of the poison, which snake's bite had been overcome.[5]

So at last, relieved by this help, the Roman soldiers wandered far and wide over the desert lands. Phoebe the Moon, having twice hidden her blaze and twice regained her light, rising and vanishing, saw Cato wandering the sands. And then, more and more, the dust began to harden for him and Libya, thickening, returned to solid ground and then the leaves of the stands of trees began to raise themselves and uncivilised huts built from straw began to arise. How much joy this better land gave the wretched men when they first saw lions face to face! The nearest town was Leptis [Minor]; in its quiet military station they spent a winter free from rains and heat.

5 The actions and remedies of the Psylli here may be contrasted with the remedies and scepticism in Celsus 1.

PLINY THE ELDER

Gaius Plinius Secundus

Rome's foremost natural historian had a distinguished military and administrative career in Germany in his younger years, and in various provinces later on under the Emperor Vespasian. He died in the famous eruption of Mount Vesuvius in AD 79 while holding the post of admiral of Rome's Western Mediterranean fleet (and so gives his name to the Plinian type of volcanic eruption). He found time to write many works, particularly under the reign of Nero when he chose to keep a low profile in politics, but his encyclopaedic *Naturalis Historia (Natural History)* in 37 volumes is the only one to survive. It covers every topic of a scientific nature and is a mine of information, but not all of which is accurate as he seems to have used his sources somewhat uncritically.

Our selection begins with extracts from his geographical survey, followed by descriptions of local animals and plants, including a vital passage describing the silphium plant. His geological studies also provide useful material on rocks and minerals of Libya, especially the carbuncles that were traded across the Sahara. The term *carbuncle* seems to apply here to various precious stones of reddish hue, particularly carnelians, although not all of them originated in Libya.

The items included in this miscellany are those which Pliny associated directly with Libya in some way, so not all animals, plants and minerals which happen to have existed in ancient Libya are included.

1 The continent of Africa

The Greeks called Africa *Libya* and the sea in front of it the Libyan Sea. It is bounded by Ægypt. No other part of the earth contains fewer bays in the length of its coasts, which slant a long way away from the west. The names of the peoples and of the towns are totally unpronounceable except in their own languages. And for the rest, they usually inhabit strongholds.

2 The Syrtes

The third gulf [the coast from Sfax to Benghazi] is divided into twin gulfs [Gulf of Gabès and Gulf of Sidra] made terrible by the shallow and receding sea of the two Syrtes. Polybius relates that it is 300 miles [450 km] from Carthage to the nearest, which is the smaller, and is itself a hundred miles [150 km] across its entrance and three hundred [450 km] in circumference. And there is a way to it by land through sandy desert wastes and reptiles by observing the stars. There follow ravines filled with a great number of wild animals and, towards the interior, the lonely haunts of elephants, then empty deserts, and on the other side are the Garamantes, separated from the Augilae by a 12 days' journey.

Beyond them there used to be the nation of the Psylli, beyond whom is the Lake of Lycomedes surrounded by deserts. The Augilae for their own part are situated in the space nearly in the middle, at an equal distance on both sides from the Æthiopia which lies towards the west, and from the tract which lies between the two Syrtes. But along the coast it is 250 miles [380 km] between the two Syrtes. In that place there are the city of Oea [Tripoli]; the River Cinyps [Wadi Caam] and its district; the towns of Neapolis [or Leptis Magna], Taphra, Abrotonum [or Sabratha]; and the other Leptis, which is called Magna ['Great']. From that place the Greater Syrtis [Gulf of Sidra] is 625 miles [950 km] in compass but 312 miles [475 km] across its entrance. The race of the Cisippades dwells by it.

In the innermost sweep of the gulf was the country of the Lotophagi [the Lotus-Eaters], whom some call the Machroae, near to the Altars of the Philaeni. These are made of sand. After these, not far from the edge of the continent, an enormous lake receives the River Triton, and its name from that river. It was called the Pallantian Lake by Callimachus and was said to be near the Lesser Syrtis [Gulf of Gabès]; in fact, it is said by many to be between the two Syrtes. The cape that confines the Greater Syrtis is called Borion [Ras Taiunes]. Beyond is the province of Cyrenaica.

3 *Cyrenaica*

Cyrenaica (the same as the district of the Pentapolis) is renowned for the oracle of Ammon [at Siwa], which is 400 miles [600 km] from Cyrene [Shahat]; for the Fountain of the Sun; and most of all for five cities: Berenice [Benghazi], Arsinoe [Tocra], Ptolemais [Tolmeta], Apollonia [Marsa Susa] and Cyrene itself.

Berenice is on the outermost point of the Syrtis. It was formerly called Hesperidum, mentioned above, the fables of Greece being variously related.[1] And not far from the town is the River Lethon and a sacred

1 Pliny placed the legendary Garden of the Hesperides near the Atlantic coast of N. Morocco.

grove where the Gardens of the Hesperides are spoken of. It is 375 miles [570 km] from Leptis. Arsinoe, called Teuchira, is 43 miles [65 km] from it; and from there Ptolemais, with its former name of Barca, is 22 miles [33 km]. Then 40 miles [60 km] away Cape Phycus [Ras Sem] extends into the Cretan Sea, being 350 miles [530 km] distant from Cape Taenarum in Laconica, and in fact 225 miles [340 km] from Crete itself. After this is Cyrene, 11 miles [17 km] from the sea. From Phycus to Apollonia is 24 miles [36 km], to Cherronesus [Ras el Tin] it is 88 miles [134 km], from where it is 216 miles [328 km] to Catabathmos. The Marmaridae live near here, extending almost from the region of Paraetonium [Mersa Matruh] all the way to the Greater Syrtis.

After them are the Acrauceles and then the Nasamonians on the coast of the Syrtis whom the Greeks formerly called the Mesammones ['Midsanders'] on the evidence of their location, lying as they do half way in the middle of the sands. The district of Cyrene for 15 miles [23 km] in extent from the coast is regarded as fertile even for trees; but, for the same distance further inland, only for agricultural produce; then for 30 miles [45 km] in breadth and 250 miles [380 km] in length only for silphium.

After the Nasamonians there live the Asbytae and the Macae; beyond them live the Amantes after a 12 days' journey from the Greater Syrtis, and are themselves surrounded by sands towards the west. For all that, however, at a depth of about two cubits [1 m], with no difficulty at all, they come upon wells there from the overflowing waters of Mauretania. They build houses from salt hewn out of mountains as if it were stone. From them to the Troglodytes is a journey of seven days in the quarter of the winter sunset [i.e. south west], and with whom the only trade is in the precious stone imported from Æthiopia which we call the carbuncle.

4 The conquest of Phazania

Phazania lies between them towards the deserts of Africa, described as being beyond the Lesser Syrtis, where we conquered the Phazani people, and the walled towns of Alele and Cilliba, and likewise Cydamus [Ghadames] in the opposite direction from Sabratha. After these, extending for a long distance from east to west, is a mountain called Ater ['the Dark Mountain'] by our own men from its nature, similar to its having been scorched or set on fire by the sun's reflection.

Beyond it are deserts; then Thelgae, a town of the Garamantes, and also Debris with a spring that flows by with waters that are boiling from the middle of the day to the middle of the night and frozen for just as many hours to the middle of the day; and Garama [Germa], the very famous capital of the Garamantes. All were vanquished by Roman troops [c. 20 BC] and triumphed over by Cornelius Balbus, a triumphal procession [19 BC] and full Roman citizenship having been granted to this foreigner alone of all men since, after having been born in Gades [Cadiz], he was given Roman citizenship with Balbus the Elder, his paternal uncle [72 BC]. And this is extraordinary: that our historians have recorded the towns mentioned above that were captured by him and that, in his triumphal procession, besides Cydamus and Garama themselves, they carried the names and images of all the other peoples and cities, which would have gone in this order: the town of Tabudium, the Niteris tribe, the town of Milgis Gemella, the tribe or town of Bubeium, the Enipi tribe, the town of Thuben, the mountain by the name of Niger ['the Black Mountain'], the towns of Nitibrum and Rapsa, the Viscera tribe, the town of Decri, the River Nathabur, the town of Thapsagum, the Tamiagi tribe, the town of Boin, the town of Pege, the River Dasibari; then, following one after another, the towns of Baracum, Buluba, Alasit, Galsa, Balla, Maxalla, Cizania; an inscription preceded Mount Gyri, 'in which precious stones are found'.

Thus far the road to the Garamantes has been impassable, the wells being covered over with sand by bandits of that people – the wells do not need to be dug deep if one has knowledge of the localities. In the last war which they waged in company with the inhabitants of Oea at the beginning of the reign of the Emperor Vespasian [AD 69], a shortcut of four days' journey was discovered. This road is called 'By the Head of the Rock.'

5 *Towards Ægypt*

The boundary of Cyrenaica is called Catabathmos, a town and a valley that inclines suddenly. From the Lesser Syrtis to this boundary, Cyrenaic Africa extends 1,060 miles [1,610 km] in length and, as far as is known, 810 miles [1,230 km] in breadth.

What follows is called Mareotic Libya, having a common border with Ægypt. It is occupied by the Marmarides, the Adyrmachidae, and then the Mareotae. The distance from Catabathmos to Paraetonium is 86 miles [131 km]. Within this tract of land Apis, a place renowned in the religion of Ægypt, is of interest. From there to Paraetonium is 62½ miles [95 km]. From that place to Alexandria is 200 miles [300 km]. It is 169 miles [257 km] in breadth. Eratosthenes records that it is 525 miles [800 km] by the land route from Cyrene to Alexandria; Agrippa that the length of the whole of Africa from the Atlantic Sea together with lower

Ægypt is 3,000 miles [4,500 km]. Polybius and Eratosthenes, considered to be very careful, assert that it is 1,100 miles [1,675 km] from the ocean to Great Carthage, and from Carthage to Canopus, the nearest mouth of the Nile, is 1,628 miles [2,478 km]; Isidorus that it is 3,599 miles [5,477 km] from Tingis [Tangiers] to Canopus; Artemidorus that it is 40 miles [60 km] less than Isidorus.

6 The island of Meninx

These seas do not encircle very many islands. The most famous is Meninx [Jerba], 25 miles [38 km] in length and 22 miles [33 km] in breadth, called Lotophagitis ['the Island of the Lotus-Eaters'] by Eratosthenes. It has two towns, Meninx [El Kantara] on the African side and Thoar on the other, the island itself lying a mile and a half [2.3 km] from the cape to the right of the Lesser Syrtis.

7 Desert peoples

But in the interior circuit of Africa towards the south and beyond the Gaetulians, with deserts lying between, first of all there reside the Ægyptian Libyans, then the White Æthiopians. Beyond them are peoples of the Æthiopians: the Nigritae, from that river mentioned above;[2] the Pharusian Gymnetes; then the Perorsi bordering on the Ocean, whom we mentioned at the limit of Mauretania. Away from all these, towards the east, there are empty deserts all the way to the Garamantes and the Augilae and the Troglodytes, with the most reasonable belief being that of those who place the two Æthiopias beyond the deserts of [the Province of] Africa, and before all men that of Homer who narrates that the Æthiopias are divided into two parts, inclined towards the east and the west.[3] [...]

The Troglodytes hollow out caves and these are their homes. Their sustenance is the flesh of reptiles. And they have a shrill sound, not voices. They are even devoid of communication by discourse. The Garamantes live with their women indiscriminately, free from marriages. The Augilae worship only the inhabitants of the infernal regions. The Gamphasantes are naked and, taking no part in war, do not associate with any foreigner. They say that the Blemmyae are missing their heads, their mouths and

2 'The Black River, which separates Africa from Æthiopia' (V, iv, 30), which may be the River Niger or a lesser wadi of North Africa.

3 Homer, *Iliad*, I, 23–24. West and East Æthiopia are more or less West and East Africa.

eyes being fixed to their chests. The Satyrs have nothing of human nature except their shape. The appearance of the Aegipanes ['Goat-Pans'] is that which is commonly depicted. The Himantopodes ['Thongfoots'] are some strap-footed men whose nature is to walk by crawling. The Pharusii, formerly Persians, are said to have been companions of Hercules when he travelled to the Hesperides.

8 Supernatural powers

There was also the similar tribe of the Psylli in Africa, as Agatharchides describes, named after King Psyllus whose tomb is in the region of the Greater Syrtis. Their bodies had an innate poison that was deadly to snakes and by whose smell they put them to sleep; in fact, their custom was to have their children set before the fiercest of these as soon as they were born and to test the chastity of their wives with this species, the snakes not fleeing children of impure blood. At any rate, the tribe itself underwent near extermination at the hands of the Nasamonians who now live in their homes; yet a race of men descended from those who had fled or who were absent when the battle was fought endures today, few in number.

The similar tribe of the Marsi are also still in evidence in Italy, whom they say are descended from a son of Circe and that for this reason this natural power was in them. And yet there is in all men a venom against snakes: they say that snakes flee a jet of saliva as they would contact with boiling water and that they even die if this gets into their throats, especially from the mouth of a person who is fasting.

Calliphanes relates that beyond the Nasamonians and adjoining them are the Machylae, androgynes of either sex, mating among themselves as either one or the other. Aristotle adds that their right breast is that of a man, their left that of a woman.

Isigonus and Nymphodorus relate that there are certain families of witches in this part of Africa whose funeral incantations make meadowland perish, trees wither and little children die. [...]

In the deserts of Africa, visions of men arise, encountering people from time to time, and vanish in an instant.

9 Selected animals

Basilisks. The power of the basilisk serpent [i.e. to kill with a glance] is also the same [as the *catoblepas* (the gnu?)]. The province of Cyrenaica gives rise to it. It is not more than 12 inches [30 cm] in size with a white mark on its head that is prominent like a sort of diadem.* It puts all snakes to flight with its hiss and does not set its body in motion by winding its many coils like the rest of the snakes do, but advances high and upright from its middle. It kills shrubs, burns green stalks and cracks rocks not only by touching them but also just by breathing on them. Its power lies in harming others. It is believed that one was once killed by a spear from a man on a horse and the potency climbed along it; not only was the horseman killed but the horse also.

And yet to a marvel such as this – for kings have often longed to see one completely dead – the poison of weasels is destruction; and so it pleases nature that nothing should be without its match. They throw the basilisks into weasels' holes, which are easily recognised by the putrefying ground. The weasels kill them with their stench and die at the same time, and nature's struggle is accomplished.

Oxen. Oxen, alone of all the animals, graze even when walking backwards; indeed, among the Garamantes they do not do this in any other way.

Mice. There are more species of mice in the region of Cyrenaica, some with broad faces, others with pointed ones and others with prickly hairs like a species of hedgehog.

Frogs. At Cyrene the frogs used to be silent. A species of these continues in existence even though croaking ones have been brought from inland.

Sponges. Sponges all grow on rocks; they feed on shellfish, fish and mud. It appears that they have intelligence because when they sense a sponge diver they contract and are removed with far more difficulty. They also do this in a surging wave. Tiny shellfish found inside them clearly show that they live on food. Around Torone [Toroni, Greece] they say that even those which have been detached feed on these and regrow on the rocks from the roots that remain. The colour of blood is also inherent in them, especially in the African ones which breed in the Syrtes.

Animals of waterless places. In Africa the greater part of the wild animals do not drink in summer through scarcity of water. For this reason Libyan mice in captivity die if they drink. The perpetually arid parts of Africa produce a kind of wild goat which, from the nature of the place, does not drink and exists for the relief of the thirsty in a remarkable way, for bladders of a very wholesome liquid are found in their bodies and Gaetulian bandits hold out through this succour.

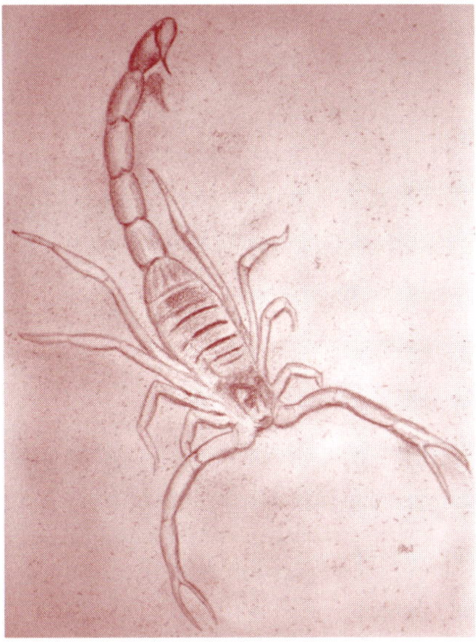

*Fig. 25 The deathstalker scorpion of North Africa (*Leiurus quinquestriatus*), of particular renown for the severity of its sting.*

Scorpions. Land scorpions, in a similar way to spiders, produce grubs with the appearance of eggs, and they die in a similar way. They are a troublesome pest with the poison of snakes except that they destroy with a suffering that is more grievous by a slow death over three days. Through their sting they are always fatal to girls and almost entirely so to women, but to men only in the morning when they have come out of their holes before they have shot their scanty poison by an accidental sting.

Its tail is always in the attitude of striking and at no time does it stop practising and never misses an opportunity; it strikes both with a sideways blow and with a blow that curves round. Apollodorus is the writer who says that they produce a white poison, having classified them into nine kinds, principally by their colours, a pointless exercise seeing that he has not previously mentioned how to tell which are the least deadly; and that some have twin stings and that the males are very fierce – for he ascribes coupling to them – and that they are distinguished by their slenderness and by their length.

They all have poison in the middle of the day when they have become warm in the sun's rays; and also, when they are thirsty, their drinking is insatiable. It is also agreed that the fiercer ones have seven joints in their tails, for there are more with six joints. The south winds even make this plague of Africa fly, lifting up their limbs like oars when they have been extended; Apollodorus also plainly states that certain ones possess wings.

The Psylli who, introducing the poisons of other countries, have almost filled Italy with foreign evils for the sake of their own profit, have also tried to import these but they have not been able to live this side [north] of the climate of Sicily.

Cicadas. Cicadas are not found where trees are far apart. For that reason they do not exist at Cyrene except around the town.

Locusts. In the region of Cyrenaica there is even a law for subduing locusts three times a year by crushing the eggs first, then the young and finally the adults, with the penalty of a deserter on the man who does nothing.

10 Notes on trees

Hammoniacum. Well then, Africa bordering on Æthiopia distils drops of *hammoniacum* in its sandy deserts. The oracle of Ammon even takes its name from this, close to which it is produced by the tree which they call *metops*. It is like resin or gum. There are two types of it: *thrauston* resembling male frankincense, which is particularly recommended; the other, which they call *phyrama*, is oily and resinous. It is adulterated with sandgrains as though they have clung to it while growing; therefore it is recommended that it be in the smallest lumps possible. The price for the best is 40 *asses** a pound.

Sphagnos. The *sphagnos* [aromatic moss] in the province of Cyrenaica lower than [i.e. north of] those places, is highly recommended. Others call it *byron*.

The elate. There is, moreover, a tree also suitable for ointments which some call the *elate*, which we call a fir, others a palm and others a *spatha*. The Ammonian is greatly commended, the Ægyptian next, then the Syrian. It is fragrant only in arid places with a dense gumdrop which is added to ointments to subdue the oil.

The citron. This tree is among the few furnishings of the more refined life and so it seems necessary to dwell upon it a little. It was known even to Homer – it is called *thyon* in Greek, *thya* by others. Consequently, he recounted that it was burned among the essences in the luxuries of Circe, whom he intended to be understood as a goddess;[4] those who interpret this word as perfumes are greatly mistaken, especially when he relates in the same line that cedar and larch were burned at the same time, by which it is clear that he was merely speaking about trees.

Theophrastus, who wrote directly after the era of Alexander the Great around the 440th year of the city of Rome [i.e. 314/313 BC], then greatly esteemed this tree, reporting that it was said that the floors of old

4 *Odyssey*, V, 60. In fact, Homer is describing the cave of the nymph Calypso rather than the palace of the sorceress Circe.

temples were made of it and that a particular imperishable quality of the genuine timber protects against all problems in roofed buildings.

Nothing is more wrinkled than its root and no other worked material is more valuable; moreover he says that this tree is of special note around the temple of Ammon and it also grows in the inland parts of Cyrenaica. However, he said nothing about tables and nobody has an earlier recollection of any before the time of Cicero.

The citrus. There is another tree with the same name, bearing fruit which some find detestable for its smell and its bitterness but which is sought after by others. Homes are also decorated with it, but it does not need describing in more words.

The lotus. Africa, where it faces towards us, also produces the remarkable lotus tree, which Theophrastus calls *celthis*, and this has been naturalised in Italy but has been changed by the soil. It is of special note around the Syrtes and the Nasamonians' country. Its size is that of a pear tree although Cornelius Nepos records that it is small. The indentations in the leaf seem something like the holm oak's but are more numerous. There are several varieties and their differences arise especially in the fruits. The size of the fruit is like a bean, its colour is like saffron but it is one colour and then another, like grapes. They grow thick-set on the branches in the same way as myrtle but not as cherry in Italy. There it is so very sweet a food that it has even given its name to a people and to a country that are too hospitable to strangers through their forgetting their native land. They say that whoever eats the fruit does not suffer disorders of the belly.

The better fruits are those without an inner kernel which, as regards the other variety, seems like bone. Also, a wine similar to mead is pressed out of it which Nepos also says does not last longer than ten days and that the berries cut up with spelt* are stored in large jars for victuals. And indeed we hear of armies being fed on it as they passed to and fro through Africa. The wood is a black colour. It is sought after for flute playing; from the root they fashion handles for small knives and other small necessities.

This is the nature of the tree there.

Christ's thorn. The region of Cyrenaica esteems its lotus below its *paliurus* [Christ's thorn]. The latter is bushier and more reddish in its fruit, the kernel of which is eaten separately; it is pleasant in its own right and sweeter in wine and, indeed, it makes wines agreeable with its juice.

The date palm. The inner part of Africa towards the Garamantes and as far as the deserts is composed of palm trees of great size and sweetness with ones of note especially around the temple of Ammon.

The poplar. There are three kinds of poplar: the silver, the black and the one which is called Libyan, very small and dark of leaf and highly esteemed for the mushrooms that sprout on it.

Propagation by rain. And not only does the nature of the soil around these trees [like the cypress] matter, or the constancy of the climate, but a temporary force as well: rainstorms generally bring some seeds and pour down with a particular kind, sometimes even an unknown kind, which happened in the region of Cyrenaica when silphium grew there for the first time, as we shall relate in the natural history of herbs. And a wood grew near that city from a thick, pitch-black rainstorm.

Almonds. In the region of Cyrenaica they plant almond trees when the etesian* winds are blowing.

11 *Libyan abundance*

Climate. But among the Bactri, in Africa and at Cyrene the mild climate makes weeding superfluous and the people do not return to the fields after sowing except for the harvest because the dryness controls weeds, the produce being nourished merely by the nocturnal dew.

Tacape. A city of Africa which is called Tacape [Gabès], in the middle of the desert for those travelling to the Syrtes and Leptis Magna, is fertile beyond all wonder from the well-watered soil. A spring overflows in every direction for about three miles. It is certainly copious but it is distributed among the inhabitants in fixed periods of time. Olive trees are set under the very large palm trees there, fig trees are set under the olives, pomegranates under the fig trees, and vines under those; under the vines they sow corn, then pulses and then vegetables, all these things in the same year, and all are maintained in the shade of another thing.

Four cubits each way of this earth in a square [4 m^2] are sold for four denarii.* (Cubits are not measured with fingers extended but drawn together into a fist.) Above all else is the fact that they gather the vintage twice a year from vines that bear fruit twice, and unless the fertility is exhausted in numerous ripenings the produce might be killed off in a single profusion. But as it is, something is in fact being gathered through the whole year and it is well known that men do not interfere in this fertility.

Pruning. Pruner, may the scars of your trees not face that way [i.e. north], neither vineyard trees nor vines, except in Africa, Cyrene and Ægypt.

12 A Libyal herbal

Misy. Similar to the truffle but fleshier, with a sweetness of scent and flavour that makes it outstanding, is the thing which they call *misy* in the Province of Cyrenaica and which they call *iton* in Thrace and which they call *ceraunion* in Greece.

Wild cucumber. Some record that at Cyrene, among the leaves and branches, there grows a cucumber like heliotrope, the size of a walnut, but that its seed is bent back like the tail of a scorpion, but it is white.

Some even call the cucumber 'scorpion'. Through its seed and *elaterium** it is very effective against the sting of a scorpion. A measure in due proportion, from a half to a whole obolus [0.25–0.5 g] is for purging the bowels of toxins; more than that and it kills. It is drunk in the aforesaid manner both against phthiriasis and by those who suffer from oedema. Anointed with honey or old olive oil it heals tonsillitis and affected windpipes.

Many think that it is what is called the *anguinus* ['serpentine'] among us and the wild cucumber by others. Mice do not touch things sprinkled with a decoction of it. The same people say that, boiled down with vinegar, they spread it for gout and for disorders of the joints as a medicine that acts fast; it even heals aches of the loins with its seed that has been dried in the sun and then ground, to the measure of 20 denarii* [70 g] in a hemina [25 cl] of water, and it heals sudden swellings when applied with women's milk. Its *elaterium** purges women but causes miscarriage in women who are pregnant. It is beneficial to asthmatics; squirted into the nostrils it is beneficial for jaundice; smeared on in the sunshine it removes freckles and spots from the face.

Rose of Cyrene. The rose of Cyrene is the most fragrant and that is why the most beautiful perfume comes from there.

Saffron. Cultivated saffron is broader and bigger and more luxuriant, but much milder [than wild saffron]. It is degenerating everywhere and is not abundant even at Cyrene where its flowers are always the most prized. [...]

On the other hand, there is a defect with the Cyrenaic variety which is darker than all other saffron and withers very quickly.

Lotus. We spoke of the lotus plant and also of the Ægyptian plant with the same name in their respective places, otherwise known as the tree of the Syrtes. This lotus, which is called the Greek bean by the Romans, checks the bowels with its berries; shavings of its wood boiled up in wine are useful for those who have dysentery, menstruation, dizziness and epilepsy, and they even keep the hair of the head from falling. It is strange that nothing is more bitter than these shavings and nothing is sweeter than the fruit. Also, medicine made from its sawdust boiled down in water of myrtle, kneaded and divided into lozenges, is very beneficial for those who have dysentery, in a dose of one victoriatus [1.75 g] to three cyathi [130 ml] of water.

13 Silphium, or laserwort

Next after these let us speak of laserwort, which the Greeks call *silphion*, very famous for its importance, found in the Province of Cyrenaica, the juice of which they call *laser*, valuable in general use and in medicines and purchased weight for weight in silver denarii.*

It has not been found in that country for many years now, since the tax collectors who rent the pastures ravage them for sheep fodder, understanding that there is more profit this way. Just one stalk has been found in our lifetime; it was sent to the Emperor Nero. If at any time a flock comes across a stalk that is hoping to grow, it is detected by this clue: when it has eaten it, a sheep sleeps on the spot and a goat sneezes.

And for a long time now no *laser* has been brought to us other than the one which grows in Persis or Media and in Armenia, growing plentifully but much inferior to the Cyrenaic one in value, and it is also adulterated with gum or *sacopenium** or crushed beans. It seems right that we should not omit that in the consulship of Gaius Valerius and Marcus Herennius [93 BC], 30 pounds [10 kg/22 lb] of laserwort were conveyed from Cyrene to Rome by the state and that, in fact, Caesar when dictator* at the start of the civil war [49 BC], brought 1,500 pounds [500 kg /1,100 lb] of laserwort out of the treasury among the gold and silver.

Among the most reliable writers of Greece we find that this grew when the ground around the Gardens of the Hesperides and the Greater Syrtis were suddenly soaked by a pitch-black rainstorm seven years before the town of Cyrene was built, which was in the 143rd year of our

Fig. 26 The silphium plant, as depicted on the reverse of gold coins of Cyrene.

own city [611/610 BC], and that this force prevailed over 4,000 stadia [700 km] of Africa; that the laserwort, a wild and obstinate thing, with a very thick root and a stalk that resembled fennel and similar in thickness, used to arise in it and, if it was cultivated, it escaped into the desert. Its leaves, very similar to celery, they called *maspetum*; the seed was like leaves, the leaf itself falling off in the spring.

Herds of cattle used to feed on it and were first purged then grew fat in a remarkable way with agreeable meat. After the leaves had fallen men would eat of this stalk cooked in all ways – boiled and roasted – also purging their bodies for the first 40 days. The juice was obtained in two ways, from the root and from the stalk, and there were these two names, *rhizias* and *caulias*, the latter cheaper than the former and rotting sooner. The rind of the root was black.

For the adulteration of these wares this juice was collected in vessels with bran mixed in and they would bring it to maturity by repeated shaking, and it would rot if they had not done it this way. The proof of its ripeness was its colour and dryness, its moisture gone.

Others relate that the root of the laserwort was more than a cubit long, that there was undoubtedly a swelling on it above the ground and that when this was cut open juice like milk used to flow out, with a stalk growing over it which they called a *magydaris*; that leaves of a gold colour existed instead of a seed, falling off from the rising of the Dog with the south wind blowing,[5] and that laserwort used to grow from these, both root and stalk completing their growth in the space of a year. These people also relate that they used to be dug around and spring up, and that cattle were not purged but were cured if sick or else died right away, which happened only occasionally. The above belief corresponded with Persian silphium.

Another type of it is what is called *magydaris*, more delicate and less potent and lacking juice, which grows around Syria, not being produced in the region of Cyrenaica; it also arises in abundance on Mount Parnassus, certain people calling it laserwort. By means of all these kinds the worth of a very wholesome and very useful thing is adulterated. The first test of the genuine one is in the slightly reddish colour and, when it is broken in two, a white colour within; then in the drop which is translucent and which melts very quickly in saliva. It has its use in many medicines. [...]

Laser, flowing from silphium in the way which I reported, and numbered among the exceptional gifts of nature, is incorporated in several compounds, but on its own it alleviates colds, and when drunk it reduces defects of the nerves. It is given in wine to women and is applied to the womb on soft pieces of wool to stimulate menstruation. Mixed with wax it removes corns of the feet which have been cut around with a blade. An amount the size of a chickpea, diluted, stimulates urination.

Andreas gives an assurance that, taken more plentifully, it does not cause flatulence and that, for old people and women, it contributes greatly to digestion; and that it is more useful in winter than in summer, and then to those who drink only water. Take care that there is no internal ulceration. In food it is effective for convalescence after sickness; in fact, given at the right time it possesses the strength of a cautery and is even more useful to those accustomed to it than to those who have never had it.

There are sure proofs of it on the outside of the body. It renders the poisons of weapons and snakes powerless when drunk. It is smeared all over these wounds with water, and with oil only for the stings of scorpions. However, for sores which have not come to maturity it is smeared on with barley flour or with dry fig. For carbuncles it is smeared on with rue or with honey, or by itself with sticky lime so that it adheres. It is also applied in this way for dog bites, with the rind of a pomegranate boiled up in vinegar for growths around the posterior, and mixed with soda for the corns which are commonly called dead corns.

With wine and saffron or pepper, and even with mouse dung and vinegar, it restores mangy hair that has previously been rubbed with vinegar.

5 This is probably the night-time rising of Canis Major in December rather than the heliacal (daytime) rising in July when the etesian* winds blew from the north.

In wine it warms chilblains and is applied after cooking in olive oil; and is applied in the same way for hard skin and for corns of the feet that have been scraped. It is of outstanding usefulness against bad waters, and unhealthy districts and weather; for a cough, the uvula, jaundice of long standing, oedema and hoarseness; it immediately cleanses the throat and restores the voice. Diluted with vinegar-drink on a sponge it soothes gout.

It is given in a broth to patients with pleurisy who will be drinking wine, and smeared all over with wax in a dose the size of a chickpea for contractions and for those with opisthotony.* For tonsillitis it is gargled. It is given with leek in vinegar to those who have difficulty breathing and for a long-standing cough, and in like manner in vinegar to those who have swallowed curdled milk; it is given with wine for consumptive defects of the chest cavity and for those with epilepsy; it is given in honey-water for paralysis of the tongue. It is applied with boiled honey for aches of the hips and loins.

I would not advise what my authorities recommend, that it be applied with wax to stop up the cavities of teeth which are aching, by the weighty evidence of the man who threw himself from a height because of this. Smeared in their nostrils it certainly enrages bulls; mixed with wine it ruptures snakes which are very eager for it. For this reason I would not advise that teeth be anointed with it although they inform us that one can do so with Attic honey. Recalling what benefits it may have when mixed with other things would be never-ending, and we are dealing with uncompounded things seeing that it appears that its natural purity exists in its simple state; in the compound state its nature is more often fallacious conjecture; nobody keeps sufficient watch on the harmony and the contradictions of nature in compounds. There is more on this topic later.

14 Minerals

Salt. King Ptolemy also found salt near Pelusium when he was setting up a camp. From this precedent they began to find it thereafter between Ægypt and Arabia even in desert places when the sand was removed, as it is also found all over the arid parts of Africa as far as the oracle of Ammon. It becomes visible with the moon by night, in fact.

But districts of Cyrenaica are made famous by Ammoniac salt and were named after it because it is found under the sand.[6] In colour it is like the alum which is called *schistos* ['split alum'], in pieces that are long but

6 False etymology. Pliny is suggesting that the district of Ammonium is named after the Greek word for sand, *ammos*.

not transparent, with a taste that is disagreeable but useful in medicine.[7] It is most approved of when it is as transparent as possible, and cleaves straight. A distinguishing feature of it is reported: within its caverns it is very light in weight but when it is brought out into the common light of day it grows heavy with a weight that is scarcely believable. The reason is plain: the moist air of the pits helps the labourers in the way that water does. It is adulterated with the Sicilian salt which we called Cocanican and also with Cyprian salt which is wonderfully similar.

Paraetonium. Paraetonium takes its name from the place in Ægypt. They say that it is the foam of the sea bound together with mud and that is why tiny shells are found in it. It also arises in the island of Crete and at Cyrene. At Rome it is adulterated with Cimolian chalk that has been boiled and thickened. The price for the best is 50 denarii* for 6 pounds [2 kg/4½ lb]. It is the greasiest of the white colours and the most tenacious for plaster on account of its smoothness.

Carbuncles. In pride of place are the carbuncles ['little coals'], so called from their resemblance to firebrands, although they themselves are not affected by fire; because of this they are called *acaustae* ['incombustibles']. There are these kinds: the Indian and the Garamantian; the latter are also called Carchedonian [i.e. Carthaginian] because of the wealth of Great Carthage. In addition there are the Æthiopian and the Alabandian, originating in Orthosia of Caria but which are finished off at Alabanda. Moreover, in all these kinds, those which sparkle more etherially are called male and those which sparkle more faintly are called female. It is also noted that among the male ones there are those which are more transparent or of a darker flame colour and some which are brilliant from their depths and which blaze more in the sun than the other kind, the best resembling the amethyst, in fact; that is, the outermost sparkle of which comes out as the violet colour of amethyst. And next best to these are those which they call Syrtitae, which shine with a feathery brightness. Moreover, they say that they can be found when the reflection of the sun is greatest. [...]

Callistratus says that the splendour of the carbuncle ought to be bright so that it exalts cloudy ones with its brightness blazing through when placed on the other side of one being looked at. Because of this the majority call it the 'bright carbuncle', and the one which shines more dully the *lignyzon* ['smoky stone']. He says that the Carchedonian ones are much smaller and are hollowed out to a capacity of one sextarius [500 ml]. Archelaus says that the Carchedonian ones have a darker

7 See Celsus 2, for example.

appearance, but in fire or in sunlight and by tilting them to one side they are kindled more dazzlingly than the others; these ones appear purple when a roof is shading them, and flame-coloured under the open sky; they sparkle against the rays of the sun, and they melt wax when they are stamped as signets however much in the shade they might be.

Many have written that the Indian ones are brighter than the Carchedonian and become dull at a different angle, and also that in the Carchedonian males a star blazes within, and that the females shed all their splendour outside of themselves. [...]

Also related is the *sandastros*, which some also call Garamantian on account of its properties. [...]

It is said that this same ability [to attract chaff and fibres, i.e. by static] is held by the Carchedonian stone, although it is much cheaper than those mentioned before. It arises in the mountains among the Nasamonians through divine rain, as the inhabitants think. They are found as a result of the moon's reflection, especially when it is full. They were formerly conveyed to Carthage.

Nasamonitis. Nasamonitis [the 'stone of the Nasamonians'] is blood red with black veins.

Syrtitis. Syrtitides [gems of the Syrtes] are found on the shore of the Syrtes and, indeed, also on the shore of Lucania, glittering with saffron yellow from a general honey colour; yet they contain faint stars within.

MARTIAL

Marcus Valerius Martialis

Martial was born around AD 40 at Bilbilis in the province of Hispania Tarraconensis (now Calatayud in Aragon, Spain). He went to Rome in 64 and joined the literary circle that included Seneca and Lucan, but these new friends and patrons died in the reprisals that followed the Pisonian conspiracy against the Emperor Nero in 65. It was a long while before Martial's fortunes picked up again but the reign of Domitian (81–96) was especially favourable. Later, however, his close association with a discredited regime prompted him to return to his native city in 98 and he died there around 104.

His poetry consists entirely of epigrams *(Epigrammata)*, more than 1,500 of them. They are a cornucopia of wit, often incisive, poignant, teasing, lyrical, scurrilous, satirical, generous, sardonic, jovial and humane, and make delightful reading.

A selection concerning our theme is given below. The first two are taken from the *Xenia (Gift Mottoes)* and the *Apophoreta (Going-Away Presents)*, published around 84–85; the remainder are from the main corpus of epigrams.

1 A suburban farm needs Libyan corn

CORN

From a Libyan farmer's harvest take three hundred pecks
Lest your estates near Rome end up as wrecks.[1]

2 Home-grown fruit

[SOFT-SEEDED POMEGRANATES AND TUBER-APPLES]

Soft-seed pomegranates and spring tuber-apples I send,
Picked from boughs near Rome; of Libyan ones make an end.

1 Martial is probably suggesting that the estates were more for leisure than for farming – a common theme with him – so grain has to be brought in for domestic use. Imported cereals came chiefly from Rome's African provinces. A peck *(modius)* was almost 8.75 litres (nearly 2 gallons).

3 *Fluffy slippers*

CILICIAN GOAT-HAIR SOCKS[2]

It was not wool but he-goat's beard that yielded
A Cinyphian garment in which your foot can lie shielded.

4 *What Libyans say of the Governor's wife is untrue*

Your wife, Gallus, has a bad reputation among the peoples of Libya,
With an ugly accusation of excessive greed.
But bare-faced lies are told. She is not accustomed to take at all.
What, then, is she accustomed to do? To give.

5 *Rudeness on return from Libya*

For five days now I've wanted to greet you, Afer,
  – from Libyan tribes you're home again.
    I come back twice, thrice ... 'He's not free,'
    Or 'he's asleep,' they say to me.
Enough already, Afer!
  You don't want greetings? Bye-bye then!

6 *A handsome youth departs for Libya*

Spendophoros, his master's armour-bearer, travels to Libyan cities.
Cupid, prepare weapons which you may present to the boy,
Those with which you transfix young men and tender girls.
Yet let there also be a swift spear in his delicate hand;
I concede breastplate to you and shield and headpiece.
So that he enter combat safely, let him go exposed –
While Parthenopaeus was unimpeded by a helmet,
No javelin, no sword or arrow injured him.
Whoever is transfixed by him will die from desire –
Oh happy the one whom such good fortune awaits!
May you return while you are a boy, while smooth of face,
And Libya not make you a man but your own city of Rome.

2 Although originally from Cilicia (Southern Turkey), this type of footwear was more commonly made in Libya, where the River Cinyps flows.

STATIUS

Publius Papirius Statius

Statius was born in Naples around AD 45–50. His father was a teacher and poet and Statius followed in his footsteps, winning poetry competitions and being much sought after as a teacher of Latin and Greek literature. His great epic, the *Thebaid*, and his incomplete *Achilleid*, were highly regarded in subsequent centuries, especially by Dante, Chaucer and other medieval poets. Like most other 'Silver Latin' poets, though, his star has waned. In addition to the epics, we have a collection of impromptu poems, the *Silvae (Raw Materials)*, composed between 89 and his death in Naples around 96.

The following is an extract from the 'Lyric Ode to Septimius Severus' in the *Silvae*. This Severus is usually identified with the paternal grandfather of the future emperor, although he may have been a cousin of that man, and was brought to Rome from Leptis Magna when very young. This item has been chosen to illustrate the close connection which Rome maintained with its citizens throughout its empire.

Septimius from Leptis is now a naturalised Italian

Did grandmother Leptis in the far-off Syrtes beget you? Presently it will produce Indian crops and take rare cinnamons away from the sweet-smelling Sabaeans.

Who does not reckon that dear Septimius crawled on every summit of Romulus? Does anyone deny that, after leaving the breast, he was nourished from the spring of Juturna?

Your excellence is not surprising. From the very first, unaware of Africa full of shallows, you entered the harbours of the Ausonians and, an adopted son, you floated on Etruscan seas.

Here, a little one among the children of the senate, you grew up satisfied with the glory of the narrow purple,* but strove for immense exertions with a noble disposition.

Not for you the Carthaginian language, nor the apparel, nor the foreign mentality – but Italian, Italian! There are in the city of Rome and in Roman squadrons those who suit Libya as foster-children.

SILIUS ITALICUS

Tiberius Catius Asconius Silius Italicus

Born probably in Northern Italy around AD 26, Silius Italicus was a senator who attained the foremost rank of consul* and became governor of the province of Asia in the troubled Year of the Four Emperors (69). After retirement from public life he devoted himself to literary pursuits before his death in 101. He owned one of Cicero's villas and restored Virgil's tomb, and greatly revered both men. He wrote Rome's longest poem, *Punica*, about the Second Punic War between Rome and Carthage (218–201 BC), taking historical facts from Livy and his style from Virgil.

There are a great many references to Libya in Silius's poem and therefore the extracts below aim to be reasonably representative. After a brief description of the Libyan continent, the poem's most significant Libyan episode is included: Hannibal's embassy to the oracle of Ammon. The third extract includes descriptions of the forces drawn from the tribes of the Syrtes and from the Greek colonies, which, as enemies of Rome, are not presented in the most flattering light. The Greeks are, however, redeemed in the two stories of asylum. The first is legendary and continues the theme of Roman and Carthaginian rivalry first stemming from the tragic love affair of Aeneas of Troy and Dido of Carthage told in Virgil's *Aeneid*. The second is historical. There are also two descriptions of Libyans – two of many – one (4) of a Libyan healer, the other (7) of a Libyan warrior, the latter in particular being rather fanciful. Further references to Libya in Silius's poem are supplied in the index of other references.

1 The dry expanse of Libya

Libya, glowing hot in the Aeolian south winds and in the torch of Phoebus, is baked, subject to heat-bringing Cancer. It is either a huge flank of Asia or it is a third part of the earth. Its boundary towards the rosy dawns is the Lagian river that reaches the sea that is swollen by its seven streams; but where it faces the Bears opposite, it is milder; it sees the plains of Europe from its neighbouring heights, separated from them by the Herculean strait that parts them; the sea blocks it on the other side and Atlas does not allow its name to be mentioned further.[1] […]

1 Aeolus was god of the winds, Phoebus god of the sun. Libya (i.e. North Africa) is described from east to west starting at the Nile where Lagus, a Macedonian general, was

But where Africa extends itself over its parched plains it is roasted, fertile only with the copious venom of snakes; where a mild tract rules fertile fields, it is fruitful and is surpassed by neither Hennaean Ceres nor Pharian farmer.[2]

2 *Hannibal sends Bostar to consult the oracle of Jupiter Ammon*

From long ago an ancient faith has been observed in the sanctuaries where horned Ammon, sitting on high among the panting Garamantes, a rival to the Cirrhaean caves, discloses the coming ages from his prophetic grove. Hannibal sought an omen for his undertakings from this place and sought to know future events before their time and to gain knowledge of the fortunes of war. [...]

Meanwhile, having crossed the sandy wastes of the Garamantes and seen the God of Thunder, Bostar came with joy bearing the oracular speeches of Jupiter and spurred their hearts on.

'O greatest descendant of Belus, who by your right hand keep servitude from your native city walls, we entered the Libyan sanctuaries. The Syrtis, drenching the stars, brought us to the gods above; the land, more violent than the seas, almost devoured us. The barren plains extend from the middle of the globe to the limit of the sky. Nature has denied the huge spaces a hill except one which a whirlwind, twisting its hollow clouds, crowded with driven sand, has heaped up; or if Africus, the South-West Wind, having ravaged the lands after breaking out of its prison, and Caurus, the North-West Wind, sprinkling the sea over the air, fall upon the plain that is large enough for their savage battles and, pouring in the dust in succession, have heaped up mountains. We extricated ourselves from these vales when we observed the stars, for daylight confuses the route, and the Little Bear, most trusted by Sidonian sailors, guides the man on foot who wanders in the vast plain, always seeing it in the middle of those regions. But when we came to the groves and leafy realms of horned Jupiter and the illustrious temple, Arisbas brought us to the abodes as welcome guests. Near to the sanctuary there is – an unusual and remarkable thing – spring water which, at the beginning of the day

progenitor of the ruling dynasty of Ægypt. The constellations of the two Bears (Ursa Major and Ursa Minor) indicate the North. The Straits of Gibraltar were formerly named after Hercules, and Atlas was a titan* (early god) who was turned into the mountain range that now bears his name in North West Africa.

2 In other words, the fertility of parts of Africa is greater than that of Sicily, where Ceres the corn goddess was worshipped at Henna, and that of Ægypt where the Pharus lighthouse stands.

and at its fading, is lukewarm and which is cold when the midday sun illuminates Olympus, and the same water boils again in the shadows of night. Then the old man showed us the places filled with the god and with a glad heart addressed us as follows:

'"Bostar, reverence with prayer these shadows of the woods and the tree tops that connect with heaven and the groves frequented by Jupiter, for, throughout the world, who has not had the gifts of Jupiter divulged to him, the twin doves that sat in the bosom of Thebes? Of the two, the one who reached the Chaonian regions on her wings fills the Dodonian oak with prophetic murmuring, but the Cytherean bird of the same colour which, borne over the Sea of Carpathus, flew into Libya on pitch-black wings, established this resting place for a temple. Here, where now you see an altar and shady groves, wonderful to tell, the bird, having selected the leader of a flock, standing firmly right between the horns of his fleecy head, sang oracles to the Marmarican peoples. Then suddenly a wood sprang up and a grove with aged oaks. And the oaks now cover the stars such as they appeared from the first day. From that time, with ancient awe, the stand of trees has had a god and is worshipped with altars always warm."

'And while we were admiring these, the doors, set in motion, opened suddenly with a creaking that was terrible, and unexpectedly a brighter light struck our eyes. The priest stood before the altars, gleaming in his snow-white robe and the people vied with each other to assemble. Then when I imparted from my breast the words entrusted to me, behold! the god suddenly entered the prophet. The trees clashed together, deep murmurings passed through the sounding grove, and then a voice greater than any known rushed forth into the air.

'"You are marching against Latium, O Libyans, and are preparing to rouse the descendants of Assaracus to war. I perceive troublesome undertakings and already savage Mars is mounting his chariot and the raging horn-footed horses are breathing out malevolent flame against the Hesperian seabord and their reins are dripping with copious blood. You who are asking for

Fig. 27 The doorways of the Temple of the Oracle at Siwa.

the results of battles and the ends of your destiny and boldly set sail on your glorious labour, invade the Iapygian plain of the Aetolian leader. You will honour your Sidonian ancestors and will leave no-one to penetrate deeper into the vitals of the Ausonian race, till at length the conquered Dardan realms shall be alarmed at you, and the people of Saturn will never set their anxiety aside while Hannibal enjoys breaths of the air of the upper world in their territories."'

Such were the oracles that Bostar brought to the joyful, and filled the men with a desire for an earlier engagement.

3 Hannibal's Libyan allies

Soldiers descended from Berenice of the waves were present, and Barca, dry with thirsty watercourses, was not forsaken, armed for the fight with rounded pikes in right hands. And Cyrene also roused to arms the treacherous inheritors of Battus from the stock of the descendant of Pelops, whom Ilertes led, he who was once praised by old Hamilcar who was lively in council but too old for war.

Then Sabratha and Sarranan Leptis sent their Tyrian populace, and Trinacrian Oea sent its colonists intermingled with Africans. [...]

Antaeus led these many peoples. Huge both in his body and in his armour, preserving Herculean fame in his deeds and in his name, he raised his head high over the corps on the march. [...]

Then the Macae of the Cinyps first learned to pitch tents in the camp in the manner of the Phoenicians. These men's faces had unkempt beards and they covered their shoulders with a bristly garment of goatskin; their hands were armed with a curved javelin. The Adyrmachidae had a short shield of various colours facing out, and a sword that, through skill, was sickle-shaped, and coverings on their left legs. But these people were austere in their meals and in their scanty victuals, for their dismal dishes were roasted on the hot sand. [...]

The Marmaridae made noise in their companies. A magical people at whose incantations the snake forgot its poison, at whose touch horned serpents would lie placid. [...]

There were seen in the camp those who are fed by the tree famous for its juice and the fruits of the sweet lotus that welcome the stranger too much. And the Garamantes who dread dipsad snakes in their vast deserts, rabid with malevolent, foaming poison. Tradition teaches that when Perseus carried off the head of the Gorgon he had slain, terrible gore flowed into Libya; from that time the land has overflowed with Medusan chelydrus snakes. Choaspes, tested by Mars, was leader of these thousands. Born in Neritan Meninx, a dart, his famous missile, always fitted out his lightning right hand. Here assembled the Nasamonians of the sea, bold enough to attack shipwrecks in the waves and take plunder from the deep. Here assembled those who live by the deep pools of the Tritonian Lake where the warlike virgin, as tradition has it, begotten of the water, besprinkled Libya first of all with the olive she had discovered.

4 A Libyan healer

After this Hannibal quickly summoned the medical skills and power of the old man Synhalus. This man surpassed all in anointing a wound with the juices of herbs and in extracting a weapon from the body by incantation and in sending sleep to a chelydrus snake he had touched, and hence his name was famous throughout the cities and shores of the Paraetonian Syrtis. Once upon a time Garamantian Ammon, the father of a former Synhalus, had given him in the beginning to know how to calm the bites of wild animals and serious wounds through healing. And when dying he then taught his son the heavenly gifts, and the son entrusted his father's skills to the repute of his heir, whom Synhalus followed, his fame not being any the slighter. Expertly he increased Garamantian teachings by his application and counted his forefather, the old companion of Ammon, on many a bust.

Then bearing ancestral medicines in his gentle right hand, his clothing drawn tight, wrapped around him according to custom, he soothed the wound with water after cleansing it of blood.

5 Dido's sister Anna finds asylum in Cyrene

When Dido was deserted by her Ilian guest [Aeneas] and their hopes were destroyed, crazed Anna hastened to the dark funeral pyre in the middle of the palace interior. Then she seized a sword, the deadly gift of the fugitive husband, determined to die. Iarbas, having been shunned for marriage, put himself in charge of the kingdom and she fled the pyre that was cooling. Who would bring succour in her needy situation after the tyrant of the Numidians had driven fear far and wide? As it happened Battus was then cherishing Cyrene with his mild rule; gentle Battus, good-natured and one to shed a tear for human misfortunes. He who, after seeing the suppliant, trembled at the fortunes of kings and stretched out his right hand, and she in the meantime remained in his abodes until the reaper twice cropped the golden ears of corn. But she was to make use of this help from Battus no longer than this, for he informed her that now across the sea Pygmalion was bringing ruin to the poor woman. She was therefore driven onto the open sea.

6 Decius also finds asylum

Poor Decius, another of Hannibal's cares, was sent away to Libyan shores, being kept to be escorted home to face his lingering wrath, if Jupiter from on high had not taken pity on the young man unworthy of punishment and turned his course to the ancient city of Battus. Here the Pellaean sceptre of Ptolemy rescued him from the threats of the men conveying him and the chains were loosened from his neck. And the same country, the guardian of his life, soon thereafter received his unviolated bones in a peaceful grave.

7 A Libyan warrior

Nabis, coming from the prophetic deserts of Ammon, joined the cruel battles unconcerned at death, as if his god was protecting him, and arrogant with conceited speech promised that Italian spoils would be fastened to his native temples. His blue garments glowed with Garamantian gems as when the scattered lamps of the stars sparkle in the sky, and his helmet was lit up with gems and his shield with gold. A fillet hanging down from his horned helmet bore sacred terrors and divine honours before it. He had a bow and a quiver and arrows dipped in the venom of horned serpents and he went through his wars armed with poison. Also, set back on the hindquarters of his horn-footed beast according to his custom, the weight of his Sarmatian pike supported on his knee, he would force it downwards on the battlefield against the enemies in front. Then after he had also thrust Sabellus through with his weapon with a great shout, through his limbs and through his armour before the consul's* eyes, he was carrying him off and was celebrating, rejoicing in Ammon and rejoicing again. The old man did not bear this provocation and so many boasts in that barbarian heart and hurled his spear towards him and, the victor now, took away from the first victor both his booty and his life at the same time.

PLUTARCH

Lucius Mestrius Plutarchus

Born around AD 46 at Chaeronea in Boeotia, where he lived most of his life, Plutarch was an influential biographer and philosopher, rewarded by emperors with administrative positions and becoming a priest at Delphi where he did much to revive the renown of the shrine.

His *Vitae Parallelae (Parallel Lives)* are noteworthy in presenting two biographies together, one of a Greek and one of a Roman, to be compared with each other. His many other works are grouped under the heading of *Moralia (Moral Essays)*.

The first extract below is from his life of Cato the Younger and is the last passage here concerning Cato's march in Libya. Plutarch's sober account may be compared to Seneca's assessment of Cato, the overdramatic version of Lucan, and with Strabo's statement that the journey took thirty days, not the seven mentioned here.

The *Coniugalia Praecepta (Advice to Bride and Groom)*, an epistle addressed to a certain married couple, contains an interesting note on practices after weddings at Leptis.

1 Cato's march

Conjecturing that Pompey the Great would escape to Ægypt or Libya and, being eager to join him, Cato set sail with all his men; but first he gave those who had no enthusiasm for the expedition leave to depart or remain behind. When he reached Libya, and while he was sailing along the coast, he met Sextus, Pompey's younger son, who told him of his father's death in Ægypt. They were all deeply distressed but, now that Pompey was dead, no one would even hear of any other leader while Cato was there. So for this reason Cato, who felt compassion for the brave men who had given proof of their fidelity and was ashamed to leave them abandoned and helpless in a foreign land, took up the command and went to Cyrene, the inhabitants of which received him although a few days before they had shut their gates against Labienus. There he learned that Scipio, Pompey's father-in-law, had been well received by King Juba and that Attius Varus, who had been appointed governor of Libya [i.e. Africa Proconsularis] by Pompey, was with them with an army. Cato therefore set out in winter by land, having got together a number of donkeys to carry water and driving plenty of cattle, and he also took chariots with him and the people called Psylli. These cure the bites of serpents by sucking the poison out and tame and charm the serpents by using incantations against them.[1] The march lasted seven days, Cato going at the head of his troops without using a horse or a beast of burden. He used to eat sitting ever since the day he learned of the defeat of Pharsalus;[2] and he would not lie down except to sleep, adding this sign of grief to the others. After wintering in Libya, he set out with his army which numbered about ten thousand.

2 Mothers-in-law of Leptis

In Leptis, the city of Libya, it is a tradition for the bride, the day after her wedding, to send to her husband's mother asking for a pot. The latter does not give it to her and says that she does not have one, so that the bride realises from the beginning the stepmother's attitude of a mother-in-law and is not angry or resentful if something worse happens later on. A wife should recognise this and try to cure its cause, which is a mother's jealous rivalry for the love of her son. The only way to cure this is to ensure the love of her husband for herself but not to divert or reduce his love for his mother.

1 Cf. the Emperor Augustus's use of them in this passage from Suetonius (*XII Caesars*, II, xvii, 4): 'Furthermore for Cleopatra – whom he particularly longed to be kept for his triumphal procession – he brought up Psylli to suck out the poisonous venom because it was thought that she had died from the bite of an asp.' For a more sceptical view of the powers of the Psylli, see Celsus 1, above.

2 Aristocratic Romans generally ate their meals lying down.

SECOND CENTURY AD

TACITUS

Cornelius Tacitus

Born into an family of *equites* (knights) in Northern Italy around AD 56, Tacitus had an outstanding political career, becoming a senator and, in due course (97), a consul,* the highest rank of the Roman magistracy.* Around 78 he married the daughter of Agricola, the governor of the province of Britain who extended Roman control deep into what is now Scotland and through all of Wales. Less content with political life under the Emperor Domitian, he spent his time writing until his death in 120.

As well as a biography of his father-in-law and a study of the peoples of Germany he wrote two great works on first-century history, the *Historiae (The Histories)* and the *Annales (The Annals)*, the former first circulated around 105–108 and covered the period 69–96, the latter circulated around 115–120 and covered the earlier period 14–68. Both are incompletely preserved, which is a great loss as Tacitus is considered one of the finest historians, the later Emperor Tacitus (275–276) even claiming him as an ancestor, it was said, and ordering a regular output of copies of his works to be made. His style, though elevated, is terse and his meaning can be hard to tease out.

Two passages below deal with the Garamantes. The first describes the role of the Garamantes during and after the war against Tacfarinas (AD 17–24) who raised the Numidians and other peoples against the Romans. The second describes the crushing of the Garamantian intervention in a local dispute in the Roman province of Africa in AD 70.

The third passage concerns the Jewish inhabitants of Africa, their possible origins and their contempt for the instigators of their exile to Palestine.

1 *The Garamantes side with Tacfarinas against Rome*

Since Tacfarinas's army, because it was unequal in strength but better at pillaging, might make incursions and outmanoeuvre them by its having more bands of men, and also attempt ambushes at the same time, the Romans prepared three lines of advance with as many columns [AD 22]. The legate* Cornelius Scipio was in command of one of these, the route by which the enemy had plundered the people of Leptis [Minor] and taken refuge with the Garamantes. [...]

Tacfarinas was still [in AD 24] plundering Africa, strengthened by Moorish auxiliary troops who, by going to war, had forsaken the royal freedmen* and servile rule during the youth of Ptolemy, the negligent son of Juba. The king of the Garamantes was the receiver of his spoils and a partner in his plundering, not to the extent of marching with an army but by sending lightly armed troops which, from a long way away, were heard to be greater than they were. [...]

Ambassadors of the Garamantes – seldom seen in Rome – also attended Dolabella. This tribe, unnerved by the death of Tacfarinas and conscious of their fault, had sent them to make amends to the Roman people.

2 *The Garamantes side with Oea against Leptis*

Later Festus settled the disagreements of the people of Oea with the people of Leptis which, from small beginnings through the seizing of produce and animals among the country people, were then carried out by war and battle. For the citizens of Oea, being fewer in number, had called out the Garamantes, an ungovernable race and rich from robbing its neighbours, from which the affairs of the people of Leptis were straitened. When their fields far and wide had been laid waste, they were in a state of trepidation within the city walls until the Garamantes were routed by the intervention of auxiliary infantry units and cavalry squadrons. All the plunder was recovered except that which they had sold to more remote peoples after wandering through inaccessible villages.

3 *Jewish origins*

They say that the Jews, fugitives from the island of Crete, occupied the furthest parts of Libya at the time when Saturn gave up his dominion, expelled by the might of Jupiter.[1] Evidence may be found in the name: Ida is a famous mountain in Crete, the neighbouring people are the Idaei, usually called the Judaei, the name having been lengthened into this barbarous one. [...]

Most writers agree that, when a plague had arisen in Ægypt, which disfigured people's bodies, King Bocchoris, seeking a cure, approached the oracle of Ammon. He was ordered to purify his kingdom and remove

1 A mythical era in which the sky god Jupiter usurped the chief position among the gods by expelling his father Saturn. The myth is a Greek one.

that race of men to other lands as they were hateful to the gods. Thus this multitude was sought out and assembled; after that it was abandoned to the desert. [...]

Nothing tormented them so much as a lack of water and they were already collapsing near to death all over the plains when a herd of wild asses moved from their pasture to a shady rock with a grove of trees. Moses followed them and, by inference from the grassy ground, revealed abundant streams of water. [...]

In order to secure his people for himself in the future, Moses introduced customs that were novel and contrary to those of the rest of mankind. They hold all things which are sacred among us as impious; on the other hand, among them is allowed what to us is sinful. In a sanctuary they consecrated an image of the animal by whose guidance they averted wandering and thirst, sacrificing a ram as an insult to Ammon.

JUVENAL

Decimus Iunius Iuvenalis

Rome's last great – and arguably greatest – satirist may have been born in Aquinum (Aquino), about 70 miles (110 km) south-east of Rome on the Latin Way, probably around AD 60. He may later have spent time in Ægypt, about which he evidently had good knowledge, possibly having been exiled there by the Emperor Domitian. He died around 130. Details of his life are, however, very sketchy, and even his full name is uncertain.

His sixteen influential *Satires (Saturae)* are an amusing yet severe critique in verse of the society of his times. The extract below is taken from his first book of satires, which was first circulated around AD 117. It is included here to illustrate a low regard in certain society for native Africans.

Your patron's best servants resent retainers like you, who have to make do with Libyan lackeys

If the master's gullet burns from wine and food, a decoction cooler than Thracian frost is requested. Did I complain a little while ago that the wines he drinks are not set before you? You drink *water* of a different kind. Beakers are given to you by a Gaetulian footman or the bony hand of a dusky Moor whom you would not want to meet in the middle of the night while you are being conveyed all along the tombs of the hilly Latin Way. Before the host there stands the best of Asia Minor, bought for a price greater than the wealth of warlike King Tullus and of King Ancus and – may I not insist with you? – all the trifles of the Roman kings. This being the case, when you are thirsty, look to your Gaetulian Ganymede. The young man purchased for so many thousands is incapable of mixing drinks for the poor, but a fine form and youth entitle him to an arrogant demeanour. When will he come to you? When will he be at hand, that solicited waiter of warm and cold water? Of course he is displeased at waiting on a retainer of long standing, because you request something, and because you are reclining while he is standing.

SUETONIUS

Gaius Suetonius Tranquillus

Born around AD 70, Suetonius rose to high rank in the imperial service and eventually ran the Emperor Hadrian's correspondence office. He also wrote a large number of books on a wide variety of subjects, but only some of his biographies survive, including his masterpiece, *The Lives of the Twelve Caesars (De vita duodecim Caesarum)*. This influential work has come down to us almost complete and provides fascinating biographies of the early emperors which contain much material that was almost certainly sourced directly from the imperial archives. Following an unspecified error of court etiquette, he was dismissed in 122 or thereabouts, but continued to write until his death in about 140.

Suetonius is also quoted in a footnote to Plutarch 1.

Vespasian's early career in Libya worked to his advantage in some ways but not in others

Through the drawing of lots[1] he assumed the quaestorship* of the province of Crete & Cyrene. [...]

Meanwhile he married Flavia Domitilla, the mistress of a Roman knight from Africa, Statilius Capella of Sabratha. [...]

Next, assigned the province of Africa [Proconsularis] by lot, he governed it very honestly and with great dignity, except that in a certain revolt at Hadrumetum [Sousse] turnips were thrown at him.[2] What is certain is that he came back no richer, so that somehow, his credit by this time being nearly exhausted,

Fig. 28 The Emperor Vespasian.

1 Senior government posts were allocated by lot.

2 Tacitus (*Histories*, II, 97, 2) states that, on the contrary, his tenure was 'infamous and detested', which might better explain the turnip riot.

he mortgaged all his estates to his brother and, of necessity, for the sake of maintaining his position, he stooped to tradesmen's ways of making money. Because of this he was called the Second-Hand Mule Salesman by the populace. It is also said that he extorted two hundred thousand sesterces* from a young man for whom he had procured the wide stripe* against his father's will, and was convicted and severely reprimanded on this account.

FLORUS

This author's full name and identity are uncertain but he may have been either a Lucius Annaeus Florus, or Publius Annius Florus, a poet and historian who was born in Africa and was a friend of the Emperor Hadrian. *The Epitome of Roman History* (generally given in full as *Epitome de Tito Livio Bellorum Omnium Annorum DCC*) is a digest of the first 700 years of Rome's history, chiefly military, culled mainly from Livy. It was first circulated probably in the 130s.

The Emperor Augustus suppresses Libyan tribal uprisings

THE GAETULIAN WAR

To the south there were disturbances more than wars. Augustus suppressed the Musulami and the Gaetulians who dwell near the Syrtes, with Cossus in command – whence his title of Cossus of Gaetulia, a name grander than the actual victory. He assigned to Quirinius [c. 15 BC] the conquering of the Marmaridae and the Garamantes. He could have returned as Quirinius of Marmarica but he was more modest in appraising his victory.

APULEIUS

Lucius Apuleius

One of the most interesting writers of the Roman Empire, Apuleius, came from Madaurus in north-eastern Numidia and described himself as 'half-Numidian, half-Gaetulian'. By profession he was an orator, philosopher and priest but he is best known for the *Metamorphoses* (or *Golden Ass*), Rome's only novel that survives essentially complete.

He married Pudentilla, a wealthy widow of Oea (Tripoli), probably around AD 155, through the encouragement of his friend and future stepson, Sicinius Pontianus. He was accused by Sicinius Aemilianus, Pontianus's uncle and brother of her rejected suitor, Sicinius Clarus, of having won her hand by sorcery and was brought to trial before the governor of the province of Africa Proconsularis, Claudius Maximus. In the hearing at Sabratha, Apuleius delivered a learned and researched speech in his defence, usually called the *Apologia*, or the *De Magia (On Magic)*, in which he ridiculed his opponents' case, amusingly and with success.

The following extracts give an account of how his marriage came about, and provide some details about the value and kind of property owned by the wealthy at the time, such as slaves, estates and dowries. We also learn something of certain religious practices in an age of great religious diversity. The final passage describes dubious attractions for the young, and hints at the linguistic diversity of the province.

1 *A marriage is arranged*

I came here, by chance or by destiny, whilst proceeding to Alexandria. By Hercules! I could have said 'would that it had never happened' if my respect for my wife did not prevent it.

It was the winter season. Through my weariness from the journey I was carried to the house of those friends of mine, the Appii, whom I name out of regard for their esteem and love, and I lay down for a considerable number of days. Pontianus came to me there. For not so very many years before, I made friends with him at Athens through certain mutual friends and associated on terms of close intimacy by sharing the same accommodation. He said everything respectfully regarding my honour, concernedly regarding my health, and skilfully regarding love. As a matter of fact, of course, it seemed to him that he had discovered a very suitable husband for his mother to whom he might safely entrust all the fortune of his house. And so, first testing my inclination by ambiguous words, since he saw that I desired to journey on and turn away from the subject of a wife, he begged me to stay, at least for a little while; and said that he himself wanted to set out with me, that I should wait for the following winter because of the heat and the wild animals of the Syrtes, because my infirmity had wasted that winter. With many entreaties he took me away from those Appii of mine so that I might be transferred to him in his mother's house. He said I should find a home that was healthier for me and, besides, from this one I would enjoy a more unrestricted view of the sea, which is very pleasing to me.

Having leant upon me with great enthusiasm, he convinced me of all these things. He recommended to me his mother and his brother – that boy there. I helped them somewhat in our mutual studies and our friendship was very much increased. In the meantime I recovered. Having been asked by friends, I gave some discourse in public. All who attended the basilica,* which was where the audience assembled in a huge crowd, exclaimed 'remarkable!' among other things, making it resound for the most part in a consistent tone and begged me to stay and become an Oean citizen. Then, when the audience had left, Pontianus accosted me with this opening, that the unanimity of the voice of the people was explained by a divine omen and disclosed that his intention, if I was not unwilling, was to join me and his mother (whom several were looking at with longing) in

Fig. 29 A basilica was a building in which much public business was transacted and very many cities of the later Roman Empire had one. The basilica of Oea, where Apuleius delivered his lecture, does not survive, but the basilica of neighbouring Leptis Magna is well preserved, although it lacks its roof. This forest of columns gives an idea of the volume and grandeur of the building.

marriage, seeing that he could trust all things to me and have confidence in me alone, he said. If I did not accept this charge because the ward being offered to me was not beautiful but of average appearance and the mother of children, and if considering these things I were to reserve myself for another match for the sake of beauty and riches, I would not be behaving as either a friend or as a philosopher. [...]

Aemilianus, you rest all your case on why the marriage records between me and Pudentilla were not signed in the town but in a suburban villa: so that fifty thousand sestertii* should not have to be poured out again and so that we should not have to dine with you or at your house. Is that a suitable case?

2 *A question of slaves*

Besides, I neither know nor care whether you have slaves to work your fields or whether you exchange labourers in common with your neighbours. But you know that I emancipated three slaves at Oea on the same day and your counsel has put this to me among other things related to him by you, and yet not much earlier he said that I had come to Oea with one slave accompanying me. I would most certainly want him to reply to me how I could have emancipated three from one alone, unless this is also magic. Should I declare that your lying has brought about blindness, or rather has become a habit? 'Apuleius came to Oea with one slave'; then after very few words you prate, 'Apuleius emancipated three slaves in one day at Oea'. Yet had I come with three and freed them all, this would not have been believable because if, for all that, I had done so, why would you rather have thought three slaves to be a sign of poverty than three freedmen* to be a sign of wealth? [...]

But after this, Aemilianus, refrain from throwing poverty against someone, you who until recently used to plough a plot of land at Zarath, which alone your father left you, on your own with one little ass over three days when there was a suitable rainstorm. For it is not long ago that the deaths of your relations one after the other bolstered you with undeserved inheritances and from which, rather than because of that supremely hideous face of yours, you have the name Charon.

3 *Religious differences*

In Greece I participated in a great many rites of religious worship. I keep carefully certain tokens and images given to me by the priests. There is nothing unusual here, I declare, nothing unknown. For example, you who attend the priests of the mysteries of Father Liber alone, you know what you hide away concealed at home and worship secretly without all the profane people. But I, as I have said, learned various religions and many a rite and diverse ceremonies through a desire for what is true and from an obligation towards the gods. I am not making this up for the occasion but it was nearly three years ago, in those first days after I had come to Oea, while discussing the greatness of Aesculapius in public, that I asserted that very same thing and I went through as many religions as I knew. This discourse is very well known, it is read everywhere, it is in all hands, not so much through my eloquence as through its being valued by the devout people of Oea through its mention of Aesculapius. [...]

Can it really seem strange to anyone who has any thought of religion that a man aware of the sacred rites of the gods keeps a certain amulet of religious worship and wraps it in linen fabric, which is the purest covering for divine objects? For wool, the refuse of the most inactive of creatures, removed from a sheep, has been unholy clothing since the statutes of Orpheus and Pythagoras. But the linen crop, the very cleanest that rises forth among the best fruits of the earth, is employed not only for apparel and clothing by the most holy priests of the Ægyptians but also for the covering of sacred objects.

But I know some people, and chiefly Aemilianus, consider it a joke to scoff at religious matters. For, as I learn from some of the Oeans who know this man, he has, to this time in his life, prayed to no god and visited no temple; if he passes any sanctuary he considers it a crime to bring his hand up to his lips as a sign of adoration. In fact, your client does not bestow any first fruits of the field or of the vine or of the flock on the gods of the country who feed and clothe him.

Fig. 30 A trailing vine with figures associated with Liber Pater, a god particularly venerated in Tripolis. Relief from a pillar of the basilica at Leptis Magna.

No shrine is situated in his villa; there is no consecrated spot or grove. What am I speaking about a grove and a shrine for? Those who have been say that they have not seen a single one on his land, or an anointed stone or garlanded branch. Two names are therefore given to him: Charon, as I said a little while ago, because of the fierceness of his countenance and disposition; but the other, which he hears more willingly, is Mezentius, because of his contempt for the gods. And therefore I can easily understand that these enumerations of so many sacred mysteries seem to be nonsense to him and perhaps because of this defiance of the divine he does not suppose that what I said is true, that I scrupulously keep so many images and memorials of divine worship.

4 A woman of property

Perhaps Aemilianus may not really believe it is so, that only three hundred thousand sestertii* were designated [as dowry] and their reversion to Pudentilla's sons was granted by the marriage contract. Take these contracts in your own hands, give them to your instigator, Rufinus; let him read, and be ashamed of his arrogant character and his vain mendacity. For, needy and poor himself, he endowed his daughter with 400 thousand sestertii* received from a moneylender. Pudentilla, a wealthy woman, was satisfied with three hundred thousand in dowry, and the husband she has, having often rejected dowries both many and large, is satisfied with the unprofitable renown of so small a dowry, otherwise valuing nothing save his wife, placing all his goods and his entire wealth in his harmony with his wife and in their great love. [...]

In fact, I was the originator, promoter and maintainer of a quiet life and of harmony and affection; not only did I not devise new animosities but I utterly eradicated old ones, too. I persuaded my wife, whose entire riches, as these men

Fig. 31 The Arch of Marcus Aurelius in Tripoli, one of the few remaining Roman structures in the former Oea.

say, I had by this time devoured, I persuaded her, I repeat, and finally convinced her that she should give the money without delay to her sons who were asking for it – about which I spoke previously – in estates valued at a low rate and as much as they themselves proposed; that beyond this she should give from her property the most productive fields and a large house sumptuously furnished, and a great quantity of wheat and barley and wine and olive oil and other produce; also not fewer than 400 slaves and animals besides, neither few in number nor of low value; so that, even that which she had allotted them from her own share would leave them free from care and would entertain a hope for the rest of the inheritance.

5 *A corrupted youth*

If you do indeed simply want the truth, Aemilianus, many are amazed at your love in respect of this boy that was so sudden after his brother Pontianus died, when earlier you were so unacquainted with him that often you did not, in fact, recognise your brother's son from his appearance. But now you show yourself so yielding to him that you are corrupting him by indulgence to such a degree that he is denied nothing, so that through these actions you make the more suspicious people credible. You received him from us an innocent boy; you immediately made him corrupt. When we were his governors he would go to his teachers. Now with great aversion he flees from them into low eating-houses; he spurns serious friends; this boy of his age holds entertainments among prostitutes with the very worst of youths. He is the governor of your home, he is the master of your slaves, he is the director of your meals. He is often seen in the gladiatorial school; indeed, he is clearly being taught the names of the gladiators and their fights and their wounds – as a respectable boy should! – by the trainer in person. He never speaks except in Punic, although he might in addition to this imitate Greek from his mother, for he is neither willing nor able to speak Latin. Maximus, you heard a little earlier – how shocking! – my stepson, the brother of Pontianus (an eloquent young man), scarcely stammering single syllables when you asked him whether his mother gave them those things which I said were given after I leant upon her.

LUCIAN of Samosata

Born around AD 120 at Samosata in the province of Syria, on the eastern frontier of the Roman Empire, Lucian received a good Greek education and attempted a number of careers: sculptor, lawyer, lecturer and, finally, administrator in Ægypt. He is, however, best known as the writer of around 80 witty satirical pieces, usually in dialogue form, in which he pokes fun at the received wisdom of his age, much to the annoyance of many religious and philosophical leaders.

The Dipsads below is unusual in being more factual. It appears to be an introduction, possibly to a larger work, in which Lucian compares the thirst of a man bitten by a Libyan dipsad, a 'thirst-snake', with his own thirst for the company of the unknown addressee. This short work gives some standard, if fanciful, views not only on the fauna of Libya but also on aspects of the life of the Garamantes.

The dipsads

The southern part of Libya is deep sand and parched earth, almost all desert, completely sterile, a vast plain devoid of shoots, grass, plants and water, unless perhaps a remnant of the rain is left standing in the hollows, but this is so turbid and stinking that not even the thirstiest of men would drink it. That is why this region is uninhabited. Who could live in a land so savage, arid, barren and consumed by drought? The very heat, the air inflamed like fire and the searing sand make the country completely inaccessible.

Only the Garamantes live on its borders, a lightly clad, agile tribe who dwell in tents and live mainly by hunting. They sometimes cross into this country to hunt, around the time of the winter solstice, after waiting for rain when the great heat has abated and the sand is moistened, making it passable. Their game animals consist of wild asses and great ostriches which stay on the ground, and especially monkeys, and occasionally elephants. These animals are the only ones that can stand the thirst and endure the ferocity of that fiery sun. Nevertheless, as soon as the Garamantes have exhausted the provisions they have brought with them, they turn back straight away for fear of the sand heating up again and becoming difficult and impassable and they and their game perishing as though caught in a trap. There is no escape if the sun draws off the moisture and rapidly dries the land, increasing the keenness of its rays which are made more vigorous by that moisture which acts as their fuel.

Yet all the things I have mentioned – the heat, the thirst, the desert, the sterility – will seem less intolerable to you than the one I am going to describe and because of which that country should be avoided altogether. Reptiles of many kinds, of enormous size and in vast numbers, of monstrous form and dripping with deadly poison, live throughout that country. Some of them hide in burrows in the sand, others crawl on the surface: toads, asps, vipers, horned snakes, stinging beetles, javelin snakes, double-ended snakes, dragons and scorpions of two kinds, one of great size and many joints that crawls on the ground and the other that flies through the air and has membranous wings like those of locusts, cicadas and bats. The number of these winged creatures makes that part of Libya inaccessible.

But the most terrible of all the reptiles that the sand breeds is the dipsad, the thirst-snake. It is not very big and resembles a viper. Its bite is powerful and its venom is thick, and which immediately brings on pain that cannot be relieved. It burns and putrefies and sets victims aflame and makes them scream as if lying on a pyre. But what torments and exhausts them most is a tremendous thirst, as indicated by the reptile's name. And what is strange is that the more they drink, the more they want to drink, their desire ever growing. Their thirst is unquenchable, even if you were to give them all the Nile or the Ister to drink. The water inflames even more, as though trying to put out a fire with oil.

The doctors say that this is because the thick venom gains fluidity when diluted by drinking, naturally becoming more liquid and spreading more widely.

I myself have never seen anyone experiencing this and I pray to the gods that I may never see a person suffering in this way, but I am glad to say that I have not set foot in Libya. However, I have heard of an inscription which one of my friends told me he himself had read on the tomb of a man who died in this way. Travelling from Libya to Ægypt his route – the only way there is – passed the Great Syrtis. There he came across a tomb on the shore by the very edge of the sea with a pillar on it representing the manner of death. On it was a man carved in the attitude of Tantalus in pictures, standing in a lake scooping up water, undoubtedly to drink it. A dipsad was wound tightly around his foot. A number of women with jars fetched water and poured it over him. Nearby lay the eggs of ostriches which, as I have said, are hunted by the Garamantes. There was also an inscription which it is worth giving:

Such, if you will, was Tantalus' pain,
His poisonous thirst unfulfilled;
In their jars the water would never remain,
Which the Danaïds constantly spilled.

There are four more lines about the eggs and how he was bitten while he was taking them but I can no longer remember them.

The neighbouring tribes do collect and prize these eggs not only for eating but so as to use the empty shells for utensils and to make cups from them. (They do not have earthenware because all the earth is sand.) If they find big ones they make hats out of them; each half is big enough for covering a man's head.

Here, then, near the eggs, the dipsads lie in ambush and when a man approaches they come out of the sand and bite the unfortunate man who then undergoes the torments I have just described, constantly drinking and increasing his thirst with no relief.

I have told you this not to rival the poet Nicander, by Zeus! nor to show you that I have not neglected the natural history of the reptiles of Libya, which praise would better suit a doctor who has to know about such things so that he can apply his skill to treatment. No, it seems to me – and for friendship's sake do not be offended by the comparison with animals – that I feel the same towards you as those who are bitten by a dipsad feel towards drinking; the more I appear in your company, the more I desire to do so. I am inflamed by unquenchable thirst and I think that I shall never have enough of this drink. No wonder: where else could I find such limpid pure water. Pardon me, then, if, bitten to the depths of my soul by a sweet and healthy bite, I drink great draughts, my head plunged into the spring. I only pray that the stream that flows from you may never fail, nor the eagerness with which you listen to me, leaving me with my mouth open and still thirsting. The thirst I have for you could, for my part, go on for ever. As the wise Plato says, you cannot have too much of a good thing.

PTOLEMY

Claudius Ptolemaeus

Arguably the world's most influential geographer and astronomer, Ptolemy's systems of geographical co-ordinates and solar system mechanics, and his atlas and star charts were the foundation of much of the science of late antiquity, the Arab classical age and the European Middle Ages until challenged, some 14 centuries later, by the explorers and astronomers of the late Renaissance.

The section on Libya from Ptolemy's *Geography* is not given here as it is simply a list of names and co-ordinates to accompany his maps, although his placing of the Libyan tribes is provided as a map. The introduction to the *Geography*, however, has some useful information on two expeditions mentioned by the explorer and geographer, Marinus of Tyre: a Roman military expedition of Septimius Flaccus, legate* of Numidia, around AD 76, and an expedition, probably for trade, led by Julius Maternus around AD 90 which accompanied the king of the Garamantes far to the south. (Septimius Flaccus may, in fact, be a confusion with Suellius Flaccus who led an expedition against the Nasamonians in 86.) The location of Agisymba is uncertain, but it was far south of the Garamantes, possibly around Lake Chad.

Two Roman expeditions to the interior

For journeys by land, counting the days of the individual stages from Leptis Magna to the land of Agisymba, Marinus reckons that the latter is 24,680 stadia [4,570 km] south of the equator. For sea journeys, using the sailing days from Ptolemais in Troglodytica to Cape Prason, he estimates that the cape is 27,800 stadia [5,150 km] south of the equator. He thus shifts Cape Prason and the land of Agisymba, which, as he himself says, belongs to the Æthiopians but is not the limit of Æthiopia to the south, to the frigid zone of the opposite side of the world, for 27,800 stadia make 55⅗ degrees on the meridian and this is as many degrees from the equator as the Scythians and Sarmatians, living north of Lake Maeotis in this kind of clime, are in the opposite direction. Marinus himself then reduces the stated number of stadia to less than half, that is to 12,000 stadia [2,000 km], which is roughly how far the winter tropic [Tropic of Capricorn] is from the equator. The only reason that he gives for the reduction is the deviation of the daily stages from a straight line and their varying lengths, omitting more essential and obvious reasons, ones that show that not only is a reduction required but that reducing by this extent is required.

Finally, concerning the journey by land from Garama to Æthiopia he says that Septimius Flaccus, who marched from Libya with his army, reached the Æthiopians after leaving the Garamantes and marching south for three months; and that Julius Maternus, having set out from Leptis Magna, and from Garama with the king of the Garamantes who was making an expedition against the Æthiopians, after marching continuously southwards for four months, came to Agisymba, the land of the Æthiopians where rhinoceros gather.

Each of these statements on its own is unbelievable, firstly because the Æthiopians are not so far as a three month journey from the Garamantes (they are more or less Æthiopians themselves and have the same king), and secondly because it is ridiculous that the king's expedition to his subjects was just in a direction north to south when the peoples extend far and wide east and west, and that he made no significant halts at all.

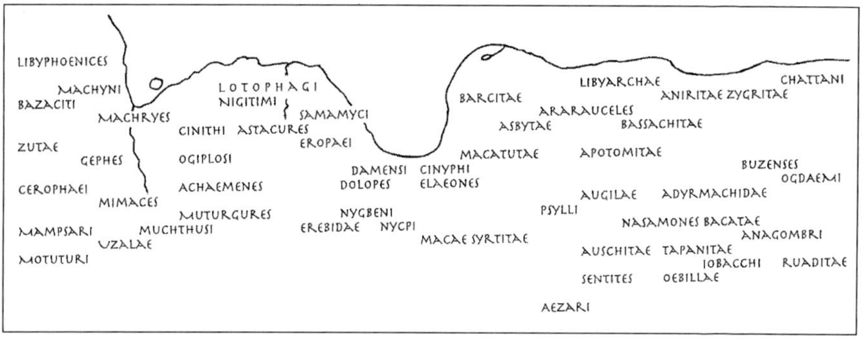

Fig. 32 Map 9: The tribes of Libya, based on Ptolemy's co-ordinates, from Book IV of the Geography. *Ptolemy does not distinguish between small tribes and larger tribal confederations.*

ATHENAEUS of Naucratis

Although born in Ægypt around AD 170, Athenaeus moved to Rome and, among other writings produced the *Deipnosophistae (The Learned Banqueters)*, an important example of symposium literature, which recorded discussions (usually imaginary) between dinner guests. About half of Athenaeus's book survives, having been first circulated probably a little before AD 200. It is a mixture of talk about literature and cookery and the extract below provides a good example. Here Athenaeus quotes directly from Polybius's *Histories* on the subject of the lotus tree. Readers may like to compare the information here with what Pliny (10, 12) says on the same subject.

The lotus

In the twelfth book of his *Histories*, Polybius of Megalopolis, who observed it himself, gives nearly the same account of the lotus of Libya as that which we have quoted from Herodotus, as follows:

> The lotus tree is not large but it is rough and thorny and its leaf is yellow-green like that of the *rhamnus* thorn but a little thicker and broader. At first the fruit resembles fully grown white myrtle berries both in colour and in size, but as it grows it becomes purple in colour, and in size about the same as round olives, and it has a very small stone. They gather it when it is ripe and some, which is meant for slaves, they pound up with groats of spelt* and pack it into jars, but that meant for free men they store in the same way, but after taking out the stones, and use it for food. As food it is rather like a fig or a date but superior in fragrance. By steeping it and crushing it in water a wine is also made from it, sweet and pleasant to the taste, like very good mead, and they drink it without water. However, it will not keep more than ten days so they make it only in small quantities as they need it. They also make vinegar out of it.

THIRD CENTURY AD

AVIDIUS

Quintus Avidius Quintianus

The small border fort of Gholaia (Bu Njem), now about 150 km south of Misurata, was built at the very beginning of the third century AD and its ruins have furnished a number of items written by its garrison, most of which are fragmentary and which were written in Latin of varying degrees of quality. The following example is perhaps the best known: a celebratory poem written on stone, probably around AD 202, by the centurion Quintus Avidius Quintianus to commemorate the provision of the bath facilities and their dedication to Salus, the Roman goddess of security and health. The first letter of each line in the Latin spells out the centurion's name, QAVIDIVSQVINTIANVS. Although in prose, the translation below aims to present some of the archaic words, alliteration and poor grammar of the original.

A dedication in the desert

Leading at the front of the soldiers in this here fort, I have thought a lot about what general votive offering to hand down to posterity for the army's return and to offer in between previous and future ones. Whilst I myself am looking for names of divinities that are worthy, at last I came across the divine designation of a goddess what to celebrate as everlasting with votive offerings in this place.

So long as there are worshippers of Salus I have made her name sacred in what way I could and have given to everyone the true waters of her deliverance from the fires so great of the south wind that wavers in the fiery flames of the sun in these perpetually sandy hills, so that by swimming in tranquillity they might soothe their bodies.

So, you who feel abundant gratitude for my achievement that the breath of your sweltering self is bolstered, do not be reluctant to render true praise with your voice of indolence to the man who wanted you to be well for your own benefit but to bear witness in particular to the love of Salus.

AELIAN

Claudius Aelianus

Although born at Praeneste near Rome, Aelian wrote in excellent Greek. His book *On the Characteristics of Animals (De natura animalium)* is a collection of facts and fantasy about animals designed mainly to entertain, though also to show how animal behaviour may often surpass that of mankind. The following passage is not to be taken seriously.

Teamworking scorpions

The ingenuity with which Nature seems to have endowed scorpions is particular to them. The Libyans, fearing their numbers and their ruses, devise all sorts of schemes to counter them: they wear closed boots, they sleep high up in raised beds, distancing the cords of their bedsteads from the walls, putting the feet of their beds in vessels filled with water, and imagine that they can then sleep in tranquillity and security.

But what sort of methods do the scorpions come up with? If a scorpion finds a place on the roof from which it can suspend itself, it clings there very firmly with its claws and lets its sting hang down. Then a second one descends from the roof, crawls down over the first and holds on to its sting with its claws and lets its own sting hang in the air. A third then holds on to that, a fourth on to the third, a fifth in line and the following ones crawl down the preceding ones. Finally the last scorpion stings the sleeper and crawls along those who are above, and the next after it, then the third from the bottom, and the rest until all are detached from one another as if undoing a chain.

OPPIAN

This poet from Cilicia, who wrote in the late second century AD, is best known for a lengthy poem, the *Halieutica (Fishing)*. A second poem, the *Cynegetica (Hunting)* is attributed to him but is probably by a Syrian imitator writing in the reign of Caracalla (211–217). This short extract from the latter gives the characteristics of the famous horses bred in Cyrene.

The fine horses of Cyrene

The particoloured breed of Moorish horses are better than all others for long courses and laborious effort. After these for completing a lengthy course come the Libyan horses, which live in Cyrene of many stones. Both are similar except that the powerful Libyan ones are larger and their bodies are longer, and since the ribs of their flanks are broader than those of others they seem bigger and run faster and endure well the burning force of the sun and the consuming assaults of noonday thirst.

IASUCTHAN

Marcus Porcius Iasucthan

Iasucthan was a centurion, probably of Libyan origin, who was based at the fort of Gholaia (Bu Njem). Like Avidius, a centurion of the generation before him, he wrote or commissioned a poem inscribed on stone which also commemorated construction at the fort, in this case the restoration of one of the gateways.

The poem is an acrostic giving the centurion's name in the first letters of each line. It is valuable in establishing the kind of Latin that may have been favoured by Libyan speakers of the language. Its erratic metre suggests that Latin in North Africa was already well on its way to having the emphasis on syllable stress rather than vowel quantity which characterises the languages which later derived from Latin. Conveying all these linguistic nuances is not possible here. Furthermore, as the meaning is sometimes unclear, the flow of thought often interrupted, and the inscription damaged, some of the translation is necessarily tentative, but it aims to give a feel for the poet's intentions.

A gateway restored

To the Emperor Caesar Marcus Aurelius [Antoninus Pius Felix Augustus,] Most Exalted [Priest], Chief Pontiff, having held Tribunician* Power [for the 5th time], Consul* [for the 4th time], Father of the Fatherland, and to [Marcus Aurelius Alexande]r, Most Noble Caesar, Augustus, [son] of our lord [Antoninus] Augustus,[1] His Excellency Flavius Sossianus, deputy governor of Numidia, restored the gateway that had fallen with age with square stone in a curved arch by the aid of a vexillation* of the

1 The imperial dedication dates the poem to early AD 222 and is addressed to the Emperor Elagabalus (better known as Heliogabalus) and his adopted son, Marcus Aurelius Alexander Severus, who succeeded him shortly after this. Elagabalus's official name was Marcus Aurelius Antoninus. Caesar and Augustus ('Majestic') were courtesy titles of the emperors. Other imperial titles such as Pius and Felix convey notions of righteousness and success. The emperor was Most Exalted Priest of the Invincible Sun Elagabalus, a religion from his homeland, Syria, and the position was hereditary. He adopted the god's name and and imposed it as Rome's most prestigious religion. The Chief Pontiff was the principal priest of Rome's religion.

3rd Augustan Faithful Avenger [Antonine] Legion,[2] men most devoted to their deity. The labour of which all their predecessors avoided, the Third, the Augustans, did with the hardy energy of warriors.

By a determined plan, with Paratus the superintendent encouraging them, the strength of a few soldiers is joined, great speed is joined to skill; stones moved under the arch from afar by an engine saving effort; the strength of the soldiers, with hempen ropes drawn tight; but now all the soldiers are straining for it to be done quickly. By their disciplined virtue they performed their everlasting work. Imitating the duties of the advanced guard they assumed distinguished qualities. They never ceased with the season of winter bearing down. More speedily did the high towers, four times divided, spring from the ground with the cry of the soldiers, the rushing worth of the 3rd Augustan Faithful Avenger Legion. So that these things got done, the soldiers transmitted their zeal to one another.

Noticing that those before them had made traces for themselves, now they likewise furnished it with the marks of their own worth and

Fig. 33 Coin of the Third Augustan Legion, which was permanently stationed in North Africa, with the legion's name and standards.

2 The Third Augustan Legion was stationed in North Africa. The Emperor Septimius Severus granted it the title Pia Vindex ('Faithful Avenger') for its loyalty in the civil wars that secured him the imperial title.

devotedness, striving that, if there were more to do, they might yet perform their labour. A certain man from the body of soldiers might have given his goodwill more. They never allowed their work to be interrupted. So great was their zeal, the great wor[th(?) ...] in happy times [...] honours [...] the immortal worth of the soldiers rejoices in the completed works.

As a gem is enclosed in gold, so does the gate adorn the camp. The flourishing Third Augustan Legion, with great merit, saw to it that it performed the acknowledgment of its devotedness to its duty. The two sceptical leaders also promptly conceded to the proud men. It had subdued the ugly remainder.

Rereading the beginnings of the lines, identify the one who presided over it.

FOURTH CENTURY AD

APICIUS

In much the same way that Hippocrates became a byword for Greek medical literature, Apicius became the name of choice of several Roman gourmets. The first Apician recipe book was probably compiled by a Marcus Gavius Apicius who lived in the early first century AD and famously committed suicide when his fortune dropped below ten million sesterces.* His work was later expanded by others using the same name, a Caelius (or Claudius) Apicius in the early second century and an Apicius Iulianus, who may have given the book its final form in the fourth century. The *De Re Coquinaria (On the Art of Cooking)* concentrates on uncommon dishes often involving rare, exotic and costly ingredients.

The extracts below give some examples of the uses of Libyan silphium in cooking (for its medicinal uses see Celsus 1 and Pliny 13, above). The fish sauce that is often mentioned is the famous *liquamen*, a sort of Worcestershire sauce liberally used in Roman cooking. Any readers wanting to try these at home, using asafoetida instead of silphium, will need to devise suitable cooking times and ingredient quantities as Apicius rarely provides such details.

1 Silphium in the kitchen

SO THAT YOU HAVE AN OUNCE OF SILPHIUM AT ALL TIMES: Put silphium in an ample glass cask, and around twenty pine-nuts, and when you need to use silphium, grind the nuts and you will be amazed at the flavours imparted to foods. Replenish the cask with the same number of nuts.

2 Silphium sauces

SILPHIUM SAUCE: Melt Cyrenaic or Parthian silphium in warm water, blended with vinegar and fish sauce, or pepper, parsley, dried mint, silphium root, honey, vinegar and fish sauce.

Another way: pepper, caraway, fennel, parsley, dried mint, silphium, aromatic leaf, malabathrum [Indian bayleaf], Indian spikenard, a moderate amount of costus, honey, vinegar and fish sauce.

3 Libyan poultry recipes

NUMIDIAN CHICKEN [GUINEA FOWL]: Cleanse, boil and wash the bird, sprinkle with silphium and pepper, and roast. Grind pepper, cumin, coriander seed, silphium root, rue, caryota date and nuts, pour in vinegar, honey and fish sauce and blend with oil. When it boils, bind with starch, pour over the bird, sprinkle pepper and serve.

SILPHIUM CHICKEN: Split a chicken from the hole, wash it, prepare it and put it in a Cumaean clay vessel. Grind pepper, lovage and fresh silphium, pour over fish sauce, blend with wine and fish sauce and put it on the chicken. If it is cooked, serve it sprinkled with pepper.

EUTROPIUS

Flavius Eutropius

Eutropius is another author about whom little is known, save that he lived in the fourth century AD and held important positions at the imperial court. He may have been a senator. He fought in the Emperor Julian's campaign against Persia in 363, and he served the Emperor Valens (364–78), becoming his official historian. He seems to have written a work on medicine but his extant book is known as *The Epitome of Roman History (Breviarium ab urbe condita)*, a short summary of the history of Rome from its foundation to his own time, using Livy and Suetonius as his chief sources. Written around 370, it is rather a dry résumé, but his style is clear and straightforward and his work was valuable to subsequent historians, being translated into Greek in his own time.

The first brief passage tells how Cyrenaica was bequeathed to Rome; the second gives a summary of the reigns of the first three emperors of the Severan dynasty from Libya. The latter passage contains a number of factual errors and anachronisms but is a readable potted biography.

1 Rome inherits Cyrenaica

At that time [of the annexation of Crete] Libya was also added to the Roman Empire [96 BC] by the will and testament of Apion who was its king. In it were famous cities: Berenice, Ptolemais and Cyrene.

Fig. 34 The Emperor Septimius Severus, who established the Severan dynasty of Roman emperors.

2 A Libyan dynasty rules Rome

After this [the deaths of the Emperors Pertinax and Julianus, AD 193] Septimius Severus took over the administration of the Roman Empire. He was born in Africa, in the Province of Tripolitana and in the town of Leptis [Magna]. He was the only emperor from Africa in all of history both before and after. He was first an attorney for the Treasury, then military tribune,* then through many and varied offices he rose as far as the administration of the whole state. He wanted to call himself Pertinax in honour of that Pertinax who had been killed by Julianus. He was very thrifty, and cruel by nature. He waged many wars, and with success. He killed Pescennius Niger, who had rebelled in Ægypt and Syria, at Cyzicus [194]. He conquered the Parthians and overcame the Arabs to such a degree that he even made a province there. For that reason he was called Parthicus and Arabicus. He repaired many things throughout the Roman world. Also under him Clodius Albinus, who had been Julianus's associate in killing Pertinax, he made Caesar in Gallia [Gaul], but he was conquered at Lugdunum [Lyons] and killed [197].

Severus, besides his military glory, was also famous for his assiduity in civic matters, and, learned in literature, he acquired a knowledge of philosophy in full. He waged his last war in Britain and, so that the

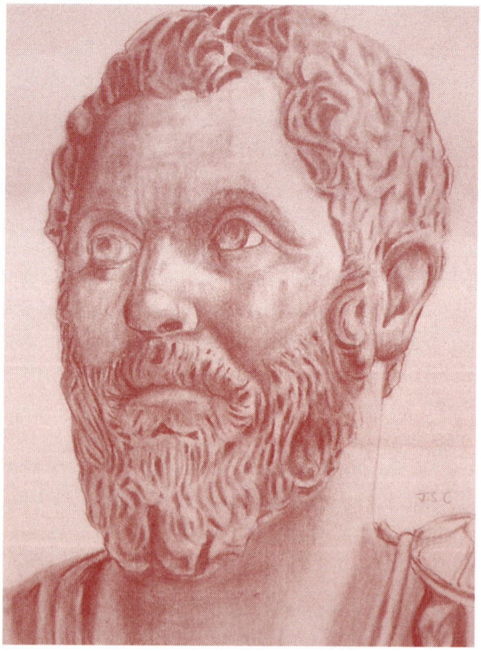

Fig. 35 Clodius Albinus, one of the claimants to the position of Roman emperor in the 190s. Both he and Septimius Severus, his successful rival, came from the Province of Africa, Clodius from Hadrumetum (Sousse, Tunisia) and Septimius from Leptis Magna (Libya).

Fig. 36 The Emperor Caracalla, who adopted the frown clearly visible in this portrait based on a contemporary bust.

recaptured provinces could be fortified with all security, he laid down a wall for 82 miles [121 km] from sea to sea.[1] He died quite old at Eboracum [York] in the sixteenth year and third month [*sic*] of his reign [4 Feb. 211] and was called 'the Divine'. But he left two sons, Bassianus and Geta, as his successors. But he wanted the name of Antoninus to be given to Bassianus by the senate. Therefore he was called Marcus Aurelius Antoninus Bassianus and he succeeded his father; for Geta, having been declared an enemy of the state, immediately lost his life [211].

Marcus Aurelius Antoninus Bassianus, then, also known as Caracalla, had more or less his father's character but was somewhat harsher and full of menace. He created one outstanding public work: the baths which are called the Antonine Baths [the Baths of Caracalla]; besides this he did nothing memorable. He was unable to control his lust so that he took his stepmother Julia for his wife. He died in Osroene, at Edessa, while undertaking an expedition against the Parthians in the sixth year and second month [*sic*] of his reign [8 Apr. 217], having scarcely exceeded his 43rd [*sic*] year of age. He was carried to his grave in a state funeral procession.

1 This was, in fact, a strengthening of Hadrian's wall.

AMMIANUS MARCELLINUS

Ammianus was born around AD 330 to a well-to-do family of Antioch. He joined the army, becoming one of the imperial bodyguard, and fought in a number of campaigns. Later he settled in Rome and wrote a history in Latin, *Res Gestae* (ususally referred to as the *Histories*), from where Tacitus had left off in AD 96, up to AD 378. The first few books are lost so what remains is a detailed and generally accurate history from 353–378.

A lengthy passage (XXVIII, 6) on attacks on Tripolitana by raiders of the Austuriani tribal confederation, and the administrative corruption associated with it, is omitted here as it is insufficiently informative about Libya itself. The short extracts below represent Ammianus's not particularly accurate attempt to describe the Pentapolis (Cyrenaica), which by his time had changed considerably and was administered as part of Ægypt. Readers are referred to the Glossary.

The Pentapolis

The Ægyptian nation is the oldest of all except that it contends with the Scythian in antiquity. On its southern [*sic*] side it is surrounded by the Greater Syrtes and the headlands of Phycus and Borion, and the Garamantes and various peoples. [...]

In former times Ægypt is said to have had three provinces, Ægypt itself, Thebais and Libya, to which succeeding generations have added two: Augustiamnica, hived off from Ægypt, and the Pentapolis, hived off from Dryer Libya. [...]

In Libya Pentapolis is situated Cyrene, an ancient but deserted city which Battus the Spartan founded, and Ptolemais and Arsinoe (which is the same as Teuchira), and Darnis and Berenice which they call the Hesperidae. But in Dryer Libya, among the few small towns, are Paraetonium and Chaerecla and Neapolis. [...]

We acquired the more arid part of Libya through the last will and testament of King Apion; we received Cyrene, with the remaining cities of Libya Pentapolis, through the generosity of Ptolemy.[1]

1 Apion and Ptolemy are one and the same person, the last king of Cyrene, who died in 96 BC, bequeathing Cyrenaica to Rome. Ammianus's account is very confused. The correct account is given in Eutropius 1, above.

THE AUGUSTAN HISTORY

The Augustan History (Historia Augusta) is a biographical work ostensibly written by six authors in the mould of Suetonius and intended to be a continuation of his *Lives of the Twelve Caesars*. This work is very inferior in quality to Suetonius's, containing much spurious and corrupted material (the creation of the Emperor Celsus on the Libyan frontier is a case in point). Furthermore, there is a considerable body of evidence to suggest that the co-authors were not six individuals writing at the time of the emperors Diocletian (AD 284–305) and Constantine (307–337) as claimed, but probably a single person writing during the reign of Theodosius I (379–395). Why this writer should choose to present himself in this way is the subject of continued debate.

The emperor Septimius Severus (193–211), 'regarded by the Africans as a god', as the author, under the pseudonym of Aelius Spartianus, says (xiii, 8), was born in Libya and, despite leaving for Rome in his youth, continued to have contact with his native land. The extracts below have been chosen to illustrate that relationship. They recount his childhood; his early political career; Libyan operations in the civil war which he fought against rival claimants to the imperial title, Pescennius Niger and Clodius Albinus (who was also from Africa); and his family's African mode of speech. As with Eutropius, many details, notably dates and family relationships, are incorrect. Readers are referred to the Glossary of names and to the Glossary of technical terms.

1 *Septimius Severus's childhood in Leptis Magna*

Once Didius Julianus had been assassinated, Severus, born in Africa, gained the imperial title. His city was Leptis; his father was Geta; his ancestors were Roman knights before citizenship was given to all; his mother was Fulvia Pia; Aper and Severus, of consular* rank, were his great uncles; Macer was his grandfather on his father's side, Fulvius Pius on his mother's side. He was himself born on 8th April in the consulship* of Erucius Clarus (second consulship*) and Severus.

In early childhood, before he was steeped in Latin and Greek literature, in which he was very learned, he engaged in no other game among the boys but Judges when he would sit in court and pass judgment, the fasces* being carried before him, a troop of children surrounding him.

In his eighteenth year he practised speaking in public. Afterwards he came to Rome in order to study.

2 Severus returns to Libya during his early political career

After his quaestorship* he received Baetica by lot and from there he made for Africa in order to settle his private affairs, his father having died. But while in Africa, Sardinia was assigned to him instead of Baetica because the Moors were ravaging Baetica.

Having performed his Sardinian quaestorship*, he received the legateship* to the proconsul* of Africa. During this legateship*, when the fasces* were preceding him, a certain fellow-citizen of his from Leptis, but a plebeian*, embraced him as an old comrade. He subjected the man to

Fig. 37 The Arch of Septimius Severus at Leptis Magna. The emperor greatly embellished his native town with monuments such as this.

cudgelling under the herald's proclamation as follows: 'Let no plebeian* person casually embrace a legate* of the Roman people.' From which it came about that even legates*, who previously used to go about on foot, rode in vehicles.

At that time, in a certain city of Africa, he consulted an astrologer when he was full of anxiety, and the astrologer, having considered his birth date, saw remarkable things. He said to him, 'State your own nativity, not another man's.' But when Severus had sworn that it was his, he told him all the things which afterwards came to pass.

3 *Rome's grain supply is secured*

On setting off, sensibly the only thing he did was to send legions to the Province of Africa in case Pescennius occupied it and oppressed the Roman people with famine. It did indeed seem that he could do this via Libya and Ægypt that are near Africa, even if the journey by land and the voyage by sea were difficult.

4 *Severus's sister's poor Latin is a source of embarrassment*

His voice was resonant but he had a somewhat African pronunciation into old age.

When his sister from Leptis, who spoke Latin with difficulty, had come to him and the emperor had been very ashamed because of her, he gave the wide stripe* to her son and many gifts to her, then bade her go back to her home town, with her son, too, who died after a short life.

FIFTH CENTURY AD

PALLADAS of Alexandria

A poet known for around 150 epigrams in the *Greek Anthology* (though not all may be by him). This is a tongue-in-cheek assessment (among several similar epigrams) of a man whose disappointment at not being made consul* as predicted led to an early grave.

Fortune's fool

In a foreign field, just before he died,
Gessius found Ammon's oracle had lied.
He cursed that science and his faith: alas!
He who trusts astrology is just an ass.

SYNESIUS of Cyrene

One of our few native writers, Synesius is possibly the most humane and readable of the authors included in this collection. A pupil of Hypatia of Alexandria, the philosopher and mathematician, for whom he held great affection and respect, Synesius was a leisured gentleman and a sound advocate of the rights of Cyrenaica, for which he felt a strong love and loyalty. He earned respect as a competent negotiator, especially when asked to approach the emperor for a reduction in Cyrenaica's tax burden, and as an organiser of defences against barbarian incursions in the region. Partly on the strength of all this he was elected Bishop of Ptolemais around AD 409 although he found his duties somewhat uncongenial and at odds with his preference for leisurely pursuits such as hunting and literature.

Synesius's literary output consists of several essays, hymns and a collection of 156 letters. The passages below are from his letters. They have been selected to illustrate aspects of life in Cyrenaica towards the end of the Roman Empire and are presented in their probable chronological order. With an elegant style, much humanity, careful observation and a marvellous sense of humour, these delightful letters range from giving plain descriptions of places such as the caverns of Bombaea to discussion of local politics. The tone changes over the years as Synesius loses his leisurely life, sees Cyrenaica subject to attacks from tribesmen and has to assume an increasingly serious role in troubled local affairs.

The first letter concerns a disastrous voyage Synesius made from Alexandria to Cyrenaica, which may have been in 401 or 407. It is both well-known and very long so only passages that are particularly relevant or funny are included. The second and third are somewhat literary yet also charming, and present Cyrenaica as a *locus amoenus*, an idyllic location. The fourth is a topographical description taken from an amusing letter about a coward in the local militia.

The tone is very much more serious in the last three extracts. The fifth letter describes the destruction wrought by tribal raiders. The final two letters show Synesius as local official: he petitions on behalf of the Hunnish mercenaries who have shown such exemplary service but who are threatened with being downgraded to the role assumed by local levies (it was only later that the Huns attained their negative reputation); and he inquires of his Church superior the answers to a number of ecclesiastical questions. Again, this last is an extract from a much longer letter and concerns the Church's attempt to have a bishop elected to a vacant see which has been temporarily occupied by another local bishop, Paul. Synesius's attempts to impose the Church's will provoke uproar.

Synesius's prose is full of quotations from Greek literature; only the most prominent have been indicated here.

1 *A voyage both tragic and comic*

TO HIS BROTHER [AD 401]

We set out from the Bendideum before first light but we had barely passed Myrmex of Pharus by midday, for our ship ran aground on the bed of the harbour two or three times. This occurrence seemed an ill omen straight away and it might have been prudent to leave a vessel that was unlucky from the outset. But we were ashamed to be laid open to an accusation of cowardice by you and so

> 'it was no longer right for us to tremble or to retreat.'[1]

So if anything befall us, we shall perish through your fault. And yet would it have been so bad for you to be laughing at us if we were out of danger? But they say of Epimetheus that

> 'he had no prudence but he did have repentance.'[2]

It is the same for us, for then we could have saved ourselves; now we are lamenting in concert on desert shores, turning our gaze, in as much as we are able, towards Alexandria and towards our motherland Cyrene. We abandoned the one when we had it but the other we are unable to reach, after having seen and suffered things that we would never have expected even in our dreams. Hear me out, then, so that you do not have the leisure for your wit.

Let us begin first of all with the composition of our crew. Our skipper was desirous of death, so indebted was he. Of those present, twelve were sailors – thirteen with the skipper – and more than half of them, including the skipper, were Jews, an infidel people and thoroughly convinced of their acting piously by sending as many Greeks as possible to Hades. The rest were a collection of peasants who, until last year, had never touched an oar. But the one sort and the other both had in common that they were

1 Homer, *Iliad*, VII, 217.

2 Line of unknown authorship.

all disabled. So when there was no danger threatening us they teased each other and called each other not by their names but by the characteristics of their misfortunes: Lame, Hernia, Lefty, Squinter... Each of them had at least one distinguishing feature and we derived no small enjoyment from this situation. But when in peril, it was no laughing matter but we lamented these very defects. [...]

But then a strong south wind carried us before it and we soon lost sight of land and came onto the route of the cargo ships with two sails which have no business with our Libya but are following another course altogether. We complained and grieved that we had distanced ourselves so far from land. Then Amaranthus, that Iapetus of ours, standing on the poop, yelled the most abominable curses at us.

'Clearly we cannot fly,' he said, 'but what can one do with people like you who fear both land and sea?'

'That's not the case, my dear Amaranthus,' I replied, 'provided that one acts correctly with regard to them both. Taphosiris is of no interest to us, for we want only to live. So what need do we have of the high seas now? Let us go directly towards Pentapolis, keeping a reasonable distance from the shore, so that if we do indeed encounter some difficulty, as often happens at sea, as you yourself say, we can at least take refuge in a nearby harbour.'

I did not persuade him at all by my discourse for the wretch turned a deaf ear. But a strong wind from the north began to blow, which raised big, swelling waves. This blast fell upon us all of a sudden and filled the sail the opposite way; from convex, as it had been, it made it concave, and the ship was on the point of being submerged by the stern. [...]

This was the day on which the Jews make the Preparation, as they call it, and they count the night with the following day and during this time they are not permitted to do any manual work. They abstain from any kind of work and so honour that day in particular. So, as soon as he supposed that the sun had departed from the earth, our steersman took his hands off the helm and, throwing himself down

> 'let trample upon him whichever sailor so desired.'[3]

We, who did not at first understand the real reason why he was lying down in this way, guessed that it was through despair. We approached him and entreated him not to abandon our last hopes as the mighty waves were indeed threatening the vessel and the sea was at war with itself. [...]

And so, against all expectation we shook off the rapacious violence of the storm that bore us along, and continued for a day and a night. When

3 Sophocles, *Ajax*, 1146.

the latter was already at the second crow of the cock, without our being aware of it, we suddenly fetched up on a rocky reef that ran out from the shore like a small peninsula. Then there was a shout when someone announced that we were running aground on the land itself. Much shouting went up but for different reasons: the sailors were worried whereas we, through our inexperience, clapped our hands and embraced each other and we could barely contain the fullness of our joy. And yet they told us that that was the greatest of the dangers which had befallen us.

Now at the break of day a man in rustic clothing signalled and pointed out with his hands the places that were dangerous and those which we could pass in safety. Then he came to us in a boat with two oars, made it fast to our vessel and he himself took the helm and our Syrian gladly gave the mastery of the ship over to him. Then, after sailing back not more than fifty stadia [9 km] he brought the ship to anchor in a delightful little harbour which is called, I believe, Azarium, and disembarked us on the beach. We proclaimed him to be our saviour and our guardian spirit. And shortly afterwards he brought another ship in, then another. Before evening our vessels numbered five saved by this worthy old man who was the very opposite of Nauplius in his actions (it was in a very different manner that the latter would welcome those who had escaped the storms). On the following day other ships arrived, several of which had left Alexandria a day before us, so today we are quite a fleet in this little harbour.

Meanwhile, provisions were running low. We were so little used to such misfortunes and we had not foreseen such a lengthy voyage so we had taken only a moderate amount of provisions and, what is more, we had not managed them well. The old man found a remedy for this as well, not by giving us anything himself (he did not even look like one who owned anything) but by pointing out to us some rocks where, he said, daily breakfast and dinner were hidden for those who were willing to take the trouble. So we fish and have been living by fishing for six days already. The grown-ups hunt eels and lobsters of large size and the children enjoy collecting gobies and shrimps. As for the Roman monk and myself, we fortified ourselves with limpets, hollow shellfish that, once attached to the rocks, stick there very firmly. At first we lived rather poorly off this fishing; everyone kept everything that he caught for himself and no-one presented anything to his neighbour, but now we have an abundance, and this is why. The Libyan women would have offered even bird's milk to the women of our party.[4] They offer them all the products of land and air that they have: cheeses, flour, barley cakes, lamb, chickens and eggs. One of them even gave them

4 Birds do not produce milk. This popular expression of the time emphasises the extent of the locals' hospitality.

Fig. 38 Venus of Cyrene.

a bustard, a very tasty bird which a peasant might mistake for a peacock at first sight. They bring these gifts on board the ship and our women accept them and share them with any others who want to.

Those who are fishing are generous now. Men and boys come one after the other, bringing me some present, a little fish caught by line, some other delicacy supplied in all cases by the rocks. I do not like to accept anything from the women through my regard for you and also to avoid any rapport with them so that I have no subsequent difficulty in denying all connection with them. Otherwise what is there to prevent my gorging myself on all these good things, so much is coming from all sides?

You will undoubtedly think that the kindness which the native women show to foreign women is due to virtue alone. This is not the case, and it is worth explaining, especially since I have so much time for leisure. The wrath of Aphrodite, one might think, has struck this land. The women of these parts suffer misfortunes similar to the Lemnian women, for their breasts are overlarge and they have chests that are disproportionate so that their infants feed not from their mothers' arms but from their shoulders where the breast is turned to. One could maintain that Ammon and the land of Ammon are equally good at raising children as raising flocks and that nature has given human beings and animals fuller and more abundant sources of milk and so, to this end, more generous breasts and reservoirs are needed. Well, these women, when they learn from men who have had contacts with others abroad that not all women are like this, are incredulous. So when they come across a foreign woman they welcome her in friendly fashion until they have made a thorough examination of her bosom. The woman who has seen her first tells another woman and they call each other like the Cicones. Then they all rush up to the spectacle and, to this end, bring presents. We had with us a young slave girl from Pontus in whom art and nature had combined to give a figure more finely chiselled than an ant's. And the most attention was concentrated on her and she gained the greatest benefits from these women, and the richest women of the neighbourhood have been asking for her one after the other for the last three days, and she is so little ashamed that she shows herself naked.

This is my story. Fortune has mixed comedy and tragedy in it and I have also done so for you in this account. [...]

2 A simple life in the country

TO OLYMPIUS [November 402]

I have neglected the duty of paying taxes, but what could I do? None of the Greeks living in Libya wants to send merchant ships to your seas. For your part, I release you from your own contribution, for the Syrians themselves never trouble to call in at Cyrenaican ports and if one were by chance to come I would not get news of it. I do not, in fact, live near the sea and I do not often go down to the harbour, but I have gone to live in the far south of Cyrenaica and my neighbours are men such as those that Odysseus went in search of when he left Ithaca to appease the anger of Poseidon according to the requirements of the oracle:

> '... men who do not know the sea
> Nor eat food mixed with salt.'[5]

But I do not think that I am exaggerating when I say that people here do not know the sea, not even for getting salt. But do not imagine that they eat their meat and their cakes without salt. We have, by holy Hestia!, at a distance southwards that is less than the distance which separates us northwards from the sea, a rock salt. We call it salt of Ammon. A crumbly rock produces it and hides it and forms a crust over it; when this is removed it is very easy to scoop out the earth to some depth, digging with one's hands or with a shovel. The lumps extracted are indeed salt, pleasing to the eye and to the taste. Do not think that it is through the vanity of a sophist* that I am describing the salt of this country. Vainglory has no place amongst rustic folk like us.

But because you are asking me to let you know everything about life here you will therefore have to put up with a chatty letter so that you pay

5 Homer, *Odyssey*, XI, 122–123.

the price for your untimely curiosity. At the same time, whatever is foreign to us is hard to believe, so it is no easy task to make a Syrian accept the existence of salt from the ground in the same way that I experience difficulties here when I reply to questions about ships, sails and the sea.

You remember once, when we were studying philosophy together, I was looking out over this very same sea and the vast great lake [Lake Mareotis] between Pharus and Canopus. There were ships there, one of which was being towed, another was making headway under sail, another was being propelled by oars. You laughed at me when I compared the last one to a centipede. Well, the people of these parts are in the same state of mind as we are when we hear tell of the world beyond Thule, whatever this Thule may be, which allows those who have passed through it to lie about it without criticism or contradiction. Even if they admit what is told to them about ships, or laugh at the idea, they vehemently refuse to believe that the sea can also nourish mankind. For them, this privilege belongs solely to Mother Earth.

Once when they refused to believe what I was saying on the existence of fish, I took a pot and, smashing it on a stone, showed them the pickled fish from Ægypt that it held in quantity, at which they said that they were the bodies of venomous snakes, leaped up and ran off, suspecting that the spines were no less deadly than the poison contained in snakes' fangs. The oldest and most intelligent man among them said that it was hard to believe that salt water could give rise to anything good and edible because the waters of springs, though excellent and drinkable, produce nothing but frogs and leeches, which not even a madman would want to eat.

Yet their ignorance is natural,

> 'for the rolling of the waves wakes them not in the night;'[6]

the sea does not, but the neighing of horses, the bleating of goats, the baaing of sheep and the lowing of bulls do and, at the first ray of sunlight, the buzzing of bees, which no other music surpasses in the pleasure it gives. Does it not seem to you that I am depicting Agemachus, such is the country in which I am living, far away from cities, from roads, and from trade and its crafty ways? Here we have time only for philosophy, not for doing evil.

All our meetings are friendly to all and we depend on each other for farming, for shepherds and flocks, and for hunting the many animals that the area offers. For neither man nor horse is accustomed to take food without sweating for it. Our lunch is barley meal, tasty to eat and tasty to

6 Line of unknown authorship.

drink, like that which Hecamede prepares for Nestor. After hard labour this beverage safeguards us from summer's heat. We also have wheat cakes; edible fruits, some cultivated, others wild, all grown in our country and full of juices from our excellent soil; also honey from our bees; and milk from goats, for it is not our custom here to milk cows. In addition, hunting with dogs and horses brings no less a contribution to our tables. I do not know why Homer did not describe it as 'glorious for mankind' and did not call 'illustrious'[7] the men who take part; yet he so praised the place of public assembly that produces only shameless and vile little men, incapable of a single decent thing, able only to cause offence and to contrive harm. This type of person makes us laugh when they happen to find themselves under our roofs for they shudder at the sight of game meat coming straight from our ovens. Why do I mention the meat of game? They would sooner taste poison than any dish of ours! They are always seeking out the lightest wine, the densest honey, the most refined olive oil and the heaviest wheat, and they praise their places of origin: Cyprus, a certain Hymettus, Phoenicia or the barbarian country [Mauretania]. Our country, even if it is inferior to each country that holds first place for a particular product, surpasses all of them for the remainder. It holds first place through its second places, as obtained by Peleus and Themistocles, who were proclaimed the best of all in all things among the Greeks. Let us indeed admit that our honey is inferior to that of Hymettus; it is, nevertheless, such that, when available, there is no need for the foreign type.

As for the olive oil of this country, it is certainly the best as long as one does not listen to people of perverse tastes, for these people judge oil by weight not quality with the idea that the lighter oil is superior. We do not have manufacturers of scales for oil but we state that, if it must be done, it would be natural to give the prize to the heavier. Furthermore, their oil, however admirable and costly, once put into a lamp is so weak that it does not manage to sustain a flame while ours is so strong as to feed a full flame and, when a lamp is needed, it produces artificial daylight. It is also useful for enriching pastries and to make the muscles of athletes supple.

The art of music native to our country is very particular also. Our followers of Agemachus play on a little shepherd's lyre, a simple thing put together by themselves, sweet in tone and fairly virile, not unsuited to the education of the children in Plato's city.[8] It is not modulated nor is it able to adapt to every inflexion but our singers adapt themselves to the simplicity of its strings, for they do not attempt refined subjects. Singing the praises of a vigorous ram is a subject suited to our tastes, and the dog with

7 Homer, *Iliad*, I, 490, and other lines; *Iliad*, IX, 441, and other lines.

8 Plato, in his *Republic* (III, 399d) shows how lyres may be useful in the ideal state.

a docked tail gets a eulogy and rightly, I suppose, because he does not fear hyenas and he chokes wolves. Nor is the huntsman the least subject for song, he who brings peace to our pastures and regales us with every kind of meat. Nor is the ewe who bears twins considered unworthy of our lyre, she who nourishes youngsters greater in number than her years. We often also sing with feeling the praises of the fig tree and the vine; but above all we sing supplications for the good of men and plants and flocks.

These are our subjects for celebration, both seasonal and traditional, the heritage of poor folk. But the emperor and his companions and the dance of Fortune, all the things we hear about when we meet and all those mere names which, like flames, rise up to the heights of glory and are then extinguished, no-one mentions them here and our ears are excused from hearing such matters. No-one doubts that there is always an emperor living (we are reminded of this each year by the tax collectors), but it is not very clear who he is. Amongst us there are some who think that Agamemnon, the son of Atreus, is still ruling, the noble and good king who advanced against Troy and whose name we hear spoken since our childhood as the ruler *par excellence*. And the good herdsmen name one of his friends as Odysseus, a bald man but very capable in dealing with affairs of state and in finding the means out of difficulties. And indeed they laugh when they speak of him, as if it was just last year that he blinded the Cyclops, and tell how that old man came out of the cave mouth under the belly of the ram, how the brute guarded the entrance and, when he realised that the head of the flock was bringing up the rear he imagined that this was through sympathy for his master's misfortune rather than the weight that he was carrying.[9]

This letter has let you be with us in spirit for a little while. You have contemplated our fields and seen the simplicity of our life. You will say that this is life such as was lived in the time of Noah, before justice was reduced to slavery.

3 *Leave unhealthy Phycus*

TO THE SAME [HIS BROTHER] [March 405]

Are you surprised that living in a place as dry as Phycus you should be shivering and toxin enter your blood? You would have found it stranger if your body had been able to overcome the heat there. Come to us here.

9 The story of how Odysseus blinded the Cyclops and then escaped from his cave by clinging to the belly of a ram is told in Homer's *Odyssey*, IX, 105ff.

With the help of God you will recover your health. You will be far from the air tainted by the exhalations of the marsh, away from that brackish water that is warm and totally stagnant – dead, one should say. What pleasure is there in lying on the sand of the seashore? That is the only pastime you have, for where else can you go? Here, on the other hand, you can go under the shade of a tree and if you don't like that one you can go to another, and even from copse to copse. You can even find a nearby stream and cross it. How delightful is the Zephyr which lightly stirs the branches. There are the various songs of birds, the colours of flowers, the bushes of the meadow. Here are the works of cultivation, there the gifts of nature. Everywhere there is a fragrance, the aromas of a healthy land. I will not praise the grotto of the Nymphs – that would require a Theocritus! But there is something finer here.

4 *The caves of Bombaea*

TO HIS BROTHER [May 405]

[...] Despite all these worries we tried to find out where on earth Johannes had got to. He had reached Bombaea without pausing for breath and had hidden himself in the cave there, holed up like a rat of the fields. Bombaea is a mountain full of caves where art and nature working in concert have formed an impregnable fortress. It has been famous for a long time, and rightly; and it has been compared to the gallery tombs of Ægypt. But today it is admitted that it is worth more for defence than any walls because even a man most attentive to his own safety (I do not use words that are too blunt, although the appropriate term would be *cowardly*) hid himself there as in the safest of refuges. When you enter this place you find a real labyrinth that is hard to traverse so that on its own it could act as a place of refuge for Johannes.

5 *I love Libya despite everything*

TO THE LADY PHILOSOPHER [May(?) 405]

Even if forgetfulness affect the dead in Hades,
Even there shall I remember[10] ...

10 Homer, *Iliad*, XXII, 389–90.

My dear Hypatia. I am surrounded by the misfortunes of my homeland and am barely able to tolerate them. Every day I see enemy forces and men with their throats cut like sacrificial victims. I am breathing air polluted by the decaying of corpses and am waiting to undergo a similar disaster myself, for how can I keep my hopes up when the sky is all covered by the shadow of birds of prey? Yet even under these conditions I love my homeland. What else can I do, Libyan that I am, born here and seeing the noble tombs of my forebears? It is only for your sake that I would be able to neglect my homeland and change my location if I had the opportunity.

6 *Hurrah for the Huns*

TO ANYSIUS [June 411]

Nothing could be of better service to the Pentapolis than to give special honour to the Unnigardae, who are excellent both as men and as soldiers, in preference to all the other troops, not only those that are called native units but also all those who have ever come into these parts as auxiliaries. In all honesty, the latter, despite their superiority in numbers, have never yet engaged an inferior enemy with any courage, whilst the Unnigardae, only forty in number, engaged an enemy of over a thousand men on two or three occasions. With the help of God and their leader they have gained the most considerable and glorious victories. The barbarians had barely advanced before them when some were killed and others put to flight. They are still patrolling the high ground, watching for enemy attacks, like dogs ready to bound out of an enclosure to prevent a wild animal from attacking the flock.

We feel ashamed when we see these brave men weeping in the very midst of their undertakings on our behalf. I am unable to read without emotion the letter which they sent me and I wish that you too should not remain unmoved by their plea. Through me they are making a request to you, and through you to the Emperor [Theodosius II], a request which we would have done well to address to you even if they had said nothing, which is that these men should not be enrolled among the native units. They would be useless both to themselves and to us if they were deprived of imperial favours and if, in addition, they were stripped of their changes of horses and their arms and the pay appertaining to troops on combat operations. I pray you who were the bravest among them to refuse to tolerate that your comrades be demoted in their status but instead let them retain the certainty of their former position and not be stripped of their honours. The latter could well be obtained if by your liaison our most benificent Emperor were to learn how useful they have been to the Pentapolis. Add in your letter another request to the Emperor on my part, that he add a hundred and sixty more to the forty there already are. Who would not admit that, with the help of God, two hundred Unnigardae, like in character and strength to these whose docility we are praising, will be sufficient for the Emperor, when commanded by you, to bring an end to the Ausurian war? What use are the many levies and the annual expense of maintaining an army here? We need hands for war, not a list of names!

7 A riotous election

TO THEOPHILUS [PATRIARCH OF ALEXANDRIA]
[late Jan 412]

It is my desire, as well as divine necessity, to consider as law everything that your holy throne ordains. So, having set aside my funeral duties and having forced my still convalescent body to action, I have crossed a dangerous region infested with enemies treating it as if it were not dangerous, and have arrived at Palaebisca and Hydrax, which are two villages of the Pentapolis on the very borders of Dry Libya. There I convened a meeting of the people. I gave them one letter and I read to them from the other (one was addressed to them, the other to me although it concerned them). I then gave a speech appropriate to an election in the hope of persuading them or, if necessary, to force them to come to a decision concerning a bishop, but I was not able to overcome this people's devotion to the most holy Paul.

Father, believe me, I never wanted to make a pointless journey. I have only offended a people who held me in respect. Some of the most prominent citizens protested at the tops of their voices; others, standing on any raised platform, harangued the crowds with their lengthy speeches. I ordered the ushers to remove them and expel them from the assembly, accusing them of corruption and conspiracy. The agitation of the crowd increased and I pacified them and called them to order, using every possible argument to exalt your patriarchal throne and seeking to persuade them that despising or honouring you means despising or honouring God. Then they invoked the blessed name of your holy person with reverence. They knelt down, calling on you with cries and groans as if you had been present. The emotion of the men, even though it was greater than I expected, was moderate; the women, on the other hand, uncontrollable as they are, raised their arms, lifted up their children and closed their eyes so as not to see the bishop's throne empty of its habitual occupant. Indeed, they almost provoked the same state of mind in us, despite our holding an opposing view. Fearful of this contagion I dissolved the assembly because I felt influenced by these emotions and reconvened it for three days from then, not without first having pronounced the most frightful execrations against anyone who, through venality, self-interest, complacency or from any personal motive, used language promoting disobedience to the Church.

The appointed day came and the people again showed themselves hostile and unruly. They did not even wait for a discussion but everything was immediately in uproar, a confused sound in which the excess of noise made it impossible to distinguish individual voices. When the heralds of the church demanded silence, the cries ended in a lament, horrible to hear: men groaning, women wailing, children crying. One was lamenting his father, another his son, another his brother, each attributing to Paul one relationship or other according to his age. Whilst I was attempting to speak, a petition was passed up to me from the middle of the crowd. Someone asked me to read it out loud. It was a request to me not to restrain them by force any more but to postpone any decision until they were able to address a petition on the issue to your Most Blessed Person and send a representative. In addition they begged me to write a statement in their favour to explain what I learned here.

SIXTH CENTURY AD

ANONYMOUS
from the *Latin Anthology*

The *Latin Anthology (Anthologia Latina)* is a collection of epigrams and short poems culled from the body of Latin verse. It was compiled later than the celebrated *Greek Anthology*, and is much inferior to it. A group of a hundred or so poems appears to relate to Libya in the later classical age, but these are very difficult to date and place exactly, although they may be by the same poet. I have here followed the view that these poems were composed under Vandal rule (around AD 500), although some have also argued, for example, for a third century date for the poem abusing the Libyan (4), seeing it in the context of raids on the Roman province by the Africans of the interior, which occurred increasingly after the Severan period.

This small selection aims to show something of life and opinions in Libya in the late classical period. Three poems relate to daily life in this settled agricultural society: a poem in praise of the months, which was a popular theme in late antiquity and which lists many of the products of Libya; an epigram celebrating the citron fruit, which grew abundantly in North Africa; and a witty epigram on Bacchus, god of wine. These are interspersed with two poems abusing native Libyans. Abusive poems in Latin have a long tradition dating back to Catullus and Martial, but these suggest a considerable contempt for native Libyans even centuries after European settlement.

1 The round of the year

IN PRAISE OF ALL THE MONTHS

Janus is resplendent, adorned with the clothing of public office,
	Designating the years by the consuls* of Romulus.
Stretching out rustic tools to the newly planted vines born of Bacchus,
	This month deserves to have the name of the god Februus.
March, practising simulations of warfare in the exercise grounds
	Brings the milky gifts of the Cinyphian flock.
Renewing the sacred rites of the Dionean mother,
	Joyful April claps with frisky castanets.

May, named in honour of the daughter of Atlas,
    Embellishes flowering thorns with beautiful roses.
June adorns summer lunches with blood-red berries;
    Lucky Juventa gives her name to it.
Formerly Quintilis, rejoicing in the shoots of Ceres,
    July has its name from great Caesar.
The heat of Phaethon thoroughly scorches August;
    A cooling-vessel, a fan and a melon refresh one who is tired.
Libra's September arranges hours of equal length,
    Carrying from the country a trapped hare with clusters of grapes.
October treads the grapes with frisky boots
    And sweet new wines froth in full vats.
Tilling November turns over the fields with fertile plough
    When the plump olive feels the polished millstones.
Sluggish midwinter commends its December to all
    When skilful dice unite masters with their servants.[1]

2 A rotten poet

ON THE POET OF THE ARZYGES

Young man, begotten of crags of cut flint,
More uncultivated than woodland arbutus,
Although you are numbed, more unpolished than a tree trunk,
You wish to fashion poems with your own verses
And to amuse yourself with various forms of metre.
But who would judge you skilful in the arts
Which a more intelligent disposition of feeling would have granted?
Only someone hewing firewood with sturdy axes,
Cutting back the hardness of your exceedingly hard soul,
Could render you into the wooden poet
Who imitated the cow with her adulterous timbers
Or who built the horse of the Greek deceit.[2]

1 At the festival of the Saturnalia, a combination of festivities towards the end of the year (and a precursor of Christmas), masters would wait on their servants on one day, and give presents and play dice and other games on other days.

2 Pasiphae, wife of King Minos of Crete, was attracted to a bull and had a hollow wooden cow constructed in which she lay and enticed the bull. The Horse of Troy was hollow and contained Greek soldiers; the Trojans were deceived into taking the horse into their city, thus unwittingly allowing enemy men within the city walls.

3 *The wonderful citron*

ON THE CITRON

Protected by thorns, the gifts of the productive fruit tree gleam;
The golden swelling of the citron pleases our mouths.
Hippomenes won his prize with such a fruit;
The grove of the Hesperides brought forth such orbs.

4 *An ugly customer*

ANOTHER ONE [ABOUT 'THE ÆGYPTIAN']

The dregs of the Garamantes has appeared in our clime
And this dark, home-born slave rejoices in a pitch-black body –
A frightening spectre who would terrify even real men by its
appearance
If the sound uttered by its lips did not signify a human being.
May the dread Underworld carry the ink-black monster off:
The house of Dis should have a keeper like that.

5 *Blood and wine*

ANOTHER ONE [ABOUT GOATS]

The temples of Lyaeus the Liberator are appeased with Cinyphian
blood,
The god to whom a flock of goats is a lawful sacrifice.
But for animals to take vengeance on gods is not permitted,
Nor is it possible to repay deities with retaliation in kind.
The goats have their revenge. Liber the Liberator is invalidated
in name:
The god, in self-contradiction, is imprisoned in a goatskin bottle.

PROCOPIUS of *Caesarea*

Born at an uncertain date at Caesarea in Palestine, Procopius became a staff officer of the great general Belisarius whose campaigns secured much of the Western Mediterranean for the Roman Empire after it had previously been lost to various Germanic peoples. These campaigns are described in Procopius's *De Bellis* (usually referred to as *The History of the Wars*), which was first circulated around AD 551. Books III and IV deal with the short Vandalic War of 533–534 which ended the Vandal kingdom in North Africa where it had been established by King Geiseric in 439.

Most of the fighting took place in what is now Tunisia and is therefore outside the scope of this book. The extracts here concern certain events which took place in Tripolitana and Cyrenaica.

Procopius wrote other works, one, the *De Aedificiis (On Buildings)*, being very flattering of the Emperor Justinian I, another, the famous *Historia Arcana (The Secret History)*, quite libellous instead. He died in 565 and is often regarded as the finest historian of late antiquity.

1 The Vandals oppress Libya

Later Geiseric devised the following plan. He razed the walls of all the cities in Libya except for Carthage in order that the Libyans themselves should not have strong positions from which to start a revolt if taking sides with the Romans, nor should anyone sent by the emperor have any hope of capturing a city to establish a garrison there and cause problems for the Vandals.

At the time it seemed that his decision was a good one and had assured success for the Vandals in the best way. But subsequently, when Belisarius captured these cities more easily and with less of a struggle, since they had no walls, Geiseric then became an object of ridicule and what at one time had seemed to him to be a good idea turned out to be foolishness. For as events unfold, men change their opinions on what has been decided previously.

All those among the Libyans who were men of consequence and property he turned into slaves for his sons Honoric and Genzon, together with their estates and all their wealth. (Theodorus, his youngest son, was already dead without ever having had children either male or female.)

He confiscated the lands of the remaining Libyans, which were numerous and very good, and distributed them among the Vandal nation, from which these lands have been called 'Vandals' estates' up to the present day. The previous owners of these lands were therefore reduced to extreme poverty whilst at the same time preserving their freedom, and they had permission to go wherever they wanted. Geiseric decreed that all the lands which he had given over to his sons and to the Vandals should be exempt from tax of any kind.

As for those lands which did not seem good to him, he left them to their original owners, but subjecting these to such a heavy tax assessment that nothing at all was left to those who kept their properties. Furthermore, many were exiled or put to death on various serious charges but the worst of all, in fact, being that of hiding one's own money. This is how the Libyans knew misfortune of every kind.

2 *Tripolitana rebels against the Vandals with Roman help*

The Emperor [Justinian I] [...] curbed his eagerness for war. But one of the priests whom they call bishops, who had come from the East, expressed a wish to speak to the Emperor. When he was introduced to Justinian he informed him that God had commanded him in a dream to go to the Emperor to rebuke him because, having undertaken to protect the Christians in Libya from tyrants, he had become afraid for no good reason. 'Yet,' God said, 'I myself will stand by him in this war and will make him lord of Libya.'

After hearing these words the Emperor could not put his plan aside. He equipped an army and a fleet, and prepared arms and victuals, and ordered Belisarius to prepare himself shortly to take command in Libya.

Meanwhile Pudentius, an inhabitant of Tripolis in Libya, raised the district in revolt against the Vandals and sent to the Emperor to ask him to send some troops for, he said, he would have no difficulty in gaining the territory for the Emperor. Justinian sent him Tattimuth and a force of no great size. Pudentius added this force to his own and, in the absence of the Vandals, took possession of the territory and made it subject to the Emperor.

3 *Peace talks at Leptis turn violent*

But in the fourth year after this [AD 543–544] it happened that their fortunes were turned around. In the seventeenth year of the reign of the

Emperor Justinian, Cyrus and Sergius, the sons of Bacchus, Solomon's brother, were authorised by the Emperor to govern the cities of Libya: Cyrus, the elder, in Pentapolis, Sergius in Tripolis.

The Moors called Leuathae came to see Sergius in the city of Leptimagna [i.e. Leptis Magna] with a great army, spreading the report that they had come so that Sergius would secure the peace by giving them the gifts and the insignia of power as was customary. Sergius, on the advice of Pudentius, a man of Tripolis, whom I have mentioned in my narrative above and who, at the beginning of the war against the Vandals, served the Emperor Justinian against them, received eighty of the foreigners, the most important ones, in the city and promised to satisfy all their demands, but he enjoined the others to remain in the suburbs. Then, after giving these eighty men assurances concerning the peace, he invited them to a banquet. But they say that the intentions of these foreigners were treacherous and that they had come into the city in order to set a trap for Sergius and kill him.

While they were in conference with him, among all sorts of grievances they particularly complained that the Romans had unjustly destroyed their crops. Sergius, paying no attention to these things, got up from his seat and wanted to leave. One of the foreigners laid hold of his shoulder to try to stop him and the others rose in commotion and were already pressing about him, but one of his bodyguards drew his sword and killed this Moor, with the result, naturally, that a great tumult arose in the hall and Sergius's bodyguards killed all the foreigners. But one of them, seeing the others being massacred, rushed out of the building where these events were unfolding, unobserved by anyone, and came to his fellow tribesmen and revealed what had happened to their companions. At this they returned in haste to their own camp and, together with all the others, took up arms against the Romans.

When they came near to the city of Leptimagna, Sergius and Pudentius advanced against them with their army. The battle was at close quarters. At first the Romans were victorious and killed many of the enemy, plundered their camp, secured their goods and enslaved a vast number of women and children. But afterwards Pudentius was killed, victim of his daring recklessness. Since it was already dark, Sergius returned to Leptimagna with the Roman army.

CORIPPUS

Flavius Cresconius Corippus

This collection ends as it began, with an epic poem. Although the age of Homer and the age of Corippus were very different indeed, and the language, style and outlook are also quite different, Corippus is writing in the same tradition begun by his poetic forebear.

Corippus was born in North Africa, possibly near Carthage, probably early in the sixth century. He started his career as a teacher and then went to Constantinople to take up a position at the imperial court. He wrote poetry, beginning perhaps with pastoral verse and ending with a panegyric, written around 567. But his greatest poem, which he recited in public at Carthage, was the *Iohannes* (or the *De bellis Libycis, On the Libyan Wars*) about the campaign of Iohannes Troglyta to suppress the tribal uprising in North Africa after the Roman conquest of the Vandal kingdom.

Most of the action of the poem takes place in what is now Tunisia, but there are lengthy passages dealing with the local tribes of Libya and their involvement in these events. The following extract is suitably representative and describes a consultation of the oracle of Ammon, the tribes who go to war, and the mustering of the Roman forces who have to face the harsh environment of Libya. This is worth comparing to similar passages in Lucan and Silius Italicus, although Corippus, as well as a contempt for the rebels also has a contempt for the local, non-Christian religion, a feeling which is largely absent in earlier pagan writers.

A prophecy of Ammon stirs up war

As soon as Bruten had perceived that the fury of his people had increased and that the rage of insane Mars was growing, he then sought the territories of the Marmaridae where horned Ammon dwells and asked for oracles of unfeeling Jupiter. The deceiver, Jupiter, he whom you question in vain, always loves to trick pitiful minds. He is frightening and rejoices in blood and seeks to ruin all nations. After a wild bull had been struck straight in the forehead by a two-edged axe so that it fell down dead, the gloomy prophetess seized a noisy tambourine and madly whirled, leaping around the altars with clashing sounds. Her neck sprang up high, her eyes flashed with fire, her hair stood out over her brow and her face vouched for the god in her ardour. Now pallor stained her cheeks, then she rolled her eyes, then her head, howling in a high pitch while she gathered the raging fires. But when she felt the god through her whole breast she looked up in the nighttime sky to the elevated moon with its blood-red light, she examined the fates, counting them; she was inflamed, she panted, she gaped, went pale, then red, sweated, then felt cold while she sought the prophetic path. At last her ungodly voice brought forth from her barbarous mouth the mysteries of the fates under Heaven.

'The Ilaguan victor, acting with cruel Mars, will throw the Latins into confusion. With great courage the Mazacians will occupy the fields of Byzacium for time everlasting. Then there will be a nourishing rest from exertion. The leader, Carcasan, nobler and calm, when he has entered the lofty strongholds of Carthage through their opened gates will be conveyed through the middle of the city by the multitude accompanying him. The African will wonder at their terrible faces. They will run bearing laurels and palms at his approach. Carthage will be called fortunate among all nations. The fear of Carcasan will make the troublesome tribes subject, and they will be thankful for treaties of peace.'

While the prophetess foretold these things, the spirit, throwing her speech into confusion, impeded and deceived their worthless minds with error. Fallacious Ammon beguiled the Massylian tribes with these delusions. While prophesying truth he covers it with fog and contrives traps. For the Moors did indeed occupy the fields of Byzacium for all time and will always occupy them with their bones which, by the power of great Iohannes, lie only broken. Carcasan the leader, grown great, passed through the middle of the lofty strongholds of Carthage accompanied by

Fig. 39 The remains of the Temple of the Oracle at Siwa, which was the second, larger temple built near the older Temple of Ammon.

his people. Then when his neck had been cut, Africa saw his head fixed on a rigid pole.

Weak in mind, he prepared savage hostilities, trusting too much in the injurious oracles. Rumour running wild, that Ammon had prophesied sovereignty for the tribes, went through all the peoples. Swift squadrons hurried away from the hot Syrtes and summoned the uncivilised tribes under the mere idea of sovereignty. A barbarian crowd assembled and increased in numbers and in weapons. Then cavalry and infantry rushed up, and those who sat on tall camels in the manner of the Moors. And not only the Ilaguas or merely the tribes who had waged previous wars met them but other men came, any rough Nasamonian who ploughed the Syrtic fields, any neighbour of the Garamantian lands who cultivated his own lands, those who drink the pools at the edge of the Nile. Who could name the tribes or number them? You might count either the waves of the sea or the raindrops in the clouds or how many sandgrains there are bathed by the seashore, or the fish or the birds that all the open sea or all the land have in them, how many ears of corn the changing meadow bears when spring is young, or how many stars adorn the whole sky.

Then the leader of their hostilities, thinking himself safe and strong with his forces and theatre of war, refreshed his effigies and standards and moved his army from the furthest regions, raging with more than his usual obstinacy, and proceeded against his enemy in the manner of Antaeus who, often overcome by the brawn of Hercules, falling voluntarily would refresh his exhausted body by touching the sand until the Tirynthian victor got to know his stratagem and, clasping his enemy with his utmost strength, he counterbalanced his body bent forward by his great weight, squeezing his barbarous throat. As he could not touch his mother earth, victorious death closed the wretch's eyes. Conquered in this way, Carcasan renewed all his powers from his own Syrtes and, not knowing that he was about to die in this way, he prepared war against his enemy. Then the terror of Mars and the great many cruel dangers of the dark night left their hearts.

See how the messenger sent by great Rufinus flew through the Libyan cities that were calm just then and terrified them with a rumour, informing them that the troops that had been conquered were waging war again, that squadrons of cavalry were even then hastening to the western borders and that they were devastating the farms of Tripolis; that with Carcasan as leader the savage tribes were going towards the walls of lofty Carthage and promising themselves the title of sovereignty. The soldier who had been sent had scarcely reached the Sidonian palace[1] bearing the commander's orders. Bitter rage struck his heart when this man was making

1 Corippus means Tyrian. Carthage was founded from Tyre (see Virgil), not Sidon.

his report. But he sought advice, the better sense of his virtuous mind winning over his fierce valour. His concerns were pondered in his breast and he did not cause his gaze to waver. His shrewdness of mind, on the watch for everything, mulled things over; with discernment he weighed matters and saw unspeakable danger on every side. Then calling his leading men according to his custom he looked for their advice and revealed his thoughts and concerns in words to this effect:

'Comrades, the conquered Ilaguas who must be conquered again are provoking hostilities, daring to join battle with our proven units. They are now bearing down upon the fields of Tripolis and the insurgents plunder their spoils, promising to march against our territories. I am preparing to strike camp, to go against so many tribes, desirous to join battle in foreign lands and overthrow our enemies far from our estates, lest Africa, agitated again by violent disasters, be destroyed even more. The costs, and the difficult roads of the place, are troubling my thoughts but I discern an unproductive crop this year. The province itself has lost its abundance through hostilities, lying too exhausted, alas. A large army would not be able to endure hunger. If we allow our enemies so much as to reach the furthest territories of Byzacium then they will want to hasten on and they will ruin everything by their plundering, and battles will again throw the worn-out country into confusion. Consider this and strengthen my irresolute mind with your instructions.'

The leader had scarcely said these things when it was resolved by his people to go far away, and they declared that they were able to endure the heat of the west of Libya and all the throng promised their fierce hands and minds and were willing to attempt great exertions on behalf of their country, and they despised the rebellious tribes and their savage dispositions.

Their leader, when he saw his armies excited by fierce valour and that they were promising that they would be brave in the hostilities, called for the standards to advance. Then the bugle groaned its strident tones through the air; its harsh sound roused the fully armed troops. At his command all the cavalry squadrons and the infantry assembled from their own quarters, and the Latin commanders and their attendants, and Cusina the general, always very loyal to Roman arms, bringing the Massylian army into the hostilities. This most resolute of leaders proceeded into the southern clime where the sky under the constellation of Cancer is master of those places that are too scorched by the sun and the fields suffer from thirst and glow in the westerly Zephyrs, for there Africus, the South West Wind, dries up all the countryside with his flaming storms, and there the thirsty African wanders in hot deserts, panting and destitute, and even searches for Stygian streams.[2]

2 In other words, water underground, like the river Styx, which flowed beneath the earth in the classical Underworld.

SUGGESTIONS FOR FURTHER READING

This reading list suggests a small selection of items for the general reader.

Texts and translations

Full details of the passages from classical writers in the text are given in the Index of Extracts on page 220.

Most of the texts in the original language are available in the Oxford Classical Texts series of Oxford University Press. The Loeb Classical Library of Harvard University Press is the most readily available source of original texts with a literal English translation alongside.

Translations into English of the best-known classical authors may generally be found in series from a variety of publishers, Everyman's Library, Oxford Classics, Penguin Classics and Wordsworth Classics being readily available.

Not all of the authors here are well-known or in print, in which case libraries will be the best resource. The Index of Extracts has some suggested sources.

Internet resources

Most of the texts and many translations are available on the internet. Normally, the author's name in a suitable search engine will provide relevant sites. Web content is subject to frequent change but, at the time of going to press, Lacus Curtius, Perseus and Project Gutenberg, for example, have a large selection.

Information on classical civilisation is readily available on a variety of sites, including Lacus Curtius above, Theoi, and others. The world's major museums all have websites with search facilities.

Inevitably, readers should be wary of accepting online information at face value.

Classical Libya

A small selection of books which cover Libya's age of Greece and Rome include:

Aubet, Maria Eugenia *The Phoenicians and the West* (Cambridge University Press, 1993)
Bates, Oric *The Eastern Libyans* (Cass, London, 1914)
Boardman, J. *The Greeks Overseas*, 4th edn (Penguin, London, 1999)
Bovill, E.W. *The Golden Trade of the Moors*, 2nd edn (Oxford University Press, London, 1965)
Brett, Michael & Fentress, Elizabeth *The Berbers* (Blackwell, Oxford, 1996)
Bulliet, Richard W. *The Camel and the Wheel* (Columbia University Press, 1990)
Goodchild, Richard *Cyrene and Apollonia* (Antiquities Dept of Cyrenaica, 1959)
Goodchild, Richard *Libyan Studies* (ed. Joyce Reynolds) (Elek, London, 1976)
Haynes, D.E.L. *The Antiquities of Tripolitania* (Antiquities Dept of Tripolitania, Tripoli, 1959)
Kenrick, Philip *Tripolitania* (Silphium Press, London, 2009)
Mattingly, David J. *Tripolitania* (Batsford, London, 1995)
Mattingly, David J. *The Archaeology of Fazzan, vol. 1* (Society for Libyan Studies, London, 2003)
Raven, Susan *Rome in Africa*, 3rd edn (Routledge, London and New York, 1993)
Thompson, Lloyd A. *Romans and Blacks* (Routledge, London, 1989)
Warmington, B.H. *Carthage* (Robert Hale, London, 1960)
Wheeler, Mortimer *Rome Beyond the Imperial Frontiers* (Penguin, Harmondsworth, 1954)
Williams, Gwyn *Green Mountain* (Faber, London, 1963)
Wright, John *Libya* (Ernest Benn, London, 1969)

Classical civilisation

Birley, A.R. *Septimius Severus the African Emperor*, 2nd edn (Routledge, London & New York, 1999)
Graves, Robert *The Greek Myths* (Penguin, Harmondsworth, 1955)
Hornblower, Simon & Spawforth, Antony (eds) *The Oxford Classical Dictionary*, 3rd edn (Oxford University Press, 1996)

Kean, Roger and Frey, Oliver *The Complete Chronicle of the Emperors of Rome* (Thalamus, Ludlow, 2005)

Lemprière, J. *A Classical Dictionary* (reprint, Bracken Books, London, 1984)

Morkot, Robert *The Penguin Historical Atlas of Ancient Greece* (Penguin, London, 1996)

Radice, Betty *Who's Who in the Ancient World* (Penguin, Harmondsworth, 1973)

Scarre, Chris *The Penguin Historical Atlas of Ancient Rome* (Penguin, London, 1995)

INDEX OF EXTRACTS (BIBLIOGRAPHY)

The following passages have been included in this collection. Authors are listed in alphabetical order by their common name. Works of certain authors do not have a standard title so those listed here are those most commonly given, with a typical English rendering such as may be found in translations. All the works below are included in volumes of the Loeb Classical Library of the Harvard University Press, except where indicated in the notes.

Aelian, *De natura animalium* (*On the Characteristics of Animals*)
VI, 23

Ammianus Marcellinus, *Res gestae* (*Histories*)
XXII, xv, 2 (part)
XXII, xvi, 1
XXII, xvi, 4–5
XXII, xvi, 24 (part)

Anon., *Anthologia Latina* (*The Latin Anthology*)[1]
(1) 108 (117)
(2) 120 (131)
(3) 158 (169)
(4) 173 (183)
(5) 178 (188)

Apicius, *De re coquinaria* (*On the Art of Cooking*)[2]
(1) I, x
(2) I, xvi
(3) VI, ix (part)

Lucius **Apuleius**, *Apologia*[3]
(1) 72, 1 (part) – 73, 4
88, 1
(2) 12, 1–5
23, 6–7
(3) 55, 8–11
56, 1–8
(4) 92, 1 (part) – 4
93, 2 (part) – 6
(5) 98, 4–9

Aristotle, *Historia Animalium* (*History of Animals*)
V, 556a (part) – 556b (part)
V, 557a (part)
VII/VIII, 606a (part)
VII/VIII, 606a (part)
VII/VIII, 606b (part)
VII/VIII, 606b (part) – 607a (part)
VII/VIII, 607a (part)
VIII/IX, 615a (part) – 615b (part)

Athenaeus, *Deipnosophistae* (*The Learned Banqueters*)
XIV, 651c (part) – f (part)

[1] Kay, N.M. *Epigrams from the Anthologia Latina* (Duckworth, London, 2006)
[2] Edwards, John *The Roman Cookery of Apicius* (Century, London, 1984)
[3] Online: e.g. www9.georgetown.edu/faculty/jod/apuleius/text.trans6.html

Quintus **Avidius** Quintianus,
Quaesii multum[4]
Callimachus,
(1) *Hymni* (*Hymns*)
II, 55–64
II, 65–96
(2) from *Anthologia Graeca* (*Greek Anthology*)
VII, 517
Gaius Valerius **Catullus,**
Carmina (*Poems*)
VII
Aulus Cornelius **Celsus,**
De medicina (*On Medicine*)
(1) V, 27, 3, A–C
V, 27, 4, A (part)
V, 27, 5 (part)
V, 27, 6–8
V, 27, 10 (part)
(2) VI, 6, 39, C
Lucius Iunius Moderatus **Columella**
(1) *De arboribus* (*On Trees*)
xxiii, 1
(cf. *De re rustica* V, x, 15)
(2) *De re rustica* (*On Agriculture*)
VI, xvii, 7–8 (part)
(3) *De re rustica* (*On Agriculture*)
XII, lix, 4 (part)
Flavius Cresconius **Corippus,**
Iohannes[5]
VI, 145–275
Eutropius, *Breviarium* (*Epitome*)[6]
(1) VI, 9 (VI, 11)
(2) VIII, 10–11 (VIII, 18–20)
Florus, *Epitome*
II, xxxi (IV, xii, 40–41)
Herodotus, *Historiae* (*Histories*)
(1) II, 31–33 (part)
II, 33 (part) – 35 (part)
(2) II, 42 (part)
(3) III, 13 (part)
III, 17 (part)
III, 25 (part)
III, 26 (part)
(4) IV, 150 (part) – 158
(5) IV, 159–167
(6) IV, 168–183
IV, 185–190
(7) IV, 191 (part) – 192
(8) IV, 197–199
(9) IV, 200–205
(10) V, 42
Historia augusta
(*Augustan History*)
(1) Severus i, 1–4, 5 (part)
(2) Severus ii, 3 (part) – 9
(3) Pescennius Niger v, 4–5
(4) Severus xix, 9 (part)
Severus xv, 7
Homer, *Odyssea* (*Odyssey*)
(1) IV, 83–89
(2) IX, 82–104
Iasucthan (Marcus Porcius Iasucthan)[7]
Juvenal (Decimus Iunius Iuvenalis), *Saturae* (*Satires*)
I, Satire v, 49–65
Marcus Annaeus **Lucanus,**
Pharsalia/Bellum civile (*Civil War*)
(1) IV, 666–686
(2) IX, 294–318
(3) IX, 348–367
(4) IX, 411–444 (part)
(5) IX, 444 (part) – 471 (part)
IX, 481–489
(6) IX, 511–550 (part)
IX, 564–586

[4]Adams, J.N. *The Poets of Bu Njem: language, culture and the centurionate* in *Journal of Roman Studies* 89 (1999) pp. 109–34

[5] Text: Diggle, J. & Goodyear, F.R.D. *Flavii Cresconii Corippi Iohannidos Libri VIII* (Cambridge University Press, 1970); translation: Shea, George W. *The Iohannis or De Bellis Libycis of Flavius Cresconius Corippus* (The Edwin Mellon Press, Lewiston, 1998)

[6] Eutrope *Abrégé d'histoire romaine* ed./trans. Joseph Hellegouarch (Les Belles Lettres, Paris, 1999)

[7] Adams, J.N. *The Poets of Bu Njem: language, culture and the centurionate* in *Journal of Roman Studies* 89 (1999) pp. 109–34

(7) IX, 604 (part) – 610
IX, 619–623
IX, 700–733
IX, 833–838
(8) IX, 839–846 (part)
IX, 890–949
Lucian *Dipsades* (*The Dipsads*)
Titus **Lucretius** Caro, *De rerum natura* (*On the Nature of Things*)
VI, 848–878
Marcus **Manilius**, *Astronomica* (*Astrology*)
IV, 597–601
IV, 658–670
IV, 778–781 (part)
Marcus Valerius **Martialis**, *Epigrammata* (*Epigrams*)
(1) *Xenia* (XIII), 12
(2) *Xenia* (XIII), 43
(3) *Apophoreta* (XIV), 141 (140)
(4) II, 56
(5) IX, 6
(6) IX, 56
Pomponius **Mela**, *Chorographia* (*Geography*)[8]
(1) I, 4, 20–23
(2) I, 7, 35 – 8, 41
(3) I, 8, 42–48
Cornelius **Nepos**, *De viris illustribus* (*Lives of Illustrious Men*)
(1) VI (Lysander), iii, 1–4
(2) XVII (Agesilaus), viii, 6–7
Oppian, *Cynegetica* (*Hunting*)
I, 289–299
Palladas, from *Anthologia Graeca* (*Greek Anthology*)
VII, 687
Pindar, *Pythionicae* (*Pythian Odes*)
IV, 1–69
Gaius Plinius Secundus, **Pliny the Elder**, *Naturalis Historia* (*Natural History*)
(1) V, i, 1
(2) V, iv, 26–28
(3) V, v, 31–34
(4) V, v, 35 – 38 (part)
(5) V, v, 38 (part) – vi, 40
(6) V, vii, 41 (part)
(7) V, viii, 43
V, viii, 45 (part) – 46 (part)
(8) VII, ii, 14 – 16 (part)
VII, ii, 32 (part)
(9) VIII, xxxiii, 78–79
VIII, lxx, 178 (part)
VIII, lxxxii, 221 (part)
VIII, lxxxiii, 227 (part)
IX, lxix, 148 (part) – 149 (part)
X, xciv, 201 (part)
XI, xxx, 86 – 89 (part)
XI, xxxii, 95 (part)
XI, xxxv, 105 (part)
(10) XII, xlix, 107 (part) – 108 (part)
XII, lxii, 134
XIII, xxx, 100 – 107 (part)
XIII, xxxiii, 111
XVI, xxxv, 85 (part)
XVI, lxi, 143
XVII, xxx, 133 (part)
(11) XVIII, l, 186
XVIII, li, 188–189
XVIII, lxxvi, 328 (part)
(12) XIX, xii, 36
XX, iii, 7 (part) – iv, 9
XXI, x, 19 (part)
XXI, xvii, 31 (part)
XXI, xvii, 33 (part)
XXIV, ii, 6
(13) XIX, xv, 38 (part) – 46
XXII, xlix, 101–106
(14) XXXI, xxxix, 78 (part) – 79
XXXV, xviii, 36 (part)
XXXVII, xxv, 92–93
XXXVII, xxv, 94 (part) – 96 (part)
XXXVII, xxviii, 100 (part)
XXXVII, xxx, 104 (part)
XXXVII, lxiv, 175 (part)
XXXVII, lxvii, 182 (part)
Lucius Mestrius **Plutarchus**
(1) *Cato* (*Cato the Younger*)
lvi

[8] Pomponius Mela *Chorographie* ed./trans. A. Silberman (Les Belles Lettres, Paris, 1988)

(2) *Moralia* (*Moral Essays*)
143A–B: *Coniugalia Praecepta* (*Advice to Bride and Groom*)
35
Procopius, *De bellis* (*History of the Wars*)
(1) III, v, 8–16
(2) III, x, 18 (part) – 24 (part)
(3) IV, xxi, 1–15
Claudius Ptolemaeus (**Ptolemy**), *Geographia* (*Geography*)[9]
I, viii
Gaius **Sallust**ius Crispus, *Bellum Iugurthinum* (*The War with Jugurtha*)
(1) xvii, 1–xviii, 2
xviii, 9–10
xix, 3
(2) lxxvii–lxxviii
(3) lxxix
Lucius Annaeus **Seneca the Younger**
(1) *Epistulae* (*Epistles*)
CIV, 33
(2) *Naturales quaestiones* (*Natural Questions*)
II, 30.1 (part)
II, 30.2
Tiberius Catius Asconius **Silius Italicus**, *Punica*
(1) I, 193–201
I, 211–214
(2) III, 6–13
III, 647–714
(3) III, 249–258 (part)
III, 262–264
III, 274–281
III, 300–302
III, 310–324
(4) V, 351 (part) – 357
(5) VIII, 50–65 (part)
(6) XI, 377–384
(7) XV, 672–692
Publius Papirius **Statius**, *Silvae*
IV, v, 29–49
Strabo, *Geographia* (*Geography*)
(1) I, iii, 4 (part)
(2) II, v, 33 (part)
(3) XVII, iii, 1
(4) XVII, iii, 17–23
Gaius **Suetonius** Tranquillus, *De vita Caesarum* (*Lives of the Caesars*)
VII (Vespasian), ii, 3 (part)
VII (Vespasian), iii, 1 (part)
VII (Vespasian), iv, 3
Synesius *Epistulae* (*Letters*)[10]
(1) V (IV) (part)
(2) CXLVIII
(3) CXIV
(4) CIV (part)
(5) CXXIV
(6) LXXVIII
(7) LXVII (part)
Cornelius **Tacitus**
(1) *Annales* (*Annals*)
III, 74 (part)
IV, 23 (part)
IV, 26 (part)
(2) *Historiae* (*Histories*)
IV, 50 (part)
(3) *Historiae* (*Histories*)
V, 2 (part)
V, 3 (part)
V, 4 (part)
Thucydides, *Historiae* (*History of the Peloponnesian War*)
VII, 50, 1–2 (part)
Valerius Maximus, *Facta ac dicta memorabilia* (*Memorable Deeds and Sayings*)
V, 6, ext. 4 (part)
Publius **Vergil**ius Maro
(1) *Georgica* (*Georgics*)
III, 339–345
(2) *Aeneis* (*Aeneid*)
IV, 31–49
(3) *Appendix Vergiliana: Moretum*
31–35

[9] Text: *Claudii Ptolemaei Geographia* ed. K.F.A. Nobbe (Lepizig, 1843); translation: *Ptolemy's Geography* ed. J. Lennart Berggren & Alexander Jones (Princeton University Press, 2001)

[10] Garzya, Antonio (ed.) *Opere di Sinesio di Cirene* (UTET, Turin, 1989)

OTHER REFERENCES TO LIBYA IN CLASSICAL AUTHORS

Readers seeking further material on Libya in the original sources may find the following references useful. The list is far from exhaustive but refers to sources that are reasonably easily obtainable. References in brackets refer to uses of Libyan terms which may not apply to the region covered in this book, as defined in the introduction.

Aelian *De natura animalium*: I, 57; (II, 7); (II, 43); (III, 2); (III, 13); (III, 31); (III, 33); (III, 36); (IV, 2); (VI, 10); (VI, 38); (VI, 56); (VII, 5); (VII, 8); (X, 36); (XII, 16); (XII, 26); (XII, 32); (XII, 44); (XIV, 11); (XIV, 14); (XIV, 17); (XIV, 19); XVI, 27–28; (XVI, 33); XVII, 6; (XVII, 10); (XVII, 27).

Ammianus Marcellinus *Res gestae*: XV, v, 36; (XVI, ix, 12); (XXII, xvi, 9); (XVII, ix, 1-3); XXVIII, vi; XXX, ii, 9–12; (XXXI, iv, 6).

Apicius *De re coquinaria*: Libyan cumin: I, xviii; III, xviii. Laser/silfi (silphium): II, i; II, ii; II, v; III, iv; III, v; III, vi; III, vii; IV, ii; IV, iii; IV, iv; V, ii; V, v; VI, ii; VI, iv; VI, v; VI, vi; VI, ix; VII, i; VII, iv; VII, v, VII, vi; VII, vii; VII, xviii; VII, xix; VIII, i; VIII, ii; VIII, iv; VIII, v; VIII, vi; VIII, vii; VIII, viii; VIII, ix; IX, iv; IX, v; X, i. Salt of Ammon: I, xiii; I, xviii; III, xv.

Apollonius Rhodius *Argonautica*: IV, 1231–1637.

Apuleius *Apologia*: 44; 45; 57–58; 59; 63; 69; 81; 94.

Caesar *Bellum civile*: III, 5.

Callimachus *Epigrammata, ex Anthologia Graeca*: VII, 524; VII, 525.

Catullus *Carmina*: XLV, 6; LXIV, 156.

Celsus *De medicina*: laser (silphium): III, 16, 2; IV, 4 (/ii, 3); IV, 6, 3 (/iii); IV, 10, 3 (/iv, 4); IV, 19, 4 (/xii). Hammoniacum: V, 5, 2; V, 18, 2; V, 18, 5; V, 18, 6; V, 18, 7, B; V, 18, 9; V, 18, 10; V, 18, 14, A; V, 18, 22; V, 18, 23; V, 18, 24; V, 18, 28; V, 18, 34; V, 19, 11, A; V, 19, 11B; V, 19, 13; VI, 6, 19; VI, 6, 25, C; VI, 6, 28. Salt of Ammon: V, 18, 2; V, 18, 7, B; V, 18, 14, B; V, 18, 16; V, 18, 17; V, 18, 28; V, 19, 14; V, 19, 15, V, 19, 17; V, 25, 13.

Columella *De re rustica*: II, x, 16; III, ii, 1; III, ii, 29; III, viii, 4; V, x, 11; V, x, 15; VII, I, 2; X, 418; XII, vii, 4.

Dio *Epitome historiae* LI, 14: LXVIII, 32.

Diogenes Laertius *Vitae*: II, viii, 59, II, viii, 65; II, viii, 85–87; II, viii, 97–99; II, viii, 103.

Florus *Epitome*: I, xli (III, 6, 3) [Cyrene]; I, xli (III, 6, 9) [Libyan Sea].

Gellius *Noctes Atticae*: XVI, xi [Psylli]; XVII, xxi, 41 [Cyrene].

Herodotus *Historiae*: I, 46; (II, 8); II, 12; (II, 15); (II, 16–17); II, 18; (II, 19); (II, 20); II, 22; (II, 24–26); II, 28; II, 50; II, 54–56; II, 65; II, 77; II, 91; (II, 99; II, 124); II, 150; II, 161; II, 181-182; (III, 12); (III, 15); III, 91; III, 96; (III, 115); IV, 29; (IV, 41–43); (IV, 44); (IV, 45); IV, 145; IV, 184; (IV, 191); (IV, 195–196); (VII, 70); VII, 71; VII, 86; VII, 165; VII, 184.

Historia Augusta: Hadrian v, 2; Severus viii, 7; xiii, 8; xxiv, 3; Clodius Albinus v, 5; Maximini xiv, 1; (Gordiani iii, 6); Gallieni 5, 4; Thirty Tyrants xxix; (Aurelian xxxiii, 4); Probus ix, 1; xii, 3; (xix, 7).

Homer *Odyssea*: XIV, 295–7.

Horace *Carmina* (I, I, 10); I, xxii, 5 [Syrtes]; I, xxiii, 10 [Gaetulian]; II, xx, 15 [Syrtes]; (II, ii, 10). *Epistulae* (I, x, 19); II, ii, 181 [Gaetulian]. *Saturae* II, iii, 101.

Josephus *Bellum Judaicum* VII, xi, 1–2.

Juvenal *Saturae*: Ammon: VI, 554–555; Gaetulian: X, 158; XI, 140, XIV 278; Libyan: V, 119; XI, 25.

Lucan *Pharsalia*: I, 367–8; I, 499; I, 686–7; III, 292–5; IV, 334; IV, 736; IX, 119; IX, 294–949 (all).

Lycophron *Alexandra*: 87 –907.

Manilius *Astronomica*: IV, 631.

Martial *Epigrammata*: I, 104, 5; II, 43, 9; II, 75, 4; III, 77, 4; IV, 30, 8; IV, 46, 10; V, 65, 3; (V, 74, 2); (VI, 42, 13); VI, 77, 8; VI, 86, 6; VII, 53, 8; VII, 95, 13 [Cinyphian]; VIII, 50, 11 [Cinyphian]; VIII, 58, 13; IX, 22, 5; IX, 35, 2; (IX, 43, 9); IX, 101, 4 [Gaetulian]; X, 14, 2; XII, 24, 6; XII, 61, 5; XIII, 42, 1; (XIII, 42, 1); XIV, 3, 2; XIV, 91, 2.

Nepos *De viris illustribus*: XXIII [Hannibal], viii, 1.

Oppian *Cynegetica*: I, 172; (II, 143); (II, 253–290); (III, 35–47); IV, 47–50; (IV, 111); (IV, 320–353). *Halieutica*: (II, 678); (IV, 630–631); (V, 453–457).

Ovid *Amores*: II, xvi, 21. *Ars Amatoria*: III, 789. *Ibis*: (198); 313; *Medicamina Faciei*: (53); 94. *Remedia Amoris*: 739; 789; (797).

Petronius *Satyricon*: 93; 119, 14-16; (120, 62); (121, 14).

Pindar *Pythicae*: V; IX.

Pliny *Naturalis historia*: I re. Lib. V; I re. Lib. XII; I re. Lib. XIII; I re. Lib. XX; I re. Lib. XXX; I re. Lib. XXXVII (x 2); II, xliv, 115; II, cvi, 28; V, iii, 25; V, ix, 49; VI, xxxv, 194; VI, xxxviii, 208–209; VI, xxxix, 212; VIII, xi, 32; VIII, lxi, 142; IX, lx, 127; XIII, xliv, 127; XV, xxxi, 105; XX, xliii, 110; XXI, xlv, 78; XXII, xlvii, 100; (XXV, lxxvi, 123); XXVIII, vi, 30; XXXI, xliii, 94; XXXII, ix, 18; XXXIV, xix, 59; XXXIV, xxvii, 114; XXXIV, xxvii, 115; XXXV, vii, 30.

Plutarch *Mulierum virtutes*: xix; xxv

Procopius *Bellum Vandalicum*: III, I, 14; III, i, 16; III, vi, 9; III, vi, 11; (III, viii, 15); III, xi, 22; IV, v, 10; (IV, xxviii, 47); and many references to Libya and Libyans (i.e. Africa, Africans).

Propertius *Elegiae*: II, ix, 33; (II, xxxi, 12); III, xix, 7; III, xxiv, 16; IV, i, 103; IV, vi, 4; (IV, ix, 46).

Ptolemy *Geographia*: IV, iii; IV, iv; (IV, v); IV, vi (part). *Tetrabiblos*: II, iii.

Sallust *Bellum Iugurthinum*: (lxxxix, 4).

Seneca *Epistulae*: XXXI, 9.

Silius Italicus *Punica*: II, 56–64; II, 117; II, 165; (II, 310); (II, 330); (II, 348); (II, 358); (II, 388); (II, 574); (III, 173); (III, 226); (III, 563); IV, 445–453; IV, 469; IV, 533; IV, 628; (IV, 799); (V, 89); V, 193–194; (V, 217–219); (V, 250); V, 287–301; V, 434–456; (V, 639); VI, 43; VI, 672–676; VI, 704–705; (VI, 712); (VII, 32); (VII, 401); (VII, 432); VII, 609–616; VII, 628–630; (VIII, 205);

GLOSSARY OF TECHNICAL TERMS

Terms explained in this glossary are marked in the text with an asterisk (*)

Aegis: goatskin cloak of protective power like a shield or breastplate, decorated with snakes, worn by certain Greek deities such as Zeus and Athena.

Asses: Roman coins (plural of *as*, see note on money).

Basilica: public building, usually in a town market place, in which business, trials and civic gatherings were held.

Censer: a receptacle in which to burn incense.

Consul, consular, consulship: the highest political office (*magistracy*) of the Roman state (though after 27 BC the post of emperor was created and took greater importance). Two 'ordinary' consuls, elected each year, took office jointly on 1 January and gave their names to the year (resignation or death led to the appointment of 'suffect' consuls for the remainder of the year).

Denarii: Roman coins (plural of *denarius*) (see note on money) and also a measure of dry weight.

Diadem: crown, band or wreath for the head.

Dictator: occasional office provided for by the Roman republican constitution. During times of severe national emergency the normal joint offices of state were replaced for a maximum of six months by a single man. Julius Caesar abused this power by being appointed dictator for ten years and subsequently for life.

Elaterium: processed juice of the wild cucumber.

Etesian: periodic winds from the north that blew towards Africa particularly in late summer.

Fasces: tied bundles of wooden rods which represented the authority to impose corporal punishment and which were carried before a Roman *magistrate*. In the provinces, an axe was added to symbolise the power to impose capital punishment also.

Freedmen: former slaves who had been granted liberty. They often continued in the service of their masters, frequently gaining considerable influence.

Gorgon: ancient female deity, originally alone but later there were several sister gorgons. Gorgo herself, or Medusa, had snakes for hair and turned to stone anyone who looked at her. Gorgon faces were deemed to ward off evil and were popular in ancient art.

Hecatomb: a sacrifice of one hundred oxen.

Hoplite: Greek infantryman armed with a shield and long spear, usually fighting in close formation (a phalanx).

Legate, legateship: Roman administrative position. A *legate* (*legatus*) could be the general in command of a legion (5,000 regulars) and in Africa, a province with only one legion, he was also the deputy governor.

Magistracy: the executive power of the Roman government, exercised by elected officials (*magistrates*) such as consul, praetor, quaestor and aedile.

Murex: shellfish crushed for purple dye.

Narrow purple: the type of stripe on the clothes of the Roman knights (*equites*), which distinguished them from the common people and from the wide purple stripe of the senators.

Opisthotony: a severe illness somewhat like tetanus.

Penteconter: longship with places for fifty oarsmen.

Plebeian: Roman citizen from a family that was not of the patrician (aristocratic) class. The distinction is imperfectly understood, but often refers generally to anyone not of the noble ruling families.

Proconsul: Roman administrator, usually the governor of a province, who had been *consul* and therefore attained appropriate seniority and experience in government.

Quaestorship: the office of quaestor, a rank in the Roman *magistracy*, which might take various forms. Vespasian, for example, was quaestor of the province of Crete & Cyrene, akin to being deputy governor.

Sacopenium: gummy juice of an unidentified plant.

Sesterces: Roman coins (*sestertii*, plural of *sestertius*, see note on money).

Sophist: initially a learned man; later a type of teacher, usually itinerant, who tended to specialise in life skills; and, later still, a specialist in rhetoric.

Spelt: variety of wheat commonly grown in the ancient Mediterranean.

Talent: a weight of coin, varying from place to place and according to the metal. Initially it represented a volume of metal of about one cubic foot. Attic (Athenian) talents were around 26 kg of silver and about 50 kg of gold. Ægyptian talents were slightly more. (See note on money.)

Thole: place for resting an oar created by means of two wooden pins inserted into the side of the boat between which the oar is placed.

Titan: one of the early gods of Greece who were supplanted by the Olympian gods (such as Zeus, Poseidon, etc.).

Tribune, tribunician: the title of various official posts in Roman civil and military administration. A military tribune was a staff officer in a legion.

Trireme: fast, versatile warship powered by oars arranged in three banks.

Vexillation: a detachment of a Roman legion usually created on an *ad hoc* basis for a particular task.

Wide stripe: Roman senators were distinguished by a wide purple stripe on their tunics (as opposed to the narrow stripe of the knights). Taking or being given the *wide stripe* meant becoming a senator.

Note on money

Currency varied considerably over the period covered by this book. The principal Greek units of currency were the *obol*, the *drachma* (or *drachm*) and the *talent*. The principal units of Roman currency were the *as*, the *sestertius* and the *denarius*. There were many other coins of various sorts over the centuries and most of their designations were also measures of dry weight.

Note on distances

Greeks measured long distances using the *stadium* (pl. *stadia*), which was 600 feet, although that length varied according to location and over time. The Attic *stadium* was about 185 metres and other places used a different measure again. There were, therefore, very roughly 6 *stadia* to 1 km. The *cubit* (about 47 cm) was the standard shorter measure. Roman *miles*, however, were a fixed distance, about 1.48 km. The Roman *cubit* was a little less than the Greek (about 45 cm). In the text, distances are always also given in kilometres.

Note on weights and measures

These take many forms (*cyathus*, *hemina*, *scrupulum*, etc.) and are always converted into metric measures in the text.

Note on winds

Whereas we designate winds by their direction, Greek and Roman winds usually had names which not only indicated their direction but often their nature, too:

Africus	=	South West
Aquilo	=	North (stormy)
Auster	=	South
Boreas	=	North/NNE
Caurus	=	North West
Eurus	=	East/ESE
Notus	=	South
Leuconotus	=	SSW
Zephyr	=	West (mild)

GLOSSARY AND INDEX OF NAMES

Abbreviations: *A.L.* = *Anthologia Latina/Latin Anthology*, b. = born, C = Century, *c.* = circa, d. = died/death in, E. = east/Eastern, fl. = flourished, *H.A.* = *Historia Augusta/Augustan History*, N. = north/Northern, pl. = plural, *q.v.* = *quo vide*/which see, r. = reigned, S. = south/Southern, trad. = traditionally, W. = west/Western

530–522 BC): Herodotus 45–46, 52, Seneca 102, 103

Cancer: constellation, sign of the Zodiac, through which the sun passes at the N. summer solstice: Lucan 106, 112, Silius 139, Corippus 216

Canis Major: constellation, the Greater Dog: Pliny 132

Cannae: battlefield of Apulia, Italy (now Canne della Battaglia, Puglia), site of great Carthaginian victory over Rome (2 Aug 216 BC): Manilius 91

Canopus: town at westernmost mouth of River Nile: Pliny 122, Synesius 198

Capella: Statilius Capella, Roman knight from Sabratha: Suetonius 153

Cappadocia, Cappadocian: region of E. Anatolia (now central Turkey): Columella 104

Capricorn: constellation, sign of the Zodiac (*see also* Tropic): Lucan 112, Ptolemy 165

Caracalla: nickname of the Roman emperor of the Severan dynasty, born Lucius Septimius Bassianus, from the caracallus, a long hooded Celtic cloak which he wore (b. AD 188, r. 211–217): Oppian 173, Eutropius 183

Carcasan: leader of tribal uprising in Roman Africa AD 546–548 (d. AD 548): Corippus 214–215

Carchedonian: Greek name for Carthaginian: Pliny 134–135

Caria: region of W. Asia Minor (now W. Turkey): Herodotus 42, Pliny 134

Carneades: philosopher from Cyrene who became head of the Academic school (*c.* 214–129 BC): Strabo 87

Carneius, Carneian: epithet of Apollo, from the Carnea festival held in his honour in Greece, especially at Sparta: Callimachus 65–66

Carpathus, Sea of: body of water between Rhodes and Crete, named after the island of Carpathus which lies between them: Silius 141

Carthage, Carthaginian:
- (I) Phoenician city of N. Africa, Great Carthage to the Romans, near modern Tunis: Thucydides 62, Sallust 73, 74, 76, Virgil 79, Strabo 82, 83, 84, 85, Manilius 91, Valerius 92, Mela 99, Pliny 119, 122, 134, 135, Statius 138, Silius 139, Procopius 210, Corippus 213, 214, 215
- (II) Carthaginians: inhabitants of Carthage and its empire: Herodotus 46, 61, Sallust 74, 75–76, Strabo 83, 84, 85, Valerius 92

Catabathmos: 'the Descent', a town and valley marking the boundary of Cyrenaica and Ægypt, now near Sollum, Egypt: Sallust 74, Strabo 83, 87, Mela 99, 100, Pliny 120, 121

Catiline: Lucius Sergius Catilina, Roman senator, governor of Africa and revolutionary (*c.* 108–62 BC): Sallust 73

Cato: Marcus Porcius Cato 'the Younger', or 'of Utica', Roman senator and general (95–46 BC): Strabo 86, Seneca 102, Lucan 106, 107, 108, 110, 111, 113, 117, Plutarch 145–146

Catullus: Gaius Valerius Catullus, Roman poet (*c.* 84–*c.* 54 BC): Catullus 71–72, Nepos 77, *A.L.* 207

Caurus: N.W. wind: Silius 140

Celsus:
- (I) Aulus Cornelius Celsus, Roman writer (1C AD): Apicius intro, Celsus 94-96, Lucan 117, Pliny 134, Plutarch 146, Apicius 179
- (II) Celsus: probably spurious claimant in Libya to Roman imperial title: *H.A.* 185

Celts: major race of W. Europe: Herodotus 44

Cephalae: 'the Heads', headland at W. point of the Greater Syrtis (now Ras el Barq, near Misurata): Strabo 84, 85, 96

Cephisus: river of central Greece: Pindar 40

Cercinna: island off the E. coast of Africa proper (now Kerkenna, Tunisia): Strabo 84

136, 137, Statius 138, Silius 139, 140, 141, 142, 143, 144, Plutarch 145, 146, Tacitus 150, Juvenal 152, Suetonius 153, Florus 155, Lucian 162–163, 164, Ptolemy 165, 166, Athenaeus 167, Oppian 173, Iasucthan 174, Apicius 179, 180, Eutropius 181, 182, Ammianus 184, *H.A.* 185, 186, 187, Synesius 194, 195, 197, 201, *A.L.* 207, Procopius 210, 211, 212, Corippus 213, 215, 216
- (II) Libya (of Ægypt): probably late Roman province of Libya Inferior (Lower Libya): Ammianus 184
- (III) Dry(er) Libya: informal name for districts of late Roman diocese of Ægypt, formerly Cyrenaica and W. Ægypt: Ammianus 184, Synesius 203
- (IV) modern state: Eutropius 182
- (V) Libyan Desert: modern name for part of the Sahara west of the Nile: Strabo 81
- (VI) Libya Pentapolis: unofficial name for late Roman province of Libya Superior (Upper Libya): Ammianus 184
- (VII) Libyan Sea: sea off the N. African coast: Mela 97–98, Pliny 118
- (VIII) Libyan(s): inhabitant(s) of Libya: Homer 37, Herodotus 43, 45, 48, 49, 50, 52–58, 59, 61, Thucydides 62, Sallust 74, Strabo 88, Pliny 122, Martial 137, Silius 139, 141, Aelian 172, Synesius 202, *A.L.* 207, Procopius 210–211
- (IX) Libyan-Ægyptians: people of W. Ægypt: Mela 98

Ligurians: people of N.W. Italy: Sallust 75

Little Bear: N. constellation (Ursa Minor): Lucan 112

Livy: Titus Livius, Roman historian (59 BC–AD 17): Valerius 92, Silius 139, Florus 155, Eutropius 181

Locri Epizephyrii: town near the S. tip of Italy (now Locri): Strabo 84

Lotophagi: the Lotus-Eaters who inhabited the Libyan coast: Homer 37, Herodotus 55, 56, Strabo 84, Mela 99, Pliny 119

Lotophagitis:
- (I) 'Lotus-Eaters' Island', also known as Meninx (now Jerba, Tunisia): Pliny 122
- (II) Syrtis Lotophagitis: the Lesser Syrtis: Strabo 84

Lotus-Eaters: or Lotophagi, inhabitants of the Libyan coast: Homer 37–38, Herodotus 55, Strabo 84, Mela 99, Pliny 119, 122

Loxias: epithet of Greek god Apollo: Herodotus 51

Lucan: Marcus Annaeus Lucanus, Roman poet, nephew of Seneca (AD 39–65): Celsus 95, Seneca 102, Lucan 106–117, Martial 136, Plutarch 145, Corippus 213

Lucania: region of S. Italy: Pliny 135

Lucian: Greek satirist (*c.* AD 120–*c.* 180): Lucian 162–164

Lucretius: Titus Lucretius Caro, Roman poet (*c.* 98–*c.* 55 BC): Lucretius 69-70, Mela 100

Lugdunum: city of Gaul, capital of Roman province of Gallia Lugdunensis (now Lyons/Lyon, France): Eutropius 182

Luke: saint and writer of New Testament gospel and *Acts* (1C AD): Mela 97

Lyaeus: 'Releaser', epithet of Dionysus or Bacchus, Greek god of wine, because of his releasing inhibitions: *A.L.* 209

Lycaean: epithet of the god Zeus as god of wolves: Herodotus 61

Lyceum: school of Aristotle in Athens: Aristotle 63

Lycomedes, Lake of: (unknown) Libyan lake: Pliny 119

Lyons: or Lyon, city of France, formerly Lugdunum: Eutropius 182

Lysander: Spartan military leader (d. 395 BC): Nepos 77

M

Macae: a people of Libya on the Greater Syrtis: Herodotus 54, 61, Pliny 120, Silius 142

May: fifth month of the Roman calendar, named in honour of Maia, daughter of Atlas and mother of Hermes/Mercury: *A.L.* 208
Mazacian(s): (member of) Libyan tribe: Lucan 107, Corippus 214
Mede(s): inhabitant(s) of Media: Herodotus 52, 59, Sallust 74, Lucan 107
Medea: princess of Colchis, sorceress and lover of Jason: Pindar 130
Media: region of Persia (now N.W. Iran): Pliny 130
Medina Sultan: location on the Gulf of Sidra, formerly Charax: Strabo 85
Mediterranean: sea dividing Europe, Asia and Africa: Homer 37, Herodotus 42, Sallust 73, Manilius 91, Mela 97, Pliny 118, Procopius 210
Medusa, Medusan: snake-haired gorgon, a monster of Greek myth so hideous that looking on her turned the beholder to stone: Lucan 114, Silius 142
Megalopolis: main city of Arcadia in the Peloponnese, Greece: Athenaeus 167
Mela: Pomponius Mela, Roman geographer (*c.* 24 BC–*c.* AD 45): Sallust 73, Valerius 92, Mela 97–101
Melanippus: a deceased young man: Callimachus 66
Memphis: city and one-time capital of Lower Ægypt: Herodotus 45
Menelaus:
- (I) king of Sparta at time of Trojan War (if real, lived late 13C BC): Homer 37
- (II) Port of Menelaus: (unidentified) town of Cyrenaica: Herodotus 53, Nepos 78, Strabo 87

Meninx:
- (I) island in the Lesser Syrtis, traditionally the home of the Lotus-Eaters (now Jerba, Tunisia): Strabo 84, Pliny 122, Silius 143
- (II) main town on Meninx Island (now El Kantara): Strabo 84, Pliny 122

Meroë: city on the Nile, capital of ancient kingdom of Kush (now near Shendi, N. Sudan): Strabo 83
Mersa (Marsa) Matruh: town of modern Egypt, formerly Paraetonium: Strabo 88, Mela 100, Pliny 120
Mesammone:s Greek name for the Nasamones ('Midsanders'): Pliny 120
Metellus: Quintus Caecilius Metellus Numidicus, Roman consul and commander (109–107 BC) in war against Jugurtha (*c.* 160–91 BC): Sallust 75
Metrodidactus: 'Mother-Taught', nickname of the younger Aristippus because taught by his mother, Arete: Strabo 87
Mezentius: legendary king of Caere in Etruria (now Cerveteri, Italy) who considered his own prowess greater than the gods: Apuleius 160
Middle Ages: period between the Ancient World and the Renaissance, roughly 8C–15C AD: Ptolemy 165
Milgis Gemella: town conquered by Balbus (possibly the oasis of M'lili in Algeria): Pliny 121
Milh, Ras el: headland of Cyrenaica, formerly Ardanis: Strabo 87
Minerva: Roman goddess of wisdom, arts and war, similar to Greek goddess Pallas Athene (*q.v.*): Mela 99
Minos: legendary king of Crete after whom the Minoan civilisation, which originated in that island, is named: *A.L.* 208
Minyans, Minyan: a pre-Greek people of the Aegean, believed to have been descended from the Argonauts: Pindar 41, Herodotus 46
Misurata: coastal town of Tripolitania at W. extremity of Gulf of Sidra: Avidius 171
Moon: celestial body worshipped as a goddess: Herodotus 57, Lucan 117
Moor(s), Moorish: inhabitant(s) of Mauretania (*q.v., and also* Maurusians): Sallust 74, Mela 98, Lucan 107, 108, Tacitus 150, Juvenal 152, Oppian 173, *H.A.* 186, Procopius 212, Corippus 214, 215

Ras: 'Cape', *see under individual names.*
Red Sea: sea between Africa and Arabia: Strabo 86
Renaissance: period of revival of classical culture in Europe (14–16C AD): Aristotle 63, Seneca 102, Ptolemy 165
Rhodius: *see* Apollonius Rhodius
Rome, Roman:
– (I) city and empire: Herodotus 54, Lucretius 69, Catullus 71, Sallust 73, 75, Nepos 77, Virgil 79, Strabo 81, Manilius 91, Mela 97, Seneca 102, Lucan 106, 107, 111, 112, 116-117, Pliny 118, 121, 126, 130, 134, Martial 136, 137, Statius 138, Silius 139, Tacitus 149, 150, Juvenal 152, Suetonius 153, Florus 155, Apuleius 156, 157, 160, Lucian 162, Ptolemy 165, Athenaeus 167, Avidius 171, Aelian 172, Iasucthan 174, Apicius 179, Eutropius 181, 182, Ammianus 184, *H.A.* 185, 186, 187, Synesius 192, 195, *A.L.* 207, Procopius 210, 211, 212, Corippus 213, 216
– (II) Roman(s): citizen(s) of the Roman state: Strabo 87, Celsus 94, Lucan 106, Pliny 130, Plutarch 145, 146, Tacitus 149, Procopius 210, 212
Romulus: founder and first king of Rome (mythical, or b. *c.* 771 BC, r. 753–*c.* 717): Statius 138, *A.L.* 207
Rufinus:
– (I) Herennius Rufinus, father-in-law of Sicinius Pontianus, who brought charges against Apuleius: Apuleius 160
– (II) Roman official (6C AD): Corippus 215
Russian: inhabitant of Russia (ancient Scythia): Virgil 79

S

Sabaeans: inhabitants of Saba (or Sheba), S.W. Arabia: Statius 138
Sabellus: Roman soldier killed by Nabis the Libyan: Silius 144
Sabratha: city of W. Libya, also called Abrotonum: Herodotus 54, Aristotle 64, Strabo 84, Lucan 112, Pliny 119, 120, Silius 142, Suetonius 153, Apuleius 156
Sagittarius: constellation, sign of the Zodiac: Lucan 112
Sahara: desert: Pliny 118
Salamis: city of E. Cyprus (now ruined): Herodotus 51
Sallust: Gaius Sallustius Crispus, Roman senator and governor of Africa Nova (Numidia) (*c.* 86–35 BC): Sallust 73-76, Valerius 92, Mela 99
Salus: Roman goddess of security and health: Avidius 171
Samians: *see* Samos.
Samos, Samian:
– (I) Greek island of the Dodecanese group in the Aegean Sea, just off the Asian coast: Herodotus 42, 47, 51
– (II) Samians: people from the island of Samos: Herodotus 46, 47
Samosata: city of Commagene (in Roman Syria) on the Euphrates, birthplace of Lucian (now Samsat, Turkey): Lucian 162
Sardinia, Sardinian: central Mediterranean island and Roman province: *H.A.* 186
Sarmatian:
– (I) of Sarmatia, extensive region of E. Europe (now Ukraine): Silius 144
– (II) Sarmatians: inhabitants of Sarmatia: Ptolemy 165
Sarranan: of Sarra, another name for the port of Tyre in Phoenicia, so named after a shellfish found there: Silius 142
Saturn: ancient Roman god of agriculture with particular affection for Italy, corresponding to Greek Cronus, whose position was usurped by his son Jupiter (Greek Zeus): Silius 142, Tacitus 150
Saturnalia: Roman festival in December in honour of Saturn, characterised by partying, social levelling and present giving: *A.L.* 208

Sfax: coastal city of E. Tunisia: Pliny 118

Shahat: modern name for Cyrene: Strabo 86, Mela 100, Pliny 119

Shaker: epithet of Poseidon as god of earthquakes: Pindar 40

Shelley: Percy Bysshe Shelley, British poet (AD 1792–1822): Lucan 106

Sicanus: Syracusan general during the Athenian invasion of Sicily of 415–413 BC: Thucydides 62

Sicily, Sicilian: large island of Central Mediterranean Sea, S.W. of the Italian peninsula: Thucydides 62, Pliny 125, 134, Silius 140

Sicinius:
- (I) Sicinius Aemilianus, who brought a lawsuit against Apuleius (2C AD): Apuleius 156, 158, 159, 160, 161
- (II) Sicinius Clarus, rejected suitor of Apuleius's wife Pudentilla (2C AD): Apuleius 156
- (III) Sicinius Pontianus, stepson of Apuleius and nephew of (I) and (II) above (2C AD): Apuleius 156–157, 161

Sidon, Sidonian:
- (I) city of Phoenicia (Lebanon): Sallust 75, Silius 140, 142, Corippus 215
- (II) Sidonian(s): inhabitant(s) of Sidon: Homer 37, Sallust 75

Sidra, Gulf of: Libyan sea gulf of Mediterranean, formerly Greater Syrtis: Herodotus 53, Strabo 84, Mela 99, Pliny 118-119

Silius Italicus. Tiberius Catius Asconius Silius Italicus, Roman poet (*c.* AD 26–101): Virgil 79, Lucan 107, Silius 139-144, Corippus 213

Sinope: city of N. coast of Asia Minor (now Sinop, Turkey): Herodotus 44

Siwa: oasis in W. Egypt, formerly site of the temple of Ammon: Strabo 81, Lucan 106, 113, Pliny 119, Silius 141, Corippus 214

Socratic: follower of philosophy of Socrates: Strabo 87

Sollum: town of W. Egypt, formerly Catabathmos, which gives its name to a sea gulf: Herodotus 53, Strabo 87

Soloeis: promontory of far N.W. Africa (possibly Cape Spartel, Morocco): Herodotus 43

Solomon: uncle of Cyrus and Sergius, governors in Libya (6C AD): Procopius 212

Sophocles: Greek tragic playwright (*c.* 496–406 BC): Synesius 194

Sossianus: Flavius Sossianus, deputy governor of Numidia in AD 222: Iasucthan 174

Sostratus: notably wealthy Greek merchant from Aegina (6C BC): Herodotus 47

Sousse: coastal city of N.E. Tunisia, formerly Hadrumetum: Suetonius 153, Eutropius 182

Southern Sea: the Indian Ocean: Herodotus 46

Spain: state in Iberian peninsula, a part of former Hispania: Sallust 74, Mela 97, Seneca 102, 104, Lucan 106, Martial 136

Sparta, Spartan:
- (I) capital city of Laconica, Greece: Homer 37, Thucydides 62, Callimachus 66, Nepos 77, 78
- (II) Spartan(s): citizen(s) of Sparta: Herodotus 61, Nepos 77, Ammianus 184

Spartianus: Aelius Spartianus, pseudonym of writer of the *Historia Augusta* (late 4C AD): *H.A.* 185

Spendophoros: young man who leaves Rome for Libya: Martial 137

Stagira: formerly Stagirus, on the Chalcidice Peninsula, N.W. Greece, birthplace of Aristotle: Aristotle 63

Statilius Capella: Roman knight from Sabratha: Suetonius 153

Statius: Publius Papirius Statius, Roman poet (*c.* AD 50–*c.* 96): Lucan 106, Statius 138

Stoic: adherent of Stoicism, Greek school of philosophy: Seneca 102, Lucan 106

Strabo: Greek geographer from Amasia in Pontus (*c.* 64 BC–*c.* AD 25): Strabo 81-88, Mela 97, Lucan 107, Plutarch 145

the water and food all around him: Lucian 163–164

Taphosiris: or Taposiris Magna, town S.W. of Alexandria, Ægypt at the far W. end of Lake Mareotis: Synesius 194

Taphra: town of Libya between Leptis Magna and Sabratha: Pliny 119

Tartessus: coastal region of S.W. Iberian Peninsula: Herodotus 47, 59

Tattimuth: commander of a modest Roman force which assisted Pudentius's revolt in Tripolitana in AD 533: Procopius 211

Tauchira, or Teuchira: town of Cyrenaica, later called Arsinoe (now Tocra): Herodotus 53, Strabo 86, 87, Pliny 120, Ammianus 184

Taurus: constellation, sign of the Zodiac: Lucan 112

Telesicrates: athlete from Cyrene, winner of the race in armour at the Pythian Games of 474 BC: Pindar 39

Tetrapyrgia: 'Four Towers', town inland of the Gulf of Sollum: Strabo 87

Teucer: ancestor of the kings of Troy: Virgil 80

Teuchira: *see* Tauchira

Thala: town in Numidia captured by Rome in 108 BC: Sallust 75

Thapsagum: (unknown) town of Phazania: Pliny 121

Thebais: late Roman province of S. Ægypt: Ammianus 184

Thebans: *see* Thebes

Thebes, Theban:
- (I) city and one-time capital of Ægypt, near modern Luxor: Herodotus 46, 56, Lucan 115
- (II) capital of Boeotia, Greece (now Thivai): Silius 141
- (III) Thebans: citizens of Thebes in Ægypt: Herodotus 45
- (IV) Thebans: citizens of Thebes in Boeotia, Greece: Nepos 77

Thelgae: (unknown) town of Phazania: Pliny 120

Themison: merchant of Thera living in Crete (7C BC): Herodotus 48

Themistocles: Athenian statesman and admiral (*c.* 528–*c.* 462 BC): Synesius 199

Theocritus: of Syracuse, greatest Greek pastoral poet (*c.* 300–*c.* 260 BC): Synesius 201

Theodorus: a son of King Geiseric of the Vandals (5C AD): Procopius 210

Theodosius:
- (I) Theodosius I: Flavius Theodosius, Roman emperor (b. *c.* AD 346, r. 379–395): *H.A.* 185
- (II) Theodosius II: Flavius Theodosius, Eastern Roman emperor (b. AD 401, r. 408–450): Synesius 202

Theophilus: patriarch (archbishop) of Alexandria, AD 385–412: Synesius 203

Theophrastus: of Eretos, philosopher and writer, best known for his works on plants and human character (*c.* 370–288 BC): Pliny 126, 127

Thera, Theraean:
- (I) city and island of the Cyclades in the Aegean Sea (also known as Santorini) which first sent colonists to Libya: Pindar 39, 40, Herodotus 46–49, 51, 61, Strabo 86, Callimachus 66
- (II) Theraeans: inhabitants of Thera: Herodotus 46-47, 48-49, 50, Sallust 74

Theras: regent of Sparta and, later, founder of Spartan colony on island of Calliste, renamed Thera: Herodotus 46

Thessalian: of Thessaly, region of N.E. Greece: Lucan 117

Theste: spring in Cyrenaica, site of battle between Cyrene and Ægypt *c.* 570 BC: Herodotus 50

Thibron: Spartan mercenary in service of Macedon, invader of Cyrenaica (d. 322 BC): Strabo 87

Thoar: town on Meninx island: Pliny 122

Thrace, Thracian: region and kingdom of S.E. Balkans: Pliny 129, Juvenal 152

Thuben: (unknown) town of Phazania: Pliny 121

THE SOCIETY FOR LIBYAN STUDIES

The Society for Libyan Studies was founded in 1969 to encourage scholarly research on the country and peoples of ancient and modern Libya. Most of the Society's resources are devoted to archaeological survey and excavations in Libya, but the Society also sponsors and co-ordinates the activities of researchers in such fields as ancient and Islamic history, geology, geography, natural history, education, linguistics and law. The Society publishes detailed reports on its field projects, popular titles (under the Silphium Press imprint) and an annual journal, *Libyan Studies* which contains articles and preliminary reports on the Society's current fieldwork. Members receive a free copy of the annual journal and are entitled to buy other publications at discounted prices. Members and friends are invited to attend the Annual General Meeting and four lectures held in London each year, on a wide range of topics relating to Libya's rich culture and heritage.

Library

The Society's library of books on Libya and related North Africa studies is housed in the Library, Ground Floor, School of Oriental and African Studies, Malet Street, London, WC1E 7HP. Members are entitled to a letter of introduction which will enable them to consult the SOAS library and to have borrowing rights.

Archive

The Society's archive of documents, photographs and drawings is stored in the Centre for Interdisciplinary Artefact Studies at the University of Newcastle upon Tyne, Newcastle, NE1 7RU. The material is open to members by arrangement with the Department.

Join the Society for Libyan Studies

The subscription year runs from 1 April. For more information on membership and the Society please consult the website http://www.britac.ac.uk/institutes/libya/ or contact the General Secretary by post.

The General Secretary
The Society for Libyan Studies
c/o The Institute of Archaeology
31–34 Gordon Square
London
WClH OPY

PUBLICATIONS OF THE SOCIETY FOR LIBYAN STUDIES

1. **Libyan Studies: Select Papers of the late R. G. Goodchild: collected articles from 1949–1967.** Edited by J. M. Reynolds. l976. xxii + 345 pp, 96 pls, index.

2. **Excavations at Sidi Khrebish Benghazi (Berenice). Volume I, Buildings, Coins, Inscriptions, Architectural Decoration.** (Supplement to *Libya Antiqua V*, vol. I). Edited by J. A. Lloyd with contributions by J. M. Reynolds, R. M. Reece, F. Sear, P. Kenrick. 1977. xxx + 311 pp, 71 figs, 32 pls. Arabic summary: 120 pp. Published in collaboration with the Department of Antiquities and Ministry of Teaching and Education, Tripoli.

3. **Excavations at Sidi Khrebish Benghazi (Berenice). Volume II, Economic Life at Berenice, Sculptures and Terracottas, Amphoras and Plain Wares.** (Supplement to *Libya Antiqua V*, vol. II). Edited by J. A. Lloyd with contributions from G. W. W. Barker, A. Wheeler, D. Webley, A. Bonanno and J. A. Riley. 1979. vi + 467 pp, 153 figs, 43 pls. Arabic summary: 19 pp. Published in collaboration with the Department of Antiquities and Ministry of Teaching and Education, Tripoli. ***Out of print.***

4. **Excavations at Sidi Khrebish Benghazi (Berenice). Volume III, part 1: The Fine Pottery.** (Supplement to *Libya Antiqua V*, vol. III.1). By P. M. Kenrick. 1985. xviii + 515 pp, 78 figs, 24 pls. Arabic summary: 12 pp. Published in collaboration with the Department of Antiquities and Ministry of Teaching and Education, Tripoli.

5. **Excavations at Sidi Khrebish Benghazi (Berenice). Volume III, part 2: The Lamps.** (Supplement to *Libya Antiqua V*, vol. III.2). By D. M. Bailey. 1985. ix + 194 pp, 19 figs, 39 pls. Arabic summary: 3 pp. Published in collaboration with the Department of Antiquities and Ministry of Teaching and Education, Tripoli.

6. **Excavations at Sidi Khrebish Benghazi (Berenice). Volume IV, part 1: The Mosaics and Marble Floors.** (Supplement to *Libya Antiqua V*, vol. IV.1). By Demetrios Michaelides. 1998. xiv +160 pp, 110 black and white figs, 16 colour pls. Published in collaboration with the Department of Antiquities and Ministry of Teaching and Education, Tripoli.

7. **Ghirza: A Libyan Settlement in the Roman Period.** By O. Brogan and D. J. Smith. 1984. 330 pp, 115 figs, 172 pls, 15 appendices, index. Published in collaboration with the Department of Antiquities, Tripoli.

8. **Cyrenaica in Antiquity.** Edited by G. Barker, J. Lloyd and J. M. Reynolds. 1985. xiv + 403 pp, 58 figs, 77 pls, 9 tables. Society for Libyan Studies Occasional Papers I, Publisher: BAR International Series 236. ***Out of print.***

9. **Town and Country in Roman Tripolitania, Papers in honour of Olwen Hackett.** Edited by D. J. Buck and D. J. Mattingly. 1985. xvi + 311 pp, 111 figs. Society for Libyan Studies Occasional Papers II. Publisher: BAR International Series 274. ***Out of print.***

10. **Libya: Research in Archaeology, Environment, History and Society, 1969–1989.** (***Libyan Studies 20***). Edited by D. J. Mattingly and J. A. Lloyd. 1989. xi + 262 pp, 45 figs, 3 pls. Arabic summary: 4 pp.

11. **Excavations at Sabratha, 1948–1951, Volume II, part 1. The Finds. The Amphorae, Coarse Pottery and Building Materials.** By John Dore and Nina Keay with contributions by H. Dodge, D. P. S.Peacock and R. H. Seager-Smith. Edited by M. G. Fulford and M. Hall. 1989. xiii + 298 pp, 72 figs, 5 tables. Arabic summary. Society for Libyan Studies Monograph no. 1. Published in collaboration with the Department of Antiquities, Tripoli and the Society for Libyan Studies.

12. **The Severan Buildings of Lepcis Magna, an Architectural Survey.** By J. B. Ward-Perkins. General Editor: G. D. B. Jones. Edited by P. M. Kenrick with drawings by R. Kronenburg. 1993. xvii + 140 pp, 42 figs (some foldout), 45 pls, maps (some foldout), Arabic summary. Society

for Libyan Studies Monograph no. 2. Published in collaboration with the Department of Antiquities, Tripoli. ***Out of print.***

13. **Excavations at Sabratha, Volume II, part 2. The Fine Wares.** Edited by M. G. Fulford and R. Tomber with contributions by N. Keay, J. R. Timby, J. W. Hayes and D. M. Bailey. 1994. xiii + 210 pp, 48 figs. Arabic summary. Society for Libyan Studies Monograph no. 3. Published in collaboration with the Department of Antiquities, Tripoli.

14. **Cyrenaican Archaeology: An International Colloquium (*Libyan Studies 25*).** Edited by J. M. Reynolds. 1994. iv + 298 pp, 38 figs, 172 pls. Arabic summary: 14 pp.

15. **Farming the Desert, The UNESCO Libyan Valleys Archaeological Survey. Volume I: Synthesis.** By G. W. W. Barker, D. Gilbertson, B. Jones, D. J. Mattingly. 1996. xx + 404 pp, 193 figs, 29 tables, index.

16. **Farming the Desert, The UNESCO Libyan Valleys Archaeological Survey. Volume II: Gazetteer 1979–1989 and Pottery.** By G. W. W. Barker, D. Gilbertson, B. Jones, D. J. Mattingly. 1996. xxiv + 393 pp, 291 figs, 9 tables, index.

17. **Excavations at Surt (Medinet al-Sultan) between 1977 and 1981.** By Geza Fehervari with contributions from 'Abbas Hamdani, Masoud Shaglouf, Hal Bishop, John Riley, Muhammed Hamid and Ted Hughes. Edited by Elizabeth Savage. 2002. viii + 120 pp, 11 figs, 45 pls (some colour), foldout plan. Arabic summary 7 pp.

18. **Christian Monuments of Cyrenaica.** By J. B. Ward-Perkins and R. G. Goodchild. Edited Joyce Reynolds with contributions by R. M. Harrison, H. M. Dodge, Sheila Gibson, John Lloyd, Joyce Reynolds and Susan Walker. 2002. 462 pp, 376 figs and plans, 2 foldout maps, index. Society for Libyan Studies Monograph no. 4.

19. **The Archaeology of Fazzan. Volume 1. Synthesis.** Edited by David Mattingly. 2003. xxvi + 428 pp, 460 figs (many in colour), 31 tables. Arabic summary. Society for Libyan Studies Monograph no. 5.

20. **The Libyan Desert: Natural Resources and Cultural Heritage.** Edited by David Mattingly, Sue McLaren, Elizabeth Savage, Yahya al-Fasatwi, Khaled Gadgood. 2006. 349 pp. Society for Libyan Studies Monograph no. 6.

21. **The Archaeology of Fazzan. Volume. 2: Site Gazetteer, Pottery and Other Survey Finds.** Edited by David J. Mattingly. 2007. xxix + 552 pp. Arabic summary. Society for Libyan Studies Monograph no. 7.

22. **The Archaeology of Fazzan. Volume. 3: Excavations of C.M. Daniels.** Edited by David J. Mattingly. 2010. xxix + 612 pp, 492 figs (many in colour), 64 tables. Arabic summary. Society for Libyan Studies Monograph no. 8.

SILPHIUM PRESS: ARCHAEOLOGY, HISTORY AND TRAVEL IN LIBYA

Silphium Press is the popular imprint of The Society for Libyan Studies. Silphium was a plant renowned in antiquity as a contraceptive, a medicinal herb and a spice. Found only in Cyrenaican Libya, it was appreciated throughout the Mediterranean world from the seventh century BC to the first century AD when it became extinct, probably through overexploitation. Our logo is inspired by images on the coins of Cyrene.

23. **Travellers in Libya.** Selected and edited by John Wright. 2005. 255 pp, 2 maps.

24. **Wheels Across the Desert: Exploration of the Libyan Desert by Motorcar 1916–1942.** By Andrew Goudie. 2008. 205 pp, 55 photographs, 12 maps.

25. **The Emergence of Libya.** By John Wright. 2008. 368 pp, 1 map.

26. **Libya Archaeological Guides: Tripolitania.** By Philip Kenrick. 2009. ix +220 pp, 113 maps, drawings and photographs.

27. **War and Politics in the Desert: Britain and Libya during the Second World War.** By Saul Kelly. 2010. 256 pp, 33 photographs, 5 maps.

28. **Travels in Classical Libya: Snakes, Sands and Silphium.** By Paul Wright. 2011. 272 pp, 29 illustrations, 9 maps.

LIBYAN STUDIES: THE JOURNAL OF THE SOCIETY FOR LIBYAN STUDIES

The annual journal of record of the Society for Libyan Studies is published in November each year. Contributions are peer-reviewed and cover a broad range of subjects, including archaeology, ancient and Islamic history, geology, geography and social sciences. The articles will appeal to readers with an interest in the Middle East and Mediterranean worlds as well as North Africa. For article submissions, please contact the Society.